THE
CHANGING PATTERN
OF
POLITICAL POWER
IN IRAQ, 1958 TO 1971

THE
CHANGING PATTERN
OF
POLITICAL POWER
IN IRAQ, 1958 TO 1971

by

Lorenzo Kent Kimball, Ph. D

Robert Speller & Sons, Publishers, Inc.
New York, New York 10010

© 1972 by Lorenzo Kent Kimball

Library of Congress Catalog Card No. 79–178827
ISBN 0–8315– 0120–0

First Edition

Printed in the United States of America

TABLE OF CONTENTS

PREFACE

PART I — POWER AND NATIONALISM

CHAPTER

PART II — IRAQ

PREFACE

The vast area known as the "Arab World" extends from the Persian Gulf in Asia to the Atlantic Coast in North Africa. The area embraces the southern shores of the Mediterranean in Africa and the eastern shorelands in Asia, extending southward to include the Arabian Peninsula and embracing all of Mesopotamia. The Western or North African area usually referred to as the Maghreb is not included when the author refers to the Arab World. Rather, the term here applies primarily to the area known as the Middle East, which encompasses all those countries of Asia lying south of the Soviet Union and west of Pakistan, and Egypt on the African continent.

The Arab peoples who inhabit this constellation of territories include the Syrians, the Lebanese, the Palestinians, the Jordanians, the Egyptians, the Iraqis, the Saudia Arabians, the Yemenites, and the inhabitants of the Persian Gulf sheikdoms. Arab nationalism represents the hopes and aspiration of some eighty million people who are striving to reconstruct the foundations of their modern life based on an historic and religious legacy after centuries of stagnation and decline. The Arabic-Islamic legacy is real in the thoughts and actions of many authoritative interpretations on which the conclusions are based.

It is recognized that there are serious divergences of opinion concerning the postulates of Arab and Western nationalism which have complicated the situation by contributing to the divisive nature of Arab nationalism itself. The author is fully aware of the strong psychological and emotional appeal of the symbols of Arab nationalism to the peoples of the Arab World and in no way intends to disparage this idealization of a hope, but the conclusion reached from the observations contained here, however, confirm that in the end practical politics and struggle for power in any given Arab country including Iraq is based on *national rather than regional interests.*

Unfortunately, there is a counter-force introduced as a result of close cultural contacts with the West during the last two centuries which has proved to be divisive in nature and may well destroy any realistic efforts to attain Arab unity. This counter-force is the secular concept of the modern nation-state system combined with the consequences of the imperial policies of Great Britain and France in the first half of the present century. The Sykes-Picot Treaty of 1916 and the mandate system of the League of Nations which resulted in the creation of a number of new and often artificial states have led to a situation in which the demand is for loyalty in terms of a local nationalism as opposed to that of Arab nationalism.

It is the conflict between these two ideas which the author explores, using the struggle for power in Iraq as the prime example of the collision of these two forces. The literature available is primarily episodic and descriptive; but the utilization of Arab Documents, of speeches of Arab leaders and of varied commentator's analyses in conjunction with the available literature on the subject has made it possible to undertake this work, which covers a combination of historical data, current events, constitutional and legal documents.

The author wishes to acknowledge the invaluable assistance of many persons who encouraged him and who gave considerable assistance in the completion of this work. First, a great deal of credit is due to Professor Khosrow Mostofi. I am deeply indebted to Professor Francis D. Wormuth for his constructive criticism; he has been a real source of scholarly inspiration over the past eight years. Next, I wish to express my gratitude to Professor Aziz S. Atiya for his constructive comments and scholarly suggestions. Special gratitude is expressed to Brigham D. Madsen, Grant Holt and Ellsworth Weaver for their support and encouraging remarks. I sincerely appreciate the time and efforts of Miss Suzan Thorley who read the entire manuscript and offered helpful suggestions, and for the highly efficient work of Mrs. Carole Swan who did the typing. Finally deep gratitude is expressed to James Patrick, Michael Ware and their mother for their patience and understanding which made the completion of this work possible. It is to them that this book is dedicated.

Lorenzo Kent Kimball
September, 1972

PART I
POWER AND NATIONALISM

CHAPTER 1
POWER

Power is a grim political reality which escapes precise definition because of its many characteristics. The concept behind this rich and untidy word, as one author calls it,[1] has been subjected to continuous and exacting examination by political thinkers from the time of the ancient Greeks to the present, and yet there is no general agreement as to its real connotations. Born in violence, "in the raw will to dominate,"[2] power has moved variously from defining the brutal act of a primitive who used to crush his enemy by hand or club to connoting the gentle act of national persuasion coalesced with the consent of the victim of such persuasion, and back again to the definition of an annihilatory force poised for action in the hands of the "primitives" of the modern world.

Further, power has moved to and through every level of institutional organization since group cohesion and aggregation became a matter of necessity or utility.[3] Power is a complex phenomenon which exists in all phases of human relationships and permeates the lives of all mankind. The conflicts and cooperation produced by the political, social, cultural and economic relations of men are a direct result of the power situation. From this has emerged the necessity, or rather the reality, of authority; and, to complicate matters, authority itself has taken most diverse and elusive forms.

To arrive at a workable solution to this difficult problem, it will be useful to review briefly some of the major attempts to define power in general and political power in particular. Dominance seems to represent the oldest social connotation of the term. Writing at the conclusion of one holocaust and on the eve of even more portentous possibilities, Bertrand de Jouvenal maintained that "Power in its pure state consists . . . of command, a command which has an independent existence." He argues that submission to command is a relatively passive factor and he rejects the notion that command is but an effect. Command is, then, power itself.[4]

> But that is not all. The idea that the rulers have been willed into ruling by the ruled is not only improbable. If regard is had to the larger formation, it is also contradictory and absurd. . . . Whereas, as history shows, communities of any size owe their existence to one thing only—to the imposition of one and the same force, and one and the same command, on divergent groups.[5]

It follows obviously that the state, as the instrument of command, has conquest as its lifeblood, and that the state is nothing more than a succession of brigands "who superimpose themselves on small, distinct societies; [who behave toward] the vanquished . . . as Power in the pure state. Power of this kind can make no claim to legitimacy. It pursues no just end; its one concern is the profitable exploitation of conquered and submissive subjects. It lives off the subject populations."[6]

Although this extreme view neglects consideration of such notions as "persuasion" and "influence" and suggests that "power" precedes the state, about which more discussion will follow, it is essential for the purposes here to set forth this idea of "domination" as being central to the thought of many of the leaders who are discussed in Part II.

The opposite view holds that

> . . . organized social power . . . [is] that type of power which is engendered and maintained by joint human activity guided by a more or less explicitly agreed upon set of rules. . . . Political power is distinct from all the other forms

of social power by reason of the function which it performs in organizing and integrating into action the inter-related activities of the inhabitants of a particular territorial area.[7]

Here the terms "integrating" and "inter-related activities" imply reciprocal action. The idea implied is opposed to the dominant command theory which supposes reaction as a secondary feature created from discipline or habit.

This leads to the relational concept of power as developed by Harold D. Lasswell and others, such as C.J. Friedrich and P.H. Partridge. According to Lasswell:

> Power is an interpersonal situation; those who hold power are empowered. They depend upon and continue only so long as there is a continuing stream of empowering responses. Even a casual inspection of human relations will convince any competent observer that power is not a brick that can be lugged from place to place, but a process that vanishes when the supporting responses cease.[8]

Here, then, the *dialectic of command* is determined by response. There is a *giving* and *taking* process involved whereby the recipient, in order to conclude the *power situation*, must respond. An order or request relayed to another must be obeyed or acquiesced to before *power* is experienced. It is a two-way street. Power cannot exist in a vacuum. This does not preclude situations where there is a refusal to act, because the refusal itself may result in deprivations or sanctions. The fact that imprisonment, fines, reprimands or loss of employment are possible leads to the pattern of expectation and thereby elicits response.[9] A power situation then is created in terms of an expectation which requires response, either of an authoritative or controlling nature, and therefore the response itself is essential to the exercise of power. This re-introduces the factors of initiative and causation of which Aristotle says, "the beginning of a chain movement is called a power. . . ." and when action is *caused* it is possible to speak of *controlling* the actions of others.[10]

Professor Oppenheim has provided another dimension beyond the ideas of influence and control. Speaking of the concept of exercising power, Professor Oppenheim points out that beyond the view that ". . . whoever performs an act of power does so intentionally . . . with the intention of determining the activities of others for the sake of achieving his own purpose."[11] Power, however, may also be exercised unintentionally. This aspect of control can be illustrated in a number of ways. Advertising on television today very often drives a prospective buyer *away* from a product, for the constant repetition of the same theme often creates revulsion. The inane programs aimed at a low mentality will drive the viewer at least to another network or conceivably to a good book. Information and discussion provided in a classroom are often translated by students into the right theory and the professor unwittingly has presented a new, unintended banner of *truth*. A casual comment by an officer can precipitate the most drastic action by a non-commissioned officer currying favor for a promotion. And, of course, neighborhood gossip can destroy reputations and cause conflicts beyond imagination.

According to another view, "Power may be defined as the production of intended effects."[12] This, however, limits the concept and does not allow for inclusion of those unintended consequences which so often occur. It must be added at this point, however, that power may be conceived in terms of command, control, and influence, either intended or unintended; power may be beneficial or destructive.

Power may be experienced as inspiring, wholesome, tolerable, or oppressive, depending on the circumstances. It may release creative energy, heightening vitality, it may destroy motivation, generating a pall of depression, or it may stimulate conflict and rebellion. It may induce a sense of freedom or a sense of tyranny.[13]

Another analysis treats power as being inter-related with the concept of influence. This, too, is posed as a *relational* concept. "Influence . . . is a relation—among individuals, groups, associations, organizations, states. We can . . . say that influence is a relation among actors in which one actor induces other actors to act in some way they would not otherwise act."[14] Dahl recognizes that, in principle, the *existence*, *direction* and *degree* of influence are measurable and essential to the analysis of power. He suggests that "influence is analogous to the concept of force in mechanics."[15] Although this analogy is not pursued very far, it neglects the subjective phenomena which Professor Wormuth has so lucidly illustrated.[16] Dahl's analysis also lacks scope and appears not to have suggested anything beyond the limited view of Russell.

Undoubtedly, power *does* include the idea of *controlling* individual or group action. This enlarges on the above concept of influence to include the idea of restraint. "To exercise control is to exercise influence or to restrain; to have control is to have influence or to prevent."[17] Further, this control can be exercised in two ways: first, by determining response through the manipulation of relative facts in such a way as to limit the choice of action; or, second, by determining the choice beforehand. The latter is, of course, influence and includes the idea of persuasion. This may also be a means of eliminating or withholding action to avoid adverse consequences. In other words, it would be preventive within the meaning of Oppenheim's definition cited here. This, the author maintains, is accomplished by narrowing the alternatives in advance. For,

> Prevention is usually not mentioned among the various forms of control and power; yet, making it impossible for others to act in a certain way constitutes the most effective device of gaining control over their actual behavior. Would-be controllers usually want to establish control over their respondents in such a way that the latter make no attempt at evading it.[18]

An additional term, force, should be introduced and distinguished at this point. The notion of force is related to both the physical and the social sciences. It can describe a purely mechanical notion as well as a social movement. It has as much relevance to physical energy as to human conduct. It is interesting that Aristotle does not distinguish between force and violence; he uses the term *bia*, which may mean both.[19] Significantly, while modern writers agree that force is associated with the exercise of power, "there is anything but agreement over the question of the proper—in both a technical and a moral sense—relation between . . . methods and the power system."[20] The most prominent views seem to be contradictory. One view, which considers "violence" as the extreme manifestation of force and the result of the failure of power, would exclude the term from a definition of power. The opposite view considers violence as a specific property of and central to the definition of "political power." It is intended in this study that force and violence both be considered as elements integral to political power.

What is "political power"? Can it be distinguished from other forms of social control? Merriam maintains that only confusion can result by trying to draw too sharp and exclusive a line between political and all other forms of organization.[21] He argues that there is a fundamental similarity in all organizational structures and functions. Be that as it may, it best suits the purposes here to stress that political power is concerned primarily with the state, that the state has been organized for the control of men and that power in this sense will utilize whatever means that might be available and necessary for the purpose. "Political power is social power focused on the state. It involves control of other men for the purpose of influencing the behavior of the state, its legislative, administrative and judicial activities."[22] It should be noted that the military use of power, while generally thought of as a part of "administrative activities," assumes added significance and is treated in Part II as an almost exclusive entity apart from the traditional functions of government.

Beyond this implied interrelationship of political power and military power, which is most crucial, is the acute problem of the relation of political power to economic power. Unquestionably, political power could not be exercised for any period of time without economic resources. We are told by the historical materialists, however, that "political power is merely the instrument of the dominant capitalist class in its program of exploitation."[23] Further, the historical materialists maintain that political and social institutions all proceed from an economic base and are merely a part of the "superstructure" of society. This view denies the possibility of there being autonomous political power, which can proceed from either its own stimulus independently or from a different base of operation, such as the military. This view also denies the possibility of power developing its own economic basis and also, as will be suggested, the possibility that it has its own lifeblood in terms of ideology, e.g., nationalism.

This is suggested, in part, by the following observation:

In the early modern period the successful exercise of

political power entailed a basic transformation of the existing economic system and was thus responsible in large part for ushering in capitalism; the capitalistic production of goods was stimulated in supplying the tremendous new market offered by the increasingly well equipped mercenary armies. To bolster its power the mercantilistic state set out, deliberately and with carefully formulated plans, to direct the progress of capitalism. Such regulation of economic activity presupposes a sufficient degree of homogeneity in the people to enable the agencies of political power to subject the territorial-social coactivities to effective control. At all periods therefore the exercise of political power has involved regulation of the economic system with a view to easing social and economic tension.[24]

It is well recognized that "political power is exercised not only by the state but also by smaller associations within it: . . . [and that] not every political power as such is state power, but, in the eyes of its incumbents at least, every political power is potentially state power."[25] This study is concerned with both aspects of political power: actual power as state power, and potential power which resides in those groups which are competing for the control of state power. Let us consider the nature of the groups who compete for control of state power and establish whether they are distinguishable or whether one man commands the obedience of all of them.

Actual power is exercised as state power by the device of "government." "Government gives one man power over others, a power no man possesses in his own right or by virtue of his own strength."[26] By what right does one man or, as will be suggested below, a group of men, rule? From what source is this authority derived?

Merriam has conveniently summarized the principal forms of belief, or "credenda of power" as he terms it, which men have clung to as the basis or, if you will, *apologia* of authority. They are as follows:

1. Political power is ordained of God or the gods.
2. Political power is the highest expression of expert leadership.
3. Political power is the will of the many or the majority, expressed through some form of consent.[27]

The first idea, that of the divinity of power, is generally

considered related to the paternal, historical and traditional nature of authority and has a rich life of its own. Although union of altar and throne has essentially disappeared from Western institutions, it is significant to note that the separation of the religious from the secular is not yet complete in many parts of the Middle East.

The second great ideology of political power is concerned with the notion of superior ability whether it be vested in one charismatic leader or in a group of leaders known as the elite. This presupposes the ignorance and incompetence of the masses, and holds that their interests are best served when they are governed by select, superior persons. As Merriam points out: "This is the central theme that echoes through Plato's *Republic*, the endless forms of aristocracy, the modern elite in Italy (1934), the German demand for *Fuhrerschaft*; and it contains a powerful theoretical appeal to those who reason about affairs political."[28] When combined with the "divinity of power" idea, this "ideology of power" finds great expression in the politics of the Middle East today. Although the combination of the two ideas is not new historically, it is essential to recognize their combination in order to understand the politics of the Middle East.

The last form of belief, that of "the will of the majority expressed through some form of consent" is the "great credendum of democracy around which the institutions of universal suffrage, of representation, and of legal responsibility have been constructed and operated during the last three hundred years."[29] With this idea, theoretically, there is a distrust of elite ruling groups and a belief that man has a basic equality, so he must "share" in the governing process both by service (holding office) and by participation (voting). This idea further recognizes "the dignity, value, and potentiality of every man" and develops institutions and procedures for the protection of the "rights" of the individual. Carried to the extreme, "It is even possible to transfer the doctrine of divine right to the mass and make the voice of the people the voice of God."[30] This idea, then is the basis for what is called democracy, and it also is a fundamental basis for socialism and communism where the worth or well-being of the individual, whether he be a capitalist or a member of the proletariat, is the ultimate value.

Further discussion of the concept of the elite is necessary because of its importance in Middle Eastern politics, if not in all politics. In responding to the "superiority" principle, MacIver makes the observation that "No man is much stronger than another, but a group of bold and cunning men can get together and make themselves masters of the rest. They take over the resources of the community, run it in their own interest, making the rest their servants or their slaves. . . . Most governments throughout history have been in the hands of ruling groups or classes."[31] Lasswell puts the idea in its simplest form, "the elite are the influential."[32] This idea assumes that "influence is unequal" and that "the most influential are called elite."[33] It is essential to distinguish which group forms the most influential elite in any political organization. Lasswell continues to postulate that". . . man seeks to maximize valued outcomes; he does something in the expectation of being better off than if he did something else."[34] In order to do this he adopts certain "institutional practices" in order to affect "resource environment." This social process is categorized into eight valued outcomes and institutions, as follows:

1. "Power" outcomes include such a final decision as winning or losing an election or a war; and the relevant institutions are specialized as government, law, and politics.

2. "Enlightenment" outcomes are the giving and receiving of information, as in disseminating or reading books; the institutions include mass media and research agencies.

3. "Wealth" outcomes are, for example, trading, borrowing, and lending: the institutions are units of production and markets.

4. "Well-being" outcomes directly involve safety, health, and comfort; the institutions include patterns specialized to medical care.

5. "Skill" outcomes are demonstrations of excellence in arts, crafts, and professions; the institutions include the procedures of training.

6. "Affection" outcomes are the giving and receiving of love and intimacy; the institutions are the practices of family and friendship.

7. "Respect" outcomes are the giving and receiving of honor and consideration; the relevant institutions include the practices of discrimination and distinction.

8. "Rectitude" outcomes are, for example, mutual characterizations as "righteous" or "sinful," "ethically upright," or "immoral"; the rectitude institutions are the ecclesiastical or secular specializations in anticipating and applying standards.[35]

Although these eight elite levels exist in the social process and obviously "interact" in the totality of the society concerned, this study primarily deals with the notions of the power outcomes as institutionalized in the Middle East and more specifically in Iraq. It is worth noting, however, that the power elite very often reaches beyond the governmental level and includes parts of, if not all, the military and economic elites in order to complete the "power complex."

In his study of the American decision-making process, C. Wright Mills maintains that: "The power elite is composed of political, economic, and military men . . ." and that "all three are involved in virtually all widely ramifying decisions."[36] It remains to be seen whether this evaluation can be applied to the struggle for power in Iraq. That is, whether sophistication in elite interaction in Iraq has developed to the extent it has in the United States. This problem will be discussed in Part II.[37]

De Jouvenal's concept of power as command, the relational concept of Lasswell and others, including the ideas of "influences" and "control," the "intentional" or "unintentional" aspects of the exercise of power, and finally the "beneficial" or "destructive" uses of power all have relevance to the struggle for power in Iraq during the period 1958 to 1971. Further, as shall be seen later, the use of "persuasion" and "coercion," including violence, is fully germane to the subject under discussion.

Consequently, instead of limiting ourselves to any single definition of power, we intend to base our arguments on a broad concept of political power within a particular system used as a pattern for action by specific individuals in a specific society. In doing so, we will also examine the methods used to control an entire nation, the objectives sought and the degree of success or failure which has marked the attempt.

NOTES

[1]Francis D. Wormuth, "Matched-Dependent Behavioralism: The Cargo Cult in Political Science," *Western Political Quarterly*, XX (December 1967), p. 814.

[2]Charles E. Merriam, *Political Power* (New York: Collier Books, 1964), p. 31.

[3]*Ibid.*

[4]Bertrand de Jouvenal, *On Power: Its Nature and the History of Its Growth* (Boston: Beacon Press, 1962), p. 98.

[5]*Ibid.*

[6]*Ibid.*, pp. 100–101.

[7]Hermann Heller, "Political Power," *Encyclopedia of the Social Sciences*, ed. Edwin R.A. Seligman (New York: Macmillan Company, 1937), XII, 301.

[8]Harold D. Lasswell, *Power and Personality* (New York: The Viking Press, 1962), p. 10.

[9]*Ibid.*, p. 12.

[10]E.V. Walter, Power and Violence,'' *American Political Science Review*, LVIII (June 1964), p. 350.

[11]Felix E. Oppenheim, *Dimensions of Freedom: An Analysis* (New York: St. Martin's Press, 1961), p. 92.

[12]Bertrand Russell, *Power: A New Social Analysis* (New York: W.W. Norton & Company, 1938), p. 35.

[13] Walter, *op. cit.*, p. 353.

[14]Robert A. Dahl, *Modern Political Analysis* (Englewood Cliffs: Prentice-Hall, Inc., 1965), p. 40.

[15]*Ibid.*, p. 41.

[16]Wormuth, *op. cit.*, pp. 816–22.

[17]Oppenheim, *op. cit.*, p. 56.

[18]*Ibid.*, p. 52.

[19]Walter, *op. cit.*, p. 354.

[20]*Ibid.*, p. 355.

[21]Merriam, *op. cit.*, p. 22.

[22]Franz L. Neumann, "Approaches to the Study of Political Power," *Comparative Politics*, ed. Roy C. Macridis and Bernard E. Brown (Homewood: The Dorsey Press, 1964), p. 65.

[23]Heller, *op. cit.*, p. 302.

[24]*Ibid.*

[25]*Ibid.*, p. 301.

[26]R.M. MacIver, *The Web of Government* (New York: The Free Press, 1965), p. 11.

[27]Merriam, *op. cit.*, p. 119.

[28]*Ibid.*, p. 121.

[29]*Ibid.*, p. 124.

[30]*Ibid.*, p. 125. This notion has its counterpart in Islam and is described by David De Santillana, "Law and Society in Islam," in *The Contemporary Middle East*, ed. Benjamin Rivlin and Joseph S. Szyliowicz (New York: Random House, 1965). As he states it: [The people or community of Muhammad] is the chosen, the holy people, to whom is entrusted the furtherance of good and the repression of evil; it is the only seat of justice and faith upon earth, the sole witness for God among the nations, just as the Prophet had been God's witness among the Arabs.''

[31] MacIver, *op. cit.*, p. 11.

[32]Harold D. Lasswell and Daniel Lerner (eds.) *World Revolutionary Elites* (Cambridge: The M.I.T. Press, 1966), p. 4.

[33]*Ibid.*, p. 5.

[34]*Ibid.*, p. 8.

[35]*Ibid.*

[36]C. Wright Mills, *The Power Elite* (New York: Oxford University Press, 1959), pp. 276–77.

[37]See Chapters 6, 7 and 8 below.

CHAPTER 2
NATIONALISM

Power has many facets. The same can be said about nationalism and, what is more, in both national and internal politics and the global struggles which mark our age the two are often inseparable. There have been numerous attempts to account for the idea of nationalism and to explain its corresponding structure and development. As with the concept of power, the views are varied and contain objective as well as subjective implications, including departures into the realm of metaphysics. Further, there is no consensus as to when or how nationalism came into being and finally, there is only limited agreement as to its current and potential influence on the affairs of men. However, what no one can deny is the fact that nationalism "spins at the center of the world's political maelstrom."[1]

Nationalism has been variously described as a doctrine, a historical process, a plurality of power, a social force, a political force, a new tribalism, and even as an ephemeral interlude. Regardless of descriptive connotations, the force itself is as real as the power it gathers and releases in the actions of men in conflict, whether these actions be in the diplomatic arena or on the field of battle.

A nation, from which any concept of nationalism must flow, is generally considered to be a people who have some objective characteristics in common who live in a particular territory which may or may not be an independent state and who share a common history. Inasmuch as most nations have either gained their independence over the past two decades or are well on their way to doing so, it will be useful to define State within the framework of international law:

> A state proper—in contradistinction to colonies—is in existence when the people is settled in a country under its own sovereign Government. The conditions which must obtain for the existence of a State are therefore four:
>
> There must, first, be a *people*. A people is an aggregate of individuals of both sexes who live together as a community in spite of the fact they may belong to different races or creeds, or be of different color.
>
> There must, secondly, be a *country* in which the people has settled down. A wandering people is not a state. . . .
>
> There must, thirdly, be a Government—that is, one or more persons who are the representatives of the people and rule according to the law of the land. An anarchistic community is not a state.
>
> There must, fourthly and lastly, be a sovereign Government. Sovereignty is supreme authority, an authority which is independent of any other earthly authority. Sovereignty in the strict and narrowest sense of the term implies, therefore, independence all around, within and without the borders of the country.[2]

The above definition of a state will, for the purposes of this study, be interchangeable with the word nation. This legalistic definition is purposely noted at this point to present the question as to whether nationalism preceded the formation of the state or whether nationalism could conceivably have resulted from the legal establishment of a state.

The traditional view of nationalism holds that as a doctrine, "It pretends to supply a criterion for the determination of the unit of population proper to enjoy a government exclusively its own, for the legitimate exercise of power in the state, and for the right organization of a society of states."[3] Further, the doctrine holds that nationalism is a natural process by which humanity is divided into nations which are known by certain recognizable characteristics, "and that the only legitimate type of government is national self-government."[4] This is briefly the doctrine of Western European nationalism as it took shape at the beginning of the nineteenth century.

Many difficulties become obvious as we attempt to differentiate the objective characteristics as they exist today which are peculiar to one particular notion of nationalism. These characteristics have usually included language, common descent, territorial residence, customs and traditions, and religion. Subjective elements have also been introduced by some writers and include such notions as mutual affection, consciousness of difference from other people, and/or the will to belong to a particular people.[5] However, some of these objective characteristics have become comparatively irrelevant as pointed out by Hans Kohn. For example, "there are many nationalities who have no language of their own—like the Swiss, who speak four different languages, or the Latin American nationalists, all of whom speak Spanish or Portuguese."[6] Also, while common descent may have great importance to primitive man, modern nationalities are admixtures of many races. Further, customs and traditions tend to be more sectionalized and nearly all religions are found in most of the so-called nation-states. The attempt to classify modern nationalism on the basis of the alleged characteristics of a people has generally been discredited.[7]

Kohn also points out two fictitious concepts which offer no real explanation of nationalism but have been accepted as having real substance. "One holds that blood or race is the basis of nationality, and that it exists externally and carries with it unchangeable inheritance; the other sees the *Volksgeist* as an ever-welling source of nationality and all its manifestations . . . . [These] refer us to mythical prehistorical pseudo-realities."[8]

In spite of the above statements, Kohn still maintains that "Nationalities are created out of ethnographic and political elements when nationalism breathes life into the form built by preceding centuries."[9] This statement, as Mostofi has so adequately pointed out, carries the concept into the realm of the metaphysical "and reduces it to a proper object for mere contemplation."[10]

Mostofi has also suggested that "nationalism [be] taken for what it is—a behavior pattern contemporaneously relevant in that it offers a solution for contemporary problems. . . . As such, nationalism becomes a collective demand motivated by personal predispositions which are the results of environment."[11] To summarize this "new approach," the environment acts as a stimulus and unifying tool through symbolic use to create a collective force of harmonized efforts of individuals who then can be called nationalists, to satisfy demands based on the needs of the individual members of society.[12] This collective force is nationalism conceived as a social force.[13]

Another author speaks of nationalism as "an actual historical process, that of establishing nationalities as political units, of building out of tribes and empires the modern institution of the national state."[14] Hayes was noting here various meanings of the word "nationalism" and added—among other things—that the term also "is to denote a condition of mind among members of a nationality . . . in which loyalty to the idea or fact of one's national state is superior to all other loyalties and of which pride in one's nationality and belief in its intrinsic excellence and its 'mission' are integral parts."[15]

Let us consider the nature of nationalism as a "political force." A fairly recent concept but one of paramount importance is the idea that nationalism itself might be one of the "foundations of power" of any given state. It is quite common today to use the term "nation-state" and thus to use the terms "nation" and "state" interchangeably. Therefore, the term "nation-state" refers not only to the center of political authority but also connotes the power available to that center of authority in all its forms. This *modern* idea is that there is an essential tie between nationalism and the state which emerged in the second half of the eighteenth century. "Its first great manifestation was the French Revolution, which gave the new movement an increased dynamic force."[16] The roots of the idea, of course, can be traced back to what was for thousands of years the basic social institution of mankind, the tribe. "All our societies have in some measure developed from the original tribal pattern and it undoubtedly foreshadows some of the characteristics of our latter-day full-blooded nationalism."[17] Therefore, as a historical movement, nationalism does have roots deep in the past. However, it is sufficient for our purposes here to note only that this emergence depended on interconnected political, economic, cultural, religious and intellectual developments which took place over a long period of time, "and proceeded at a different pace in . . . various countries."[18] Kohn relates this thought to the ideas of popular sovereignty and the rise of the third estate. In this sense, then, his generalization about "various countries" must be interpreted to mean only western Europe. It will be argued below that it is misleading to link all nationalist movements with the middle class, since the middle class did not play significant roles in Turkey, Egypt or subsequently in Iraq.

The French Revolution succeeded in destroying, to a great degree, the monarchy and the traditional social order in France. The destruction was completed by Napoleon, who then extended the Revolution to all of Europe.

> So much turbulence and so much violence from 1789 to 1815 could not fail to have far-reaching consequences. It revived old enmities and created new ones; classes of society which had never dreamt of exercising power tasted of it by proxy, and would never again relapse into obedient tameness; hopes were kindled, passions aroused which were impossible to extinguish.[19]

It is significant to note that Napoleon's policies, even at an early stage, were conducive to the later spread of nationalism. In 1796-97, when General Bonaparte invaded Italy and occupied Venice,

> . . . he sent emissaries to the Ionian Islands, then under Venetian rule . . . to "manufacture manifestos" in order to "to stir up the shades of Sparta and Athens," to raise up the inhabitants against their masters by reminding them of the ancient glories of Greece, and exhorting them to resuscitate these glories."[20]

He continued the same tactics as Emperor when

> . . . he issued a proclamation to the Hungarians saying: "You have national customs and a national language; you boast of a distinct and illustrious origin: take up then once again your existence as a nation. Have a king of your choice, who will rule only for you, who will live in the midst of you, whom only your citizens and your soldiers will serve."[21]

This stirring of nationalist fervor, as released by the Revolution and extended by Napoleon, coupled with the Industrial Revolution with its concomitant transformation of the methods of production which disturbed traditional social relations and created new wealth, prevented the victorious powers from returning to the *status quo ante bellum* in 1815. The age of nationalism in all its dubious glory had arrived.

While the concept of nationalism itself may remain cloudy it is clear that the development of nationalism in the West is a recognizable historical process. For undoubtedly nationalism happened in certain countries, originally in western Europe, and it created a force or mood which became embodied in the "national idea." The "idea" obviously has spread throughout the world as evidenced by the great influx of new "nation-states" admitted to the United Nations since its inception. This organization expanded in a little over two decades from an original fifty nations to a current membership of one hundred and thirty-two sovereign states which are committed to the principle of self-determined nationhood. This process involved, among other things, the secularization of values. In discussing the development of nationalism as a social force in Egypt, Mostofi states:

> Simultaneous with economic decline and subsequent to the establishment of contact with the highly advanced material culture of western Europe, there came a general rise in the material aspirations of the Egyptian people. This change, which indicates the beginning of a transition from a predominantly religious to a predominantly secular culture, was by no means peculiar to Egypt or even to the Middle East. The process began in Europe subsequent to—and partly as a result of—the Crusades and has continued ever since. Ascendence of secular values and their gradual substitution for religious values were, perhaps, the most significant aspect of the Renaissance movement.[22]

The force of this change was the "raised material aspirations of a growing number of the people coupled with a general decline in the economic standards of the country. . . ."[23] When "raised material aspirations" cannot be met, social restlessness, which aims to eliminate the causes of frustration, arises. In this instance, "foreign domination" and the "ruling class" were the subjects of attack by those whose goals were being denied them. The resultant nationalism then became "a social force motivated by earthly—and observable—causes within Egyptian society. This social force is generated by the collective demand of a considerable number of Egyptian people, arising from the personal predispositions of individual Egyptians under the impact of environmental factors."[24] This, then, cannot be considered a metaphysical force, a "breath of life" as envisioned by Kohn.

Another, and perhaps more complicated, example of the forces of nationalism at work is that of German fascism, which represents the concept carried to its extreme limits. This involves the idea of "mass insecurity, induced by the instability of domestic societies and leading to emotional outbursts in the form of fervent mass identifications with aggressive foreign policies and wars."[25] Here three elements combined to produce nationalistic extremes; social disintegration, personal insecurity and modern nationalistic power drives. Various elements of the environment certainly provided the stimulus for action: defeat in World War I, attributed to domestic treachery and foreign enemies; inflation in the early twenties; and the economic crisis of 1929 which threatened the loss of social, moral and economic security. These environmental forces presented fears and frustrations upon which national socialism could easily focus to produce an extreme nationalism. This is not to say that German nationalism did not exist before the rise of national socialism. This example merely serves to illustrate the potential of such a force as nationalism in an already established state. It is not difficult to think of other examples of the force of this idea on other established nation-states. The American Revolution established a government in the United States based on the concept of freedom, not nationalism. Yet, the United States has unquestionably developed a nationalism of its own which would be unrecognizable to a number of its Founding Fathers.

The Russian Revolution of 1917 was based on a universal ideology in which it was believed, at least by Lenin and Trotsky, that the revolution would be unsuccessful unless it spread simultaneously, at least throughout all of Europe, if not world-wide. Stalin's later concept of "socialism in one country" with the passage of time, radically transformed a universal ideology into an "immense patriotic fervor of an older Russian nationalism."[26] This suggests the power and drive of what has become the "most pervasive force of our day."[27]

Pervasive as nationalism may be, we must consider to what end it prevails and what might be the consequences of such a diversified nation-state system. This might be the point to begin arguments for a return to universalism based on some "new" religious or ideological concept, but it will be left for others to renew the attempts already made. It is sufficient at this point to note that

> Europe's ghastly feuds, which we might well call the tribal wars of modern man, have led to a disgust with the extreme forms of nationalism. A new and absorbing struggle is in progress between the old concept of France, of Germany, of Italy, of Holland, and of Belgium as separate, sovereign, absolutely autonomous states and a new concept of supranational communities; a new sense that they must work together if they are to survive.[28]

But what of the Middle East? Has a supranational community already been established there for the fulfillment of material expectations and release of "mass insecurities and mass frustrations" or is this vast area merely entering into the nationalistic phase of its history? Further, and more germane, is the question of whether a new type of nationalism was evolved by an artificial process quite different from the historical development of the idea in the West. Finally, it is also important to consider whether this new nationalism is quite different and distinct from the Arab nationalism which theoretically permeates the life of the Arabs in the Middle East.

* NOTES

[1]Barbara Ward, *Five Ideas That Changed the World* (New York: W.W. Norton and Company, Inc., 1959), p. 42

[2]L. Oppenheim, *International Law: A Treatise*, ed. H. Lauterpacht (New York: David McKay Company, Inc., 1955), I, 118–19.

[3]Elie Kedourie, *Nationalism* (London: Hutchinson and Co. Ltd., 1960), p. 9.

[4] *ibid.*

[5]Karl W. Deutsch, *Nationalism and Social Communication: An Inquiry Into the Foundations of Nationality* (New York: John Wiley & Sons, Inc., 1953), p. 3.

[6]Hans Kohn, *The Idea of Nationalism: A Study in its Origins and Background* (New York: The Macmillan Company, 1961), p. 14.

[7]See Khosrow Mostofi, *Aspects of Nationalism: A Sociology of Colonial Revolt* (Research Monograph No. 3., Salt Lake City: Institute of Government, University of Utah, 1964), pp. 7–13.

[8]Kohn, *op. cit.*, p. 13.

[9]*Ibid.*, p. 16.

[10]Mostofi, *op. cit.*, p. 8.

[11]*Ibid.*, p. 14.

[12]The environment includes territory, language, material culture, spiritual culture and history.

[13]Mostofi, *op. cit.*, p. 15. See also Appendix.

[14]Carlton J.H. Hayes, *Essays on Nationalism* (New York: The Macmillan Company, 1928), p. 5–6.

[15]*Ibid.*

[16]Kohn, *op. cit.*, p. 3.

[17]Ward, *op. cit.*, p. 15.

[18]Kohn, *op. cit.*, p. 3.

[19]Kedourie, *op. cit.*, p. 92.

[20]*Ibid.*, p. 94.

[21]Mostofi, *op. cit.*, p. 17.

[22]Mostofi, *op. cit.*, p. 17.

[23]*Ibid.*

[24]*Ibid.*, p. 18.

[25]Hans J. Morgenthau, *Politics and Nations: The Struggle for Power and Peace* (4th ed., New York: Alfred A. Knopf, 1967), p. 102.

[26]Ward, *op. cit.*, p. 27.

[27]*Ibid.*

[28]*Ibid.*

CHAPTER 3
NATIONALISM AND POWER IN THE ARAB WORLD

"The Arabs are haunted by their history."

—Tütsch

Any attempt to define Arab nationalism and to delineate the relationships between the concept of nationalism itself and the exercise of power in the Arab world presents innumerable difficulties. For, as Tütsch has noted, "Arab nationalism means different things to different groups; it is by no means a simple movement."[1] The problems include a determination of (1) the genesis of Arab nationalism; (2) the factors or elements which constitute or make up the idea of Arab nationalism; (3) the import of foreign influences or external factors; (4) the systems of power developed by the contemporary and secular nation states; and (5) the principal forms of nationalism that have emerged in the area. Before any specific discussion of these problems as they relate to Iraq—a task undertaken in Part II of this study—some attention should be given to Arab nationalism in general.

There are three main sources usually cited as being the roots of contemporary Arab nationalism. These correspond to three principal periods of Arab history. The first is the pre-Islamic era, which came to a close in the seventh century. This period includes the early development and division of the Semitic races, the emergence of two highly developed civilizations in South and North Arabia which, according to some historians, were related to one another even though the existence of such an affinity is not generally recognized. This is the most important period of *al-jahilijah,* or "the state of ignorance." The term ignorance, it should be noted, "does not mean 'ignorance' as much as 'wildness' and its antithesis is not *ilm* ('knowledge') but rather *hilm* ('temperance')."[2] The importance of this period insofar as Arab national development is concerned is that it represents the era during which the Arabs struggled for survival in an inhospitable environment. From this struggle developed a bond of *asabiyah,* or solidarity, in a communal sense. Their new solidarity, plus a consciousness of race and a common language, resulted in at least a semblance of national consciousness.

> The poems, the proverbs, the traditions, the legends and mythologies, expressed in spoken literature and transmitted by oral tradition, greatly influenced the development of an Arab national consciousness; they molded the minds of the Arabs, fixed their character, and made them morally and spiritually a nation long before Muhammad welded the various conflicting groups into a single organism animated by one purpose.[3]

There is a reluctance to designate the early pre-Islamic period as one of Arab nationalism because of "the primacy of tribal affinities and loyalties," but it did assume "a distinct and effective character when the Arabs began to carry the message of Islam."[4] The advent of Islam, then, marks the second and more important period.

Islam is, of course, first and foremost a religion. It has such a body of doctrines and beliefs which are centered on the principle of *ummah,* or community. Hence, there exists a possible foundation for the concept of Arab unity. As a religion, however, it teaches that Allah (God) is an ultimate spiritual basis of all life and is universal in application. Further, as

> Ibn 'Umar has said: Islam is built upon five things: on confessing that there is no deity save *Allah,* performing prayers (*salāt*), giving the legal alms (*zakāt*), going on

pilgrimage to the House (i.e., the Kaba at Mecca), and fasting during . . . *Ramadān*. Thus did the apostle of Allah hand it on to us, but beyond that there is holy war (*jihād*), which is an excellent thing.[5]

Islam is considered as meaning basically surrender to the will of Allah.

As a creed with a message for all mankind, Islam could well be viewed as "unequivocally hostile to the sort of divisive contentions that are an endemic feature of nationalism."[6] However, Islam came to mean much more than a doctrine or belief. Within a very short span of time it became a polity—an Islamic community which embraced the greater part of the then (seventh century, A.D.) known world. The Islamic period of conquest and expansion is long and complex and no attempt will be made here to outline this period of history. However, it is essential to note the forces which can be referred to as being an influence upon modern Arab nationalism.

In the process of conquest and expansion, the Islamic movement achieved unification of the Arabs for the first time in their history. Whether this expansion was a result of Semitic migration or economic pressures is not at issue here, but the fact of accomplishment, i.e., unification, is of paramount importance. It cannot be denied that Islam provided a unifying factor and without its dynamic leadership, the movement very likely would not have succeeded. Originally, then, based on common goals, a unifying process overcame conflicting tribal loyalties, and the terms Arabic unity and Islamic unity became synonymous. "The first contribution of Islam . . . was the nationalization of Arab life within the fraternity of the Muslim community."[7]

Within the context of an Islamic community was born a nation. It was relatively easy to progress to the status of an organized state. Ideologically, for Islam, this was no problem. The state, for a Muslim, provides the means whereby each individual is governed in his everyday affairs. This involves the Muslim conception of law which is much more comprehensive than it is in the modern Western world. "The state, from the Islamic standpoint, is the means whereby the Islamic concepts of life are realized in a definite human organization. The ultimate reality . . . is spiritual, but the life of the state consists in its temporal activity."[8] In its complex structure, Islam embraces all phases of daily life, giving rules for behavior, organizing social arrangements through religiously sanctioned law (the *Shari'a*), thus demonstrating the ideal for mankind. "A division of religion and politics, of religion and science, or religion and law remains unthinkable as long as Islam is a living force, as long as Islam operates as the single, exclusive motivating force of its creation."[9]

From a sound ideological basis, it was a relatively easy step to centralization of authority and development of a bureaucratic structure to administer the edicts of the Caliphs in power. The period of conquest was brief and extensive: Following Muhammad's death in 632, the sword of Islam conquered Syria and Iraq in A.D. 633-37; Egypt fell in A.D. 629-42;[10] and an Arab Kingdom was established in A.D. 661 with seizure of power by the first Umayyad, Mu'āwiya. This was an important landmark for the theory of Arab nationalism. It marked the transformation from an Islamic theocracy under the first four Caliphs (632–661) to what in the eyes of historians was no more than a monarchy, an Arab Secular State, even though officially the title remained Caliph and the institutions were Islamic. The process of centralization began with the transfer of the seat of government to Damascus where it remained until the accession of the House of Abbas in A.D. 750. Later Arab historians noted this process of secularization when they spoke of the "Kingship (*Mulk*) of Mu'āwiya and the rest of the Umayyads with the sole exception of the pious 'Umar II (717–720), who alone is granted the title of Caliph."[11] It was on this foundation that the new rulers sought cohesion of an Empire:

> The new moral bond which was to replace the lost religious bond was fashioned from the loyalty of the Arab nation to its secular head. The sovereignty exercised by Mu'awiya was essentially Arab.[12]

Islam, in the process of conquest, expansion and development, therefore, created first a community based on solidarity and then established a state based on loyalty. The Islamic episode did even more, however, because it developed a legacy to which modern nationalists repeatedly appeal in support of their theories. It is of interest that this legacy includes other nationalities as power changed hands among the Arabs, Persians, and Turks in subsequent dynastic conflicts. In other words, the historical legacy for the

modern Arab includes the Muhammadan period, (622–32), the era
of the four Orthodox Caliphs of Medina (632–61), the Umayyads of
Damascus (661–750), the Abbasid period of Baghdad (750–1258),
the Abbasid and Fatimid period of Cairo (750–1517), as well as the
period of the Umayyads and their successors in Spain (750–1492).
This historical legacy does not end in fact until the Ottoman
conquest in 1517. These are all a part of the heritage of the modern
Arab nationalist.

> The attitude of an Arab nationalist is that the entire legacy of
> Islam, insofar as it was expressed in Arabic and arose in an
> Arab Milieu, is his heritage. He makes no distinction between
> the philosopher Al-Kindi, a pure-blooded Arab, and Al-
> Farabi, of Turkish stock, or betwen them and Ibn Sina of
> Persian stock. All contributed to a common culture.[13]

Unquestionably, the Arab-Islamic legacy provides a source of
strength, a sense of usefulness in a historical context, and a
psychological basis for modern Arab nationalism.

However well Arab nationalism may have progressed in the first
two periods discussed above, it regressed and lay dormant for many
centuries. "By the eleventh century the world of Islam was in a
state of manifest decay."[14] Economic decline, lavish extravagance
of the court, an inflated, corrupt bureaucracy, an inequitable tax
system, and a series of onslaughts by internal and external forces
revealed the weakness of the Empire. "The Christian Crusades and
the Counter-Crusade further revealed the weaknesses and strengths
of a dying Empire."[15] In addition to the Crusaders, another wave of
invaders came from Central Asia—the Turks; and finally the most
dangerous threat of all arose from far away Eastern Asia when the
Mongol hordes began their destructive move westward, culminating
in the destruction of Baghdad in A.D. 1258.

> On February 13, 1258, Hulagu and his troops entered
> Baghdad, and began forty days of pillage and massacre;
> 800,000 of the inhabitants, we are told, were killed.
> Thousands of scholars, scientists, and poets fell in the
> indiscriminate slaughter; libraries and treasures accumulated
> through centuries were in a week plundered or destroyed;
> hundreds of thousands of volumes were consumed. Finally the

Caliph and his family, after being forced to reveal the hiding place of their secret wealth, were put to death. So ended the Abbasid caliphate.[16]

The long-lasting period of stagnation, however, was revived under the stimulus of Western influence. Contact with Western Europe was not entirely extinct through the decadent years. Trade and commerce, especially during the sixteenth century, opened Arab lands to penetration by the French, English, and Italians. The greatest change, however, came with the invasion and occupation of Egypt in 1798 by Napoleon Bonaparte. This ushered in the third period of our discussion, that of the so-called modern Arab nationalism.

The brief Napoleonic episode ended in the future Emperor's defeat at Alexandria in 1801 and resulted in the evacuation of French troops from Egypt. The aftermath of the expedition, however, had grave consequences. Europe's attention was again directed toward "the somewhat forgotten land route to India and set in motion a chain reaction which made the Near East the storm centre of European intrigue and diplomacy."[17] The immediate result of this threat from abroad

. . . was the general Arab awakening which it kindled. . . . A second result . . . was the introduction of the printing press, which gave impetus to the revival of Arabic classics and culture and hence to national consciousness. A third result was the introduction of the European idea of nationality.[18]

This view of the origin of modern Arab nationalism is shared by other writers and much of the credit is attributed to the efforts of Muhammad Ali, an Ottoman soldier of Albanian origin, who successfully installed himself as the virtually independent ruler of Egypt following the defeat of Napoleon. Muhammad Ali's economic and educational reforms stimulated this idea of a national consciousness. This consciousness is alleged to have extended beyond the confines of Egypt because his expeditions extended into Syria. Although the ambitious Muhammad Ali had obtained rule over Egypt, Central Arabia, Syria and even the Sudan by 1840, "his, nonetheless, was not essentially an Arab nationalist movement. National consciousness and nationalist sentiment for independence and unity were still feeble, if not entirely lacking."[19] This episode is perhaps more appropriately described as being a decisive phase in the decline of the once great Ottoman Empire. In this respect, the process of detaching Arab provinces from the central authority of the Sultan in the Sublime Porte had been set in motion. This process of dismemberment was to be a continuous one precipitated primarily by British and French intervention. This culminated in the collapse of the Ottoman Empire at the end of World War I and resulted in the introduction of the Multiple-Mandates System.[20]

> Divisive European regimes replaced the unified Ottoman regime; and even the Arab domains which had remained under Ottoman rule during the Nineteenth and Twentieth Centuries, and had continued to live under one political system, were now fragmented into a mosaic of political entities.[21]

George Antonius in his thorough study of the modern Arab world holds that "The story of the Arab national movement opens in Syria in 1847, with the foundation in Beirut of a modest literary society under American patronage."[22] Antonius dismisses the attempts of Muhammad Ali and his supporters as motivated more by personal ambition to acquire an empire rather than a bid to create a national Arab movement. In fact, he maintains that the lack of an Arab national consciousness was a negative factor which led, in part, to Ali's failure to create his empire.[23] The start, in Antonius' view, was founded on the religious and educational efforts of American and French missionaries who influenced the formation of the aforementioned society. This involved the activities of two Christian Arabs, Nasil Yaseji (d. 1871) and Butrus Bustani (d. 1883), whose teaching and literary output instigated the formation of many learned societies. The most notable of these was formed in 1847 in Beirut, under the name of the *Society of Arts and Sciences*. The importance of this event is described by Antonius:

> Within two years of its foundation, the Society had fifty members, of which the majority were Christian Syrians domiciled in Beirut. There was no Moslem or Druze membership. It had a modest but useful library, of which Yaseji was librarian. The secretary was Bustani. Meetings of

the Society at which papers would be read by one or other of the members were held once a fortnight at first, and less frequently as time went on. . . .

This was the first society of its kind ever established in Syria or in any other part of the Arab world. The idea of promoting knowledge by an organized collective effort was foreign to the individualistic nature of the Arab whose method of approaching higher learning was akin to that of Plato's Greece, ... But it turned out to be a fruitful innovation. Other societies were formed after its pattern, which were to play an important part in the growth of the Arab national movement.[24]

One of these societies, the *Syrian Scientific Society* which was founded in 1857, included leading Arab personalities of *all* creeds. It followed the objectives, methods and even statutes of its predecessor. It survived the religious massacres of 1860 and operated on an even wider scale, expanding its membership even to Constantinople and Cairo. Antonius comments:

For the first time, probably in the history of Syria, certainly for the first time in the 350 years of Ottoman domination, a common ideal had brought the warring creeds together and united them in an active partnership for a common end. An interest in the progress of the country as a national unit was now their incentive, a pride in the Arab inheritance their bond. The foundation of the Society was the first outward manifestation of a collective national consciousness and its importance in history is that it was the cradle of a new political movement.[25]

The success of these societies would not have been possible without the introduction and expanded use of the printing press. Although the Turks had begun printing in Constantinople in 1729, it was Napoleon who brought the Arabic press with him to Cairo. Muhammad Ali established the first Moslem printing press in the Arab world. The religious missionary rivals of France and America also took full advantage of the press.

Mission-educated Syrian Christians established newspapers and periodicals in Egypt as well as Syria, and reached a wider public as more and more of the population were affected by economic and social change. It was in this period that Arab nationalism was born.[26]

A number of factors contributed to this emergence of the thought of "Arab nationalism" at this particular time. They were Arab dislike and distrust of Turkish rule, the introduction of the European idea of nationality, a revival and spread of the Arab language and culture through the use of the printing press, and of equal if not greater importance—the coming of direct foreign control; at first it was control by the French in Algeria (1830), later by the British in Aden (1839), and then the British in Egypt, the very heart of the Arab world (1882). "The occupation led to an intensive development of the nationalist movement in Egypt."[27] Of great significance is the fact that these nineteenth century nationalist movements within the Arab world were initiated and originally sustained by Christian Arabs, based mostly on economic change and under Western cultural influence. The nationalist movement was then expressed in political rather than religious terms—it had become secularized. This is not to say that the old religious forms of social expression had disappeared. Perhaps the most notable example of this is the re-emergence of the revivalist *Wahhabi* movement which eventually resulted in the creation of the new kingdom of Sa'udi Arabia.

Arab disaffection with Turkish rule received further impetus directed toward their own concept of nationalism by the emergence of a Turkish nationalist movement which progressed under the banner of Pan-Turanianism. This movement also began as a secret association called the Committee of Union and Progress. The leaders, or the so-called Young Turks, originally shared with the Arab movement one thing in common—a hatred for the ruling Ottoman despot of the moment, Abdul-Hamid (1876–1908). The revolution against Hamidian despotism was successful on July 24, 1908, and the Young Turks assumed control, temporarily at least, of the Ottoman Empire. The Turco-Arab honeymoon, however, was short-lived and regionalism based on different races and cultures soon overcame aspirations for an Ottoman-Arab fraternity. This was not the only problem which faced the new regime.

It might be said in fairness to the Young Turks that the legacy they inherited from the Hamidian regime was not only damnable in itself; they had come into it at a particularly inauspicious moment. The separatist forces at work in the Balkan provinces were in the ascendant, the covetousness of two European Powers lurked menacingly behind a thin diplomatic veil, and a series of disasters occurred before the Young Turks had had time to prove their worth: the annexation by Austria-Hungary of Boznia and Herzegovina in October, 1908, the simultaneous secession of Bulgaria, Italy's aggression in Libya in the Autumn of 1911 and the Balkan War of 1912. In these few years, the Ottoman Empire lost all its provinces in Europe.[28]

World War I completed the dismemberment of the Ottoman Empire.

Arab nationalism has emerged, then, from a pre-Islamic, an Islamic, and a modern basis in the sense that modern Arab nationalists call on all of these sources to explain, justify or defend their idea of a substantial, recognizable movement which permeates the life of the Arab world and motivates its behavior today. From this concept of Arab nationalism then derives the idea of Arab unity which is based primarily on a community of language, race and consciousness, history, and culture within a certain territorial configuration, all resulting from the unity of religion.

The importance of the Arabic language in the legacy of the Arab world is unquestionable.

> For many centuries in the Middle Ages it was the language of learning and culture and progressive thought throughout the civilized world. Between the ninth and twelfth centuries more works, philosophical, medical, historical, religious, astronomical and geographical, were produced through the medium of Arabic than through any other tongue. The languages of Western Europe still bear the impress of its influence in the form of numerous loan-words. Its alphabet, next to Latin, is the most widely used system in the world.[29]

Today the Arabic language is generally thought of as the medium of expression of some hundred million people. This is rather misleading, however, as such a reference applies only to the so-called classic Arabic of the Qu'ran. Further, this classic language during the period of Turkish domination was known only to the literate, a small minority, while a great variety of dialects developed throughout the entire area. Even today, by their own admission, an Egyptian Arab has difficulty in making himself understood in Morocco, for example. In addition to this, many Muslim minorities have never accepted Arabic as their language, notably the Turkomans, the Armenians and the Indo-European Kurds.

The importance of language as a factor in developing a national consciousness is well recognized and the above-mentioned disparities have been an inhibiting element in the aspirations of modern-day nationalists. The spoken word characteristically impresses the Arab mind to a much greater degree than is commonly understood in the West. Resonant speech has an almost unreal power which may conquer, in the Arab mind at least, the greatest of practical realities. "Beautifully turned words put an Arab into ecstasy; words are taken for the full reality. Western reality is based on facts, Arab reality may be based on words alone."[30]

Language, specifically the Arabic of the Qu'ran, has had a pronounced unifying effect and yet in its daily usage it has tended to localize, to give a feeling of community. Thus, at least insofar as local dialects are concerned, language has had some divisive influence on Arab nationalism.

A consciousness of race is much more difficult to defend in support of modern Arab nationalism. According to Arab genealogists, the Arabs supposedly have followed two separate lines of descent from Shem, the son of Noah. These two Semitic races were early divided between the North and South of Arabia and differed considerably in their character and way of life.[31] Historical expansionism, especially during the Islamic era, created an admixture of laws in the various parts of the Empire, so that the consciousness of racial heritage is predominantly regional, if not local.

Historical consciousness is not a sound basis for Arab nationalism when the modern nationalist must continuously look backward to the glorious times of the Prophet and the Umayyad and Abbasid Empires and must disregard the dissensions after the eighth century and the period of decay of the Arab Empire. In other words, despite the unifying effects of the Arabic language and culture noted above, the fact is that unified Arab Empires have existed only on the basis of Islamic solidarity, which has long since ceased to exist. Consequently, the Arabs are dominated by a distant past which must be stretched to modern times in any new attempt toward Arab solidarity. Further,

> Few attempts have been made by Arab historians to set the Arab past in world-wide perspective. It is mythologized or warped for political purposes. . . . Reading Arab political writers . . . one has to remind oneself time and again that history is not exclusively a continuous set of personal intrigues and conspiracies. The personalization of history clouds the real issues and hides the battles of ideas going on everywhere in the world.[32]

It thus follows that historical consciousness as an element of Arab nationalism is on solid grounds solely when this is based on Islamic unity. Since this unity has ceased to exist, and, what is even more significant, since modern nationalism is essentially a secular movement and secularization is the current trend in the Arab world, it is difficult to speak of a Pan-Arab nationalism in absence of its obvious religious foundations.[33]

This introduces the third major feature of this chapter: the impact of Western culture and political-economic influences. It is often maintained that modern Arab nationalism was born as a result of ideas imported from the West, that these ideas originated primarily in French political thought of the eighteenth century and that their introduction into the region dated from the Napoleonic invasion of 1798. However, since this time, nationalist movements, with the exception of Pan-Islamic movements (*Wahhabism*, the Muslim Brotherhood and the attempts of Jamal ed-Din al-Afghani and Muhammad 'Abdu),[34] have been particularized and centered in the modern nation-state system. For example, the Pan-Turanianism movement of the Young Turks was eventually limited in its scope and with the coming of Ataturk was completely abandoned in favor of modern Turkish nationalism.

Arab nationalism which would embrace all of the Arab world in its ambitions is not logical, especially, if as claimed, it is based on Western ideas. The impact of the West has been nothing less than divisive. Western technology, economic competition, and cultural penetration all contributed more to particularization than to a politically and socially unified Arab world. This is not to discount the great influence that the activities of the British and French had in helping the growth of the feelings of Arab nationalism, in revolt against colonization of foreign control after World War I. In the practical struggle for independence, the political objectives of the Arab nationalists were necessarily limited to the country within which they operated. Egyptian nationalists attained formal independence from Great Britain. Syrian nationalists attained freedom from French rule. And an independent Iraq was established through the efforts of Iraqi nationalists.

In the struggle for political control which followed the termination of direct European domination of the Arab world, four systems of power can be differentiated: the patriarchal system, the "palace" system, the multiparty system, and the single party system.[35]

Under the patriarchal system, best exemplified by Sau'dia Arabia and Kuwait, the head of state is simultaneously the head of the community in which family ties, personal loyalties and strict adherence to the Shari'a and tradition are rigidly enforced. Strong central control through loyal relatives in key administrative positions precludes independent legislation. The subjects of the ruler have no individual rights and, in fact, "the ruler and his family do not merely dominate the state, but in a very real sense own it."[36]

We will consider the "palace" system at some length in our discussion of Iraq. However, it should be noted that this system also evolved in Egypt and is the current method of control in Jordan. Here power is wielded by a king directly within a form of constitutional monarchy. These have not been limited constitutional monarchies in the British sense, because the king has always exercised more control than is authorized in the constitution. This includes manipulation or pressure to influence the outcome of elections followed by domination of the elected parliament. Rather than being based on family, the ruling group in this system is composed of the privileged class comprised primarily of large land-owners, big merchants, the old established families and traditionalist elements committed to the preservation of the *status quo*. This group is reinforced by their claim of religious legitimacy.[37] The Hashemites of Jordan and their relatives formerly ruling in Iraq based their claim to authority on their descent from the Prophet Muhammad's family.

In this system of power, the army, as the principal instrument of political control, plays a significant role. This is not new in the Middle East, since "the original propagation of Islam was largely due to the employment of military force. Moreover, this method was used by the Prophet Muhammad. . . . This point is surely of essential importance."[38] The result has been the development and general acceptance of authoritarian forms of government which rely more on the loyalty of the army than on the consent of the people. Conversely, the army has provided the main source of opposition to the rulers in the "palace." In this respect it is essential to understand "that when a military dictator assumes control of an Arab country, he does not necessarily do so against the will of a public, who are yearning for democratic institutions."[39] This thought is a dream of Western statesmen. The duty of the ruler in a Muslim country in the eyes of the Islamic faithful is to govern in accordance with Muslim law and failure to do so can result in overthrow by the use of force. In a sense, then, "the army becomes the guardian of the nation's morals."[40] The army is more than an instrument of external defense in the traditional Arab state. It is employed in and is a part of Arab internal politics.

Multiple political party systems have been attempted under parliamentary monarchical regimes, but have been relatively successful only in Lebanon and Syria. In both of these countries, groups and parties formed around the parliamentary systems during the mandates period, but with the coming of independence, power became concentrated within the presidential and parliamentary blocs.

> In both countries the parliamentary blocs represented feudal and semi-feudal families, the big merchants, and the urban rich. As political parties, they had no firm popular base, nor any clear political doctrine or program; they constituted the so-called "bloc" parties, i.e., parliamentary groups whose principal concern is sectional, group, and individual interest these are distinguished from "mass" or "doctrinal" parties, which are ideological, national organization with rigid party discipline aiming at mass recruitment.[41]

In order to maintain themselves in power, those in the presidential bloc, especially in Lebanon, attempted to maintain their balance between the competing parliamentary groups.

The single-party system of power is characterized by personalized leadership and monopoly of power by the single party. Egypt, Syria and Iraq have experienced this phenomenon. Here constitutional powers are often exceeded by the leadership; this is accepted by the masses because of the charismatic appeal of the highly personalized leadership. This system is relatively successful in retaining power if the ruling elite establishes legitimacy through a political party on a constitutional basis. Failing this, it is essential to fall back on the coercive power of the army to maintain power. And even here it is possible to revert to a position where factions within the army may eventually overthrow the regime. It should be noted that

> The strongest feature of the single-party system is that government centralization and a leadership with charismatic appeal have instituted revolutionary social reform and economic development. It is the single-party regime that has come to symbolize the revolutionary wave in the Arab world.[42]

This power system has dominated Iraq, as will be seen, following the overthrow of the traditional "palace" system in 1958. However, contrary to the social and economic development implied above, regression may occur under this type of political power system.

As mentioned at the beginning of this chapter, Arab nationalism means different things, and, in fact, it can be said to have taken three distinct forms. First of all, it takes form as a uniform movement throughout the Arab world with the single goal of Arab unity. This concept of Arab nationalism "originates from the feeling, widespread in the Arab world, of belonging together, of being part of a great community held together by common language, history, law and religion, in short of a cultural unit, the Arab nation."[43] It is assumed here that the Arab nation has existed since at least the time of Muhammad, if not earlier, and the unity that once existed has been projected into the present and future. This study suggests that the continuous existence of an Arab nation is purely mythical and without foundation in fact. This study is based on the arguments suggested above against the unifying ingredients of language, history, and culture. This is not to discount the mystique and appeal of such an idea, since the concept is "so strong that all Arab leaders have to pay public homage to it—even when they are working against it."[44] Arab nationalism mythologizes Arab unity.

A second possible form for Arab nationalism is regional nationalism which would unite several "artificial" Arab states into regional groupings. The idea is not new and has as its basis both historical economic interaction and dynastic aspirations. Four well-defined regions which have historical similarities and common interests and which would lend themselves to this form of nationalism are:

(1) The Fertile Crescent with Iraq, Syria, Jordan, Lebanon, and, if the Arabs had their way, that part of Palestine which has become the state of Israel;[45]

(2) The Arabian Peninsula with Yemen, Saudia Arabia, Kuwait, and the dependent coastal principalities of the Persian Gulf;

(3) The Nile Valley with Egypt and Sudan;

(4) The Maghreb with Libya, Tunisia, Algeria, Morocco, and Mauretania (not included as a part of this study).

The desirability of regional plans gave way to practical realities realized in local nationalism, the third form considered above. This seems to indicate that among the three, local nationalism has emerged as the dominant type which makes it the most dynamic political and social force in the area.

Egyptian nationalism is the paramount example of what is meant here by local nationalism. And here nationalism is held to be "a collective demand motivated by personal predispositions which are the results of environment."[46] In spite of attempts of unification on a regional basis, first with Syria, then Iraq, including co-operation in the fields of economies, education and defense, the drive for unity has collapsed each time. Military exploits on a joint basis in the war against Israel have been less than successful. Historical fact contradicts President Nasser when he states:

In 1956 we saw how the entire Arab nation stood with us. This is the nature of the authentic Arab people. In every Arab country there is an authentic people. All the conspiracies and forces of imperialism and reaction have not been able to divide them. They cut up the Arab nation into small states and establish border lines, but the Arab people are one. Every Arab feels that what happens in any Arab country is related to him and affects him.[47]

Egypt, or the United Arab Republic as the country is officially known since its ill-fated union with Syria in 1958, is the strongest Arab state. Modern Egyptian nationalism, as noted before, originated in the events of 1798–1801. The rise of Muhammad Ali to power, the reform measures introduced during his long reign (1805–41) and the country's virtual independence from the Ottoman Empire created a favorable atmosphere for the growth of a feeling of national consciousness which began to develop under the combined influences of Islamic culture and the glorious heritage of Ancient Egypt. The latter, long forgotten and virtually unknown at the time, was revealed to the world subsequent to the discovery of the Rosetta Stone which resulted in the foundation of a new science, Egyptology, by 1820. These remarkable developments, followed by the international events which surrounded the construction of the Suez Canal (1831–69; 1875–82) further strengthened the cause of nationalism both through increased cultural contacts with the West and a negative reaction to imperial policies of England and France. The latter, reaction to colonialism, solidified the feeling of nationalism and by 1882, when Egypt had fallen under the full economic, political and military domination of Great Britain, the battle cry of the nationalists became "Egypt for Egyptians" which would have had little or no meaning in previous decades. President Nasser's exhortations notwithstanding, particularism, inherent in the European conception of "the nation," actually began to prevail over Pan-Arab nationalism at least as early as 1882 if not earlier.[48]

Arab unification in the form of a confederation, a federation, or a complete union has been and remains the explicitly expressed goal of President Nasser, whose attempts for this purpose have met with failure in the face of localized interests. While Nasser's drive for Arab unity continued to mark Egyptian foreign policy, the individual Arab countries to which he appealed have pursued their own separate courses with little or no response to this appeal. Consequently, the drive for unity resulted in the clash of interests in which "the main struggle in the Arab world takes place between Gamal Abdel Nasser and his adherents on one side and the local nationalists in a dozen Arab countries on the other side."[49]

Although Egyptian nationalism is the paramount example of local nationalism, it is with the development of Iraqi nationalism, the struggle for power and its consequences in that country which must now be discussed.

NOTES

[1]Hans E: Tütsch, *Facets of Arab Nationalism* (Detroit: Wayne State University Press, 1965), p. 31.

[2]Hazem Zaki Nuseibeh, *The Ideas of Arab Nationalism* (New York: Cornell University Press, 1956), p. 4.

[3]*Ibid.*, p. 13.

[4]Munif al-Razzaz, *The Evolution of the Meaning of Nationalism*, trans. Ibrahim Abu-Lughad (New York: Doubleday and Company, Inc., 1963), p. 11.

[5]Arthur Jeffery, *Islam: Muhammad and His Religion* (New York: The Liberal Arts Press, 1958), p. 81.

[6]Nuseibeh, *op. cit.*, pp. 18–19.

[7]*Ibid.*, p. 21.

[8]*Ibid.*, p. 23.

[9]Tutsch, *op. cit.*, p. 33.

[10]It should be noted that Islamic conquest reached beyond the areas mentioned to include nearly all of non-Arab Persia to the East, and across Africa, exending into Spain up to and beyond the borders of modern France.

[11]Bernard Lewis, *The Arabs in History* (New York: Harper & Row, 1960), p. 65.

[12]*Ibid.*

[13]Nuseibeh, *op. cit.*, p. 29.

[14]Lewis, *op. cit.*, p. 144.

[15]See Aziz S. Atiya, *Crusade, Commerce and Culture* (Bloomington: Indiana University Press, 1962).

[16]Will Durant, *The Age of Faith* (New York: Simon and Schuster, 1950), p. 340.

[17]Philip K. Hitti, *History of the Arabs* (New York: St. Martin's Press, 1967), p. 722.

[18]Nuseibeh, *op. cit.*, p. 35.

[19]Fayez A. Sayegh, *Arab Unity: Hope and Fulfillment* (New York: The Devin-Adair Company, 1958), pp. 25–26.

[20]The effect of this division as it relates to Iraq will be discussed in Part II, below.

[21]Sayegh, *op. cit.*, p. 28.

[22]George Antonius, *The Arab Awakening* (London: Hamish Hamilton, 1938), p. 13.

[23]*Ibid.*, pp. 51–52.

[24]*Ibid.*

[25]*Ibid.*

[26]Lewis, *op. cit.*, p. 173.

[27]*Ibid.*

[28]Antonius, *op. cit.*, p. 105.

[29]Hitti, *op. cit.*, p. 4. Note: The process of Arabization worked everywhere during the early conquests except in Persia. This exception is attributed to the advanced civilization of that country, the rich literary heritage of the Persians, and the use of the Persian language and administrative system in the conduct of Arab imperial affairs. See Edward G. Browne, *A Literary History of Persia* (Cambridge: The University Press, 1956). Kurds, of course, are descendants of Medes, and hence may, too, fall under this exception. The Turks were converted too late to be Arabized.

[30]Tütsch, *op. cit.*, p. 37.

[31]Nuseibeh, *op. cit.*, p. 11.

[32]Tütsch, *op. cit.*, p. 45.

[33]*Ibid.*, p. 49.

[34]See Edward G. Browne, *The Persian Revolution of 1905–1909* (Cambridge: The University Press, 1910) for a full discussion of the doctrine of nationalism as seen by al-Afghani. See also a critique of the life and works of Afghani and 'Abdu in Elie Kedourie, *Afghani and 'Abduh* (London: Frank Cass Co., Ltd., 1966).

[35]Hisham Sharabi, *Nationalism and Revolution in the Arab World* (Princeton: D. Van Nostrand Company, Inc., 1966), p. 47.

[36]*Ibid.*, p. 48.

[37]*Ibid.*, p. 49.

[38]Sir John Bagot Glubb, "The Role of the Army in the Traditional Arab State," *Modernization of the Arab World*, ed. Jack H. Thompson and Robert D. Reischauer (Princeton: D. Van Nostrand Company, Inc., 1966), p. 54.

[39]*Ibid.*, p. 56.

[40]*Ibid.*

[41]Sharabi, *op. cit.*, pp. 50–51.

[42]*Ibid.*, p. 54.

[43]Tütsch, *op. cit.*, p. 77.

[44]*Ibid.*

[45]The Fertile Crescent or Greater Syria Plan was advanced by Iraqi leaders prior to 1958 and is discussed in Part II. See Appendix C.

[46]Khosrow Mostofi, *Aspects of Nationalism: A Sociology of Colonial Revolt* (Research Monograph No. 3, Salt Lake City: Institute of Government, University of Utah, 1964), p. 14.

[47]Address by President Nasser of the United Arab Republic on the Third Anniversary of the Beginning of the Construction of the High Dam at Aswan (Excerpts), *Arab Political Documents*, ed. Walid Khalidi and Usuf Ibish (Beirut: Political Studies and Public Administration Department of the American University, 1963), p. 7.

[48]Tütsch, *op. cit.*, p. 117.

[49]*Ibid.*, p. 124.

PART II
IRAQ

CHAPTER 4
IRAQ
A HISTORICAL SURVEY

Iraq was one of the earliest known centers of civilization in the world and its ancient history dates back to the fourth millenium B.C. There was a progression of societies based primarily on irrigation and agriculture. These included the Sumerians, who were conquered by the Akkadians, who gave way to the Elamites. Under one of the greatest kings of antiquity, Hammurabi, Iraq attained a high degree of splendor.[1] This, in turn gave way before new invaders from the north and the east; chief among these were the Kassites. Subsequent conquerors included the Mitannians, the Hittites of Asia Minor, and the war-like Assyrians. This relentless, cruel chain of events eventually gave way to Persian domination which made Iraq one of the Imperial provinces and a buffer zone between Persian and Roman empires. The land finally became an arena for prolonged warfare between Byzantium and Persia, who were to exhaust themselves to the point of being unable to meet the formidable danger which was to come from the south.[2]

Arabic Conquest

The religious and political organization that Muhammad developed at Mecca and Medina aroused and released in Arabia powerful latent forces which sought outlets in neighboring territories.

The death of Muhammad on June 8, 632 created several problems, not the least of which was the question of who was to be his successor. Competition and conflict arose and contending groups quickly developed. The major parties involved were the so-called "companions" of the Prophet, which included the Kuraish emigrants who accompanied Muhammad on the *hijra* (immigration) to Medina and those Medinese supporters or helpers (*Ansar*) who gave the emigrants asylum. The former maintained "the right of succession on the basis of blood kinship and priority in belief."[3] While later, the Medinese supported the claim of Ali, Muhammad's paternal cousin and husband of the Prophet's only surviving daughter, Fatimah. They further contended that the line of succession should then continue to Ali's sons by Fatimah, Hasan and Husayn, thereby establishing the germ of hereditary rule.[4]

The first group argued successfully, or rather it persuasively executed, "a kind of coup d'etat"[5] which installed the first of the so-called orthodox caliphs (from *Khalifat Rasul Allah*—successor of the apostle of God, a name frequently used to describe the first caliph, Abu Bakr).[6] The orthodox phase included the first four caliphs, Abu Bakr (632–634); Umar (634–644); Uthman (644–656); and Ali (656–661). The Orthodox phase is considered the patriarchal stage of the caliphate, during which time Muhammad's life and teachings continued to influence the thoughts and actions of the four caliphs.

Following a period of internal conflict when Abu Bakr was compelled to "reconvert" or to militarily subjugate Arabian dissidents, the age of Islamic conquests proceeded, primarily under Umar. The sword of Islam was extended from Arabia eastward to penetrate India and westward to conquer North Africa and Spain. The first move toward the north from central Arabia began with raiding parties; but as the raids became more successful, and the plunders more lucrative, the scope of military operations began to expand. Once the lines of communication lengthened, major decisions and initiative were necessarily left with the field commanders and conquest of neighboring lands became inevitable.

Excursions into Syria, Palestine, Egypt and Iran were conducted almost simultaneously and, strange as it may seem, with no particular master plan for such an invasion. The conquest of Iraq, then a part of the Persian Empire, began under one of the greatest Arab generals, Khalid ibn al-Walid in 634. Arab tribes on the borders of Iraq, who found themselves facing Muslims in the south and Persians to the north, chose to accept Islam and engage in a joint assault on Persian territories. The decisive battle was fought at Qadisiya in 637 when 20,000 Persians were defeated by a far smaller Arab force. This led to the fall, later in the same year, of the Persian capital, Ctesiphon, and with the capture of Mosul in 641, the conquest of Iraq by the forces of Islam was complete. Kufa and Basra were created as great garrison cities from which the conquered territory could be administered.[7]

The first period of conquests was completed to a great extent during the reigns of the first two orthodox caliphs. The third caliph, Uthman, was an older man who in comparison with his predecessors, was both weak and mediocre. Preferring luxury and comfort to the austere life of the first two Caliphs, and guilty of nepotism in all major appointments, Uthman forced his critics into rebellion which ended by his assassination in 656. His murder precipitated civil war between Ali, his elected successor, and Mu'āwiyah, a relative of Uthman, who had been appointed governor of Syria. Mu'āwiyah assumed the position of avenger of his kinsman, Uthman. Ali, who had maintained a position of neutrality concerning the murder of Uthman, succeeded to the caliphate. Mu'āwiyah, well-situated in his provincial capital of Damascus, "exhibited the 'martyred' caliph's blood-stained shirt together with the chopped-off fingers of his wife who tried to defend him, and with shrewd eloquence aroused Moslem emotions."[8] Ali was given the choice of either producing the assassins or accepting the role of accomplice. Ali had made Kufa in Iraq his second capital, and he rallied to his banner the Iraqis and the Arabs of the Hejaz. The Syrians, where either Christians or Neo-Muslims, joined forces with Mu'āwiyah as did South Arabian tribes for historical and dynastic reasons. Consequently, not so much the assassination of Uthman but rather a political conquest between Iraq and Hejaz on the one side and Syria and Southern Arabia on the other.

The decisive battle was fought at Siffin on the west bank of the Euphrates in July 657. As it became obvious that the supporters of Ali were going to be victorious, the able lieutenant of Mu'āwiyah and conqueror of Egypt, Amr ibn al-As, devised a ruse which stopped the battle. As the forces of Ali attacked they were faced with the sight of the Qu'ran hoisted on the lances of the opposing forces. This was seen as an appeal to decision by the word of God rather than by force of arms. This led to arbitration, by which Ali suffered the greater defeat. The mere fact of agreeing to arbitration lowered Ali's position to that of being a mere pretender to the caliphate. The issue was not fully resolved, however, until the murder of Ali two years later. This cleared the way for Mu'āwiyah to become caliph.[9] Ali was buried at a spot near Kufa, which is currently known as the "Mashhad (shrine of) Ali at Najaf, [and] has become one of the greatest centers of Muslim pilgrimages."[10]

Ali became the patron saint of the first great schismatic sect of Islam. The *Shi'ites*, followers of Ali, have venerated him equally with, and on occasion more than, Muhammad. He has been "declared sinless and infallible, even the incarnation of the Deity."[11]

On the other hand, a new caliphate, the Umayyad, was founded by Mu'awiyah in Damascus, Syria, in 661 which continued until its rise of the Abbasids in 750. The new Caliphate was primarily monarchical and worldly, despite the claim of Mu'āwiyah and his successors to legitimacy based on *ijma'* (consensus) and *bay'a* (allegiance).[12] Mu'āwiyah consolidated his position by executing an agreement with Hasan, Ali's son, whose "interest lay more in the Harem than on the throne,"[13] and, once secure, he organized a new state based primarily on revenue and taxes obtained from conquered territories and from the *jizya*, or poll-tax, payable by those who did not accept the faith of Islam.

Umayyad rule was centered in Damascus, and Iraq became the center of *Shi'ism*. It is of interest that even in its early days *Shi'ism* experienced an important schism of its own. The arbitration agreed to at Siffin was opposed by an important group of Ali's followers on the ground that this reduced Ali also to the role of a pretender. They revolted against him and had to be forcibly suppressed. "They were known as the *Kharijites (Khawarij)*, 'those who go out,' and were to reappear many times in the later history of Islam."[14]

The problem of the poll-tax resulted in a strengthening of the *Shi'ite* position in Iraq. New Islamic converts, or *Mawali* as they were known, demanded full equality with the Arabs, as was guaranteed all Muslims by Muhammad. It soon became obvious that the Arab aristocracy meant to retain certain exclusive rights and privileges. The *Mawali* began to demonstrate allegiance to the Shi'a cause and contributed substantially to the transformation of that sect from a reactionary movement into a religious order which began to embrace ideas from the Christian, Jewish and Zoroastrian traditions. Attempted financial reform by successors of Mu'āwiyah (*circa* 717–720) failed to conciliate the *Mawali*. Disillusionment among the non-Arab elements, which was especially strong in Iraq, gave birth to an efficient propaganda machine which disseminated extreme *Shi'ite* ideas. Known as the *Hashimiya*, it became an effective tool of Muhammad ibn 'Ali ibn al-'Abbas, who was descended from an uncle of the Prophet. He centered his activities in Khurasan, a province in northeast Persia. It was here that the standard of revolt was raised against the Umayyads in 743.[15]

The Umayyad Caliphate had destroyed the theocratic caliphate and had built instead a secular state, of which Mu'āwiyah was the first temporal sovereign. He modeled his kingdom on a Byzantine framework and guaranteed family succession to the throne. The wave of military conquests continued under the Umayyads and reached Kabul (today's capital of Afghanistan), Khurasan in Persia, and the Punjab and Sind to the southeast in India. The Umayyads conducted continuous operations against the Byzantines and laid seige at the gates of Constantinople on three occasions without success. Their excursions were directed westward also and North Africa and Spain were soon an integral part of the kingdom. They could not avoid the temptations of Gaul and the reported rich treasures of the monasteries and churches in the "land of the Franks."[16] The invasion across the Pyrenees was not stopped until the armies of Abd al-Rahman al-Ghafiqi met Charles Martel at Poitiers-Tours in 732. This first centennial of the death of the Prophet marks the extreme westward penetration by the faithful of Islam.

Moving from his stronghold in Khurasan in 747, Abu al-Abbas directed his well-organized army under the Persian, Abu Muslim, into Iraq and captured the city of Maru in 749. Abu al-Abbas was recognized as caliph in Kufa and then turned to meet the Umayyad forces early in 750 on the shores of the Zab river, a tributary of the Tigris. "The great Abbasid victory opened all Syria, and Damascus surrendered in April, 750."[17] There was an immediate attempt to eradicate all members of the Umayyad family. Eighty members of the royal family were treacherously murdered at the infamous banquet of Jaffa. They were invited guests of the Abbasids.[18] Only one person was reported to have escaped this widespread massacre. He was the nineteen-year old Abd al-Rahman, a grandson of the tenth caliph, who fled to Spain and established in Cordoba the Spanish Umayyad dynasty.

Abu al-Abbas founded the Abbasid dynasty of Islam which proved to by the most celebrated and longest lived (750–1258). The capital of Islam was moved from Damascus in Syria to Kufa in Iraq—the center of the Abbasid Empire. The fact that Abu al-Abbas assumed the title of al-Saffah (the blood pourer) foreshadowed the pattern of power that was to be pursued by this regime. Although rule by divine right was established and new prominence was given to theologians and canon lawyers, "its piety was assumed and its religiosity feigned. The Baghdad caliphs were no less worldly than their predecessors of Damascus."[19]

The real founder of the dynasty was the second caliph, al-Saffah's brother, Abu Ja'far 'Abd Allah al-Mansur, who succeeded to the throne in 754. (He was actually called al-Mansur-billah, "whom God has made victorious";[20] royal appellations of pious connotation became habitual for all the Abbasids.) In addition to liquidating the internal opposition, consolidating his power, and gradually pacifying the realm, al-Mansur erected an enduring monument to himself by building the city of Baghdad on a strategic site, lying in a valley on the west bank of the Tigris. Within a short time the city became a world center of trade and industry. Political and cultural activities gained primary importance. The system of government was influenced by and in great part patterned after that of the Persians. In fact, Persian customs and dress even became fashionable. The only remaining Arabian influences were the religion of Islam, which became the state religion, and Arabic, which was retained as the official tongue. Perhaps one of the most important governmental innovations was the establishment of the vizirate, which eventually became the most powerful position in the realm. It was the vizir who was to exercise the chief executive authority of the state. The incumbents of this office were able to amass fabulous fortunes and on occasion demonstrated generosity and political acumen to the point of becoming "popular" and perhaps dangerous. Under the strong willed Harun al Rashid (786–809), the magnificent Barmakids (a vizirial family) met their demise; "the severed head of the family leader was impaled on one of the Baghdad bridges and the two halves of his corpse on two other bridges. Other influential members of the family were apprehended and imprisoned for life; their property was confiscated. The family became extinct, but the institution continued."[21]

The apogee of the Abbasids was actually reached under this same Caliph, Harun al-Rashid and his son, al-Ma'mun (813–833). "History and legend have conspired to make of the court of Harun al-Rashid and his son Al-Manun the most glamorous one in Islam."[22] Although there was no lack of internal uprisings, control was effectively exercised through local governors and financial superintendents. Local government was kept under general surveillance by the central government. The army of the caliph consisted of both regular and volunteer troops, the core of which were the Khurasani guards. In later times volunteer forces were replaced by especially trained slaves known as *Mamluks* of central Asian Turkish origin. These slaves were destined to play a dominant part in the decline of the caliphate.

"The Glory that was Baghdad," however, stems from more than just the fabled luxurious scale of living, victory in the field of battle, and effective administration. The intellectual awakening under the Abbasids made this era one of the most momentous periods in the history of mankind. Much of the intellectual legacy of Greece came to the western world through translations accomplished during this epoch from Persian, Sanskrit, Syriac and Greek. Islam was enabled to transform its own primitive character into one which combined features of the Semitic, Persian, and Hellenistic civilizations. These concepts and ideas were absorbed and embellished with Muslim contributions and subsequently made their way to Europe through Spain and Sicily, thereby contributing directly to the Renaissance in Europe.

Contributions included the astronomical tables of al-Khwarizmi, which were a synthesis of Indian and Greek systems of astronomy, to which his own observations were added; the first algebra (from Arabic *al-Jabr*) text-book was also produced by Al-Khwarizmi; Persian literature reached Europe through Arabic translation; and the game of chess was first introduced to Europe through Spain. "Greek medicine, represented by Galen; mathematics and allied subjects, for which Euclid and Ptolemy stood; and philosophy, originated by Plato and Aristotle . . . , these [only] served as starting points on the Arab voyage of intellectual discovery."[23]

Such was the real "glory of Baghdad."

The Abbasid rule during the tenth and eleventh centuries saw deep degradation of the caliphate occur and the Commander of the Faithful became little more than a puppet of, first, the Buwayhid Dynasty, who were able to appoint and dismiss caliphs at will, and later the Seljuk Sultans of Khurasan, who recognized the caliph in name only as the head of state. The Seljuk Sultans were *Sunni* Muslims. There were also internal conflicts which produced local claimants to authority who became powerful figures in their own right in Iraq. One of the most notable dynasties to develop from this rivalry who established principalities of their own was the Zangid dynasty of Mosul, which played an important role in the Islamic defense against the Christian crusaders of the twelfth century.[24]

In this struggle to resolve the "Eastern Question" of the Middle Ages, the Zangis gave way to one of the most renowned figures of history, Saladin, who successfully disposed of Christian rule in the Holy Land during the latter decades of the twelfth century.[25] (Saladin completed his conquest on October 2, 1187, when Jerusalem surrendered.) This event is notable for the contrast in the treatment of the conquered by Saladin as opposed to the actions of the Crusaders when they first captured the Holy City in the summer days of 1099. An eyewitness to the earlier event, Archbishop William of Tyre, relates that "it was not alone the spectacle of headless bodies and mutilated limbs strewn in all directions that roused horror in all who looked upon them. Still more dreadful was it to gaze upon the victors themselves, dripping with blood from head to foot, an ominous sight which brought terror to all who met them."[26] When his turn came the great Saladin displayed "chivalry, humanity, and magnanimity; . . . [which underlined] his devotion, righteousness, asceticism, and mystic mind."[27] Saladin established the Aiyubid dynasty, another example of an independent operation under the Seljuk Sultans in Iraq, the last of which was Tughril (1177–94) who was defeated by the Turkish ruler of Khwarizm (region of Khiva, south of the Aral Sea).

The power of the Khwarizm rulers was subsequently demolished by the Mongol hordes who advanced out of the east. The "Scourge of God," Jenghiz Khan, overran all of Transoxiana before his death in 1227. A brief respite was realized until the grandson, Hulagu moved through Persia, Syria and Iraq; he captured Baghdad in January 17, 1258, as cited in Chapter 3, above.

Ottoman Rule

The establishment of Mongol rule essentially marked the destruction of the medieval Muslim world. With the transfer of power, wealth, and government to the east, the major portion of the Middle East was split into a variety of provinces. The final blows were administered by the Mongolian Turks under the leadership of Timur Leng (Tamerlane), who overran the entire area in barbaric fashion (1380–1405). To Timur belongs the dubious credit of constructing pyramids of human heads after each conquest; "at Alleppo twenty thousand heads were built into such markers."[28]

Out of this fragmentized chaos emerged the Ottoman Turkish state which dominated the Middle East scene from the early fifteenth century until the end of World War I. The Ottoman Turks had their ultimate origin in Mongolia, later mixed with Iranian tribes in Central Asia, then proceeded to Asia Minor where they gradually superseded and absorbed their Seljuk cousins. They were initially led by the grandfather of 'Uthman (1299–1326) and then by him in establishing themselves firmly in Anatolia. 'Uthman, from which the name Ottoman was derived, is considered the founder of the dynasty which was to rule the empire. "For about two-thirds of a century after its establishment in Anatolia . . . the Ottoman state was but a frontier amirate. . . . The conquest in 1453 of Constantinople . . . formally ushered in a new era, that of the empire."[29]

The Ottoman political system was headed by a sultan. His government was called the Sublime Porte ("presumably because edicts and decisions emanated from the principal gate of the palace").[30] His authority was derived not only from military power under his direct command, but from a high degree of reverence and obedience from his subjects, probably as a consequence of the constitutional position of caliph, a position also acquired through the conquest of Egypt by the Ottomans in 1517. The institutions of the state were established by Sacred Law (which followed the orthodox Hanafite school of Islam) and by the so-called *Kanuns*, the decrees published by the Sultan as supplementary to the Sacred Law. All were accepted "as emanating from God or from the sultan's supreme will."[31]

Iraq turned out to be a most difficult and expensive proposition for the Ottomans. In the first place, religious animosities were a constant source of trouble. The Ottoman Turks, who had their ultimate origin in Mongolia, became mixed with Iranian tribes and subsequently absorbed their Seljik cousins, becoming *Sunni* Muslims. While northern Iraq and Kurdistan largely followed the same faith, Baghdad was divided in its allegiance between *Sunni* and *Shi'a* Islam, and southern Iraq had become dominated by the influence of *Shi'ism*. Further, native tribes of the delta marshland and mountain regions adjoining Persia sporadically revolted against the administration. Finally, Iraq became a battle-ground in the conflict between the Ottomans and the native Safavid dynasty (1502–1736) of Muslim Persia. In fact, under Shah Abbas (1587–1629) the Safavids were able to conquer Baghdad in 1623, and they held much of Iraq until counter-conquest by the Ottomans recovered the fabled city in 1638. Local chieftains in the Basra and Delta marshlands were able to maintain independent rule against the Ottomans for two lengthy periods, 1625 to 1668 and 1694 to 1701, an indication of the decline of the power of the Ottoman sultans.[32]

In spite of a strong power base, privilege, indolence and corruption combined to contribute to the destruction of one of the greatest of modern empires. By the middle of the sixteenth century the Ottomans had extended their rule to the Danube in Europe, and they controlled the Levant, Iraq and Egypt, as well as the entirety of the Anatolian plateau. The hero of this expansion was Suleiman the Magnificent (1520–1566), under whom the empire reached its zenith. His capital, Istanbul, was adorned with palaces, mosques and public works, including schools, hospitals, public baths, and burial chapels. One architect alone was credited with three hundred and twelve buildings.[33] Although evidences of decay appeared several decades earlier, the decline began in the latter part of the sixteenth century. There followed ''a century and a quarter of disgraceful and despicable Ottoman history. A dozen sultans ruled during this period. Four were under sixteen years old when they succeeded to the throne, and most of the rest were undisciplined young men. The wealth, splendor, and ease of the court sapped their energy and morals. . . . ''[34] Sultans gave themselves up ''to hunting and to the harem,'' and numerous military calamities descended upon the empire. The defeats of the seventeenth century sapped the Ottoman institutions, especially the military, and from the beginning of the eighteenth century onward, Ottoman armies and navies proved no match for European soldiers. That stage was effectively being prepared for western incursion.[35]

Iraq stood on the periphery of the great contest taking place in Europe and Asia during the eighteenth century in that the province was ruled throughout the era by a series of *Mamluk* governors who raised and trained their own successors. "From 1704 to 1831 the Sultan failed to enforce at Baghdad an appointment of his own choice."[36] This century was a period of conflict again with Persia with both Baghdad and Mosul being under siege. These wars caused great suffering in Iraq and the province often fell into a state of anarchy with rival tribesmen in frequent revolt and competing for power. At length, internal strife and frontier war were suppressed by the greatest of the *Mamluks*, Suleyman the Great. By 1780 he had assumed control over the government of Baghdad and Basra, only to see a new formidable enemy appear in the form of the recently founded *Wahhabi* state in central Arabia. In addition, Kurdish tribesmen in the north and the powerful Muntafiq confederation in the south created even greater confusion. The Sublime Porte in the meantime was undergoing considerable reform and in 1831 one 'Ali Ridha Pasha was sent to Iraq "to end the *Mamluk* system and regain direct possession of Iraq."[37]

The nineteenth century saw great attempts on the part of the Ottomans to consolidate their rule over the province. Between 1831 and 1850 Kurdistan and the Persian frontier provinces were brought under control, but internal reforms were superficial and often ill-considered. European penetration, however, became the decisive factor in the future of Iraq. Steamboats were soon seen on the rivers of Iraq, telegraph lines appeared after 1861, railroad proposals were being developed and reform along western lines became more evident. Newspapers, schools, hospitals, tramways, army conscription, postal services, and administrative councils, although advancing slowly, were concrete evidence of European influence. A process of fundamental change, albeit negligible at the time, had begun and no regime could possibly reverse the trend.

British Occupation

World War I proved to be the fatal blow to the Ottoman Empire.

Sentiments were mixed regarding the war. The majority of influential men desired neutrality, believing that Turkish interests would be best served by such a policy; another group, strongly influenced by the liberal traditions of France and Great Britain, inclined toward the *Entente* Powers, although the inclusion of Russia disturbed them considerably; and a third group, the hard core military leaders, were impressed by German military genius. Involved military and diplomatic considerations saw Turkey subsequently join the Central Powers in the war against the *Entente*. The English, French and Russians saw no military threat from the Ottomans and it was probably considered more convenient to have Turkey join the Germans and thereby be more readily exposed to partition upon victory. "How else would Russia ever obtain her coveted Constantinople and the Straights?"[38]

The course of the war in the Middle East saw Mesopotamia become one of the areas of major hostilities. The British, long concerned about a "life-line" to the Orient, actually occupied Basra before the official entry of Turkey into the world-wide conflict. They proceeded northward but met defeat south of Baghdad in 1915. The British, subsequently regrouped and with the aid of Indian divisions were finally able to re-establish their hold on southern Iraq and they captured Baghdad in March of 1917. They had advanced halfway to Mosul by the time of the armistice in 1918. As Turkish troops were withdrawn from Mosul, the British promptly occupied the city.[39]

British involvement in Iraq's affairs had been long developing. British policy during the nineteenth century followed a rather insincere and ambiguous course dedicated to the preservation of the Ottoman Empire, yet hedged with qualifications and reservations. Positive penetration was evidenced by the establishment of an English-controlled land and river route through Mesopotamia to India between 1883 and 1887. Other examples are Britain's consistent interest in Egypt, and the acquisition of Malta (1815), Cyprus (1878) and Aden (1839)—all at the expense of the Ottoman Empire. British diplomatic performance during the course of World War I was no less devious, as is shown by the numerous secret partition agreements concluded with the various allied powers. The most significant of these as relates to Iraq was the bargain formalized on May 16, 1916, known officially as the Sykes-Picot agreement.

Under the provisions of this agreement:

(1) Russia was to obtain the provinces of Erzerum, Trebizand, Van, and Bitlis (known as Turkish Armenia) as well as territory in the northern part of Kurdistan.

(2) France was to obtain the coastal strip of Syria, the vilayet of Adana.

(3) Great Britain was to obtain southern Mesopotamia with Baghdad, as well as the ports of Haifa and Acre in Palestine.

(4) The zone between the French and British territories was to form a confederation of Arab states or one independent Arab state. This zone was to be further divided into a French and a British spheres of influence.[40]

The above agreement was later revised after the British occupied the Mosul area. In the Clemenceau-Lloyd George agreement of December 1918, France consented to the inclusion of the Mosul area in Britain's sphere of influence in compensation for British military action in Mesopotamia. This essentially consolidated the British position in Iraq when the statesmen of the *Entente* met in Paris to discuss the peace settlement. However, the work of peace moved slowly and the conflicts, with their attendant frustrations, were considerable. Not only was President Wilson annoyed by the secret wartime agreements; he refused to even consider them. According to his position, the acceptance by the allies of the Fourteen Points annulled all such agreements. The new principles of nonimperialism and national self-determination were to prevail. Extreme tension developed during the conference proceedings, and in order to break the deadlock in discussions, President Wilson proposed that a joint Allied Commission be sent to the Middle East to survey the situation and to determine what "the people" wanted. Out of this developed the King-Crane Commission, whose report, after a six-week tour of the area (May–July 1919), recommended an American mandate for Syria, with Britain as an alternative, and a British mandate for Mesopotamia. The report, however, was not discussed by the Paris Peace Conference—not rejected, just buried in the archives of the American delegation. The fact that President Wilson was back in the United States defending his position on the League of Nations Covenant against strong domestic opposition may have caused the demise of the report. It is more likely, however, that the opposition of France was the primary reason for its failure to be considered. With President Wilson gone, the field was open for France, Great Britain and the Zionists (concerned with the Balfour Declaration of 1917) to resolve Middle East problems in accordance with the wartime agreements. Actually, the matter of final settlement on Mesopotamia was delayed until the spring of 1920.[41]

On April 24, 1920, the peace delegates met again at San Remo on the Italian Riviera. It was clear by this time that the ''partition'' of the Middle East would proceed according to British and French interests. At San Remo, France was granted a mandate over Syria, and the British were given mandatory power over Iraq and Palestine. Under the provisions of the League of Nations Covenant, the supervision of the mandatory powers was to be of a temporary nature only, with the ultimate goal being complete independence for the areas concerned.[42]

The period immediately following the San Remo Conference was marked by violent reaction on the part of Iraqi nationalists and serious insurrection by tribesmen in the south against the British. On the other hand, British administrators assigned to the area brought their families, evidently believing the territorial acquisition was anything but temporary. The rebellion lasted from May to October 1920. It was considered a real war and ''reportedly cost the British nearly L.40,000,000.[43]

Sir Percy Z. Cox, who had been a British political representative in the Persian Gulf area for years and civil commissioner in Iraq during the war, was recalled from Tehran to resolve the problem. Sir Percy quickly organized a provisional council of state with a native prime minister (Sayyad Abd al-Rahman al-Gailani) and distributed portfolios amongst the most influential families and religious sects. However, to each was assigned a British adviser, who in effect, supervised the functions of the council.[44]

It was obvious, then, that complete independence was not an immediate part of the British program. ''Cox himself and his advisers, however, sympathetic to Iraqi aspirations, were convinced that the intended substitution of Iraqi for British government, must, for soundness and permanence, be gradual and progressive; indeed, the actual British administration visibly operating in every department . . . was a reality which no politics could, for the moment, dissipate.''[45]

Mandate to Independence

Iraq was the first Arab state to rise to the dignity of independence. The course was not an easy one, but was mastered under difficult conditions. Military rule under the British was formally terminated in October, 1920, and a native Council of State was formed to be responsible for the administration of the country, with the advice of British officials. Sir Percy Cox found that half the country was still in disorder. As he stated it:

> Though . . . the back of the rebellion was practically broken by the time I reached Basrah, a good many sections of the tribes in the Baghdad Vilayet were still 'out' and it was not until February that the rising could be said to have been finally cleared up. . . . As an immediate expedient therefore, I determined to institute at once a Provisional Government which, under my control and supervision, should be responsible for the administration and political guidance of the country until the general situation had returned to normal and a start could be made with the creation of national institutions.[46]

Sir Percy appealed to the Naqib of Baghdad to preside over the Council of State so established. The Naqib headed the Council, which was comprised of eight portfolios, Interior, Finance, Justice, Defense, Public Works, Education and Health, Commerce and Religious Bequests. Such problems as the organization of a civil administration under Iraqi control; the drafting of an electoral law; and the development of a plan for the formation of an Iraqi army proceeded "with surprising efficiency and absence of friction."[47]

However, the most immediate problem concerned the question of who was to rule Iraq. The British were convinced that "it could only maintain its influence in Iraq if it were to put a monarch at the head of this government."[48] Consequently, a process of elimination was inaugurated in which it was decided that a non-Iraqi and preferably one of the family of the Sharif of Mecca (King Hussein of the Hijaz) would command the most support from the population. In London, a new Colonial Secretary, Mr. Winston Churchill, had been selected, and one of his first actions was to convene a conference at Cairo to "decide, once and for all, the many outstanding Middle Eastern questions."[49] The agenda at this

conference included the selection of a ruler for Iraq. It was
determined that Prince Faisal, one of King Hussein's four sons, was
acceptable to the king-seekers at Cairo. The British encouraged
Faisal to visit Iraq and offer himself as King. Faisal arrived in Basra
on June 23 and proceeded to Baghdad, where he was cordially
received on June 29, 1921. "It was as the result of the popular
tributes that he received during the first fortnight of his presence in
Iraq that His Highness the Naqib . . . proposed to the Council [of
State] on July 11th a resolution, which was unanimously approved,
that Amir Faisal should be declared King, on condition that his
government should be a constitutional, representative and democratic one."[50] This selection was ratified by "a sort of people's
assembly" and Faisal was proclaimed King on August 23, 1921, by
Sir Percy Cox.[51]

The next step was the negotiation of a treaty to settle Anglo-Iraqi
relations.

The goal of the British was to replace the mandatory document by
a treaty, under which government would be possible with less cost
and less friction than under direct administration. This would also
serve as a method of establishing the new King as a contracting
party with sufficient administrative power, yet not enough power to
render him dangerous to British interests. The treaty, then,
amounted to a method of control from the British point of view. To
the Iraqis, a treaty meant the abolition of the detested Mandate,
which had been the source of great friction. It was further regarded
as a step toward national independence.[52]

The treaty was concluded on October 10, 1922, and together with
a number of subsidiary agreements, it confirmed British control, but
in a manner palatable, at least temporarily, to Iraqi nationalists.
Originally, scheduled to operate for twenty years, its period was
later reduced to four years with subsequent treaties being concluded
on January 13, 1926, December 14, 1927, and June 30, 1930, the
last of the series. Each one marked further relaxation in British
control, and the treaty of December 14, 1927, contained a promise
of British support for Iraq's candidacy to the League of Nations.[53]

The final treaty, dated June 30, 1930, was concluded by the
British High Commissioner and the Iraqi foreign minister. It
provided for a twenty-five year alliance between the two countries
and confirmed British support of Iraq's admission to the League of
Nations; it promised that Iraq's full independence and the

termination of the British mandate would be effective on the date of Iraq's entry into the League of Nations on October 23, 1932. Iraq was so admitted after having given "guarantees for the protection of minorities; the rights of foreigners; respect for human rights, and the recognition of debts and treaties concluded by the mandatory power."[54]

As can be seen from the events reviewed in this chapter, the struggle for power in Iraq began early in the history of the Islamic Empire. The establishment of the Abbasid dynasty in 750 A.D. resulted in the "Glory that was Baghdad" and gave to Mesopotamia an historical legacy of greatness in terms of military strength, intellectual excellence, and cultural grandeur. Internal religious struggles which divided the empire weakened the regime, allowing foreign forces from Persia and Asia to compete for control of the land between two rivers: the Tigris and the Euphrates.

Under the suzerainty of the Ottoman Turks, internal reforms and economic development were only partially successful and the area was subsequently subjected to British penetration and occupation. The British also successfully installed an Arab King of their own choice and under cover of the mandate granted by the League of Nations the British were able to continue *de facto* control over the internal and external affairs of the country then established as the state of Iraq. It was against this unpalatable control that the forces of Iraqi nationalism rebelled.

NOTES

[1]See Europa Publications, *The Middle East and North Africa* (12th ed., London: Europa Publications, Ltd., 1965), p. 220.

[2]*Ibid.*

[3]Philip K. Hitti, *The Near East in History* (New York: D. Van Nostrand Company, Inc., 1961), p. 206.

[4]*Ibid.*

[5]Bernard Lewis, *The Arabs in History* (New York: Harper & Row, 1960), p. 51.

[6]M. Th. Houtsma, *et al.* (ed.), *The Encyclopedia of Islam* (London: Luzac & Co., 1936), II, 881.

[7]Lewis, *op. cit.*, p. 55.

[8]Hitti, *op. cit.*, p. 216.

[9]See Houtsma, *op. cit.*, IV, pp. 350–58 and Sir Percy Sykes, *A History of Persia* (London: Macmillan and Co., Ltd., 1951), I, pp. 542–44 for discussion of the variant *Shi'a-Sunni* versions of the succession to the Caliphate at this important juncture in the history of Islam.

[10]Hitti, *op. cit.*, p. 217. Note: According to Houtsma, *op. cit.*, III, p. 467 *Mashhad* means literally "sepulchral chapel" primarily of a martyr belonging to the family of the Prophet.

[11]*Ibid.* See Edward G. Browne, *A Literary History of Persia* (Cambridge: The University Press, 1956), I, pp. 130 ff. on the Persian political doctrine of Divine Kingship.

[12]See E. I. J. Rosenthal, *Political Thought in Medieval Islam* (Cambridge: The University Press, 1962), p. 31. In technical terms, the election of the Caliph takes place by *bay'a*, investiture with the electors' oath of loyalty, to be followed by *bay'a* in public, expressing the *ijma'* of the community.

[13]Hitti, *op. cit.*, p. 218.

[14]Lewis, *op. cit.*, p. 63.

[15]See Browne, *Literary History of Persia, op. cit.*, pp. 231–240.

[16]Hitti, *op. cit.*, p. 225.

[17]Sydney N. Fisher, *The Middle East: A History* (New York: Alfred A. Knopf, 1959), p. 81.

[18]*Ibid.*

[19]Hitti, *op. cit.*, p. 240.

[20]Carl Brockelmann, *History of the Islamic Peoples* (New York: Capricorn Books, 1960), p. 107.

[21]Hitti, *op. cit.*, pp. 241–242.

[22]*Ibid.*, p. 243.

[23]*Ibid.*, p. 246.

[24]Sykes, *op. cit.*, II, pp. 24ff.

[25]Atiya, *op. cit.*, p. 80.

[26]*Ibid.*, p. 62.

[27]*Ibid.*, pp. 80–81.

[28]Fisher, *op. cit.*, p. 141. See Sykes, II, *op. cit.*, pp. 118–135 for a vivid description of these tragic events.

[29]Philip K. Hitti, *History of the Arabs* (New York: St. Martin's Press, 1967), p. 709.

[30]Fisher, *op. cit.*, p. 208.

[31]*Ibid.*, p. 209.

[32]Europa Publications, *op. cit.*, p. 223.

[33]Hitti, *The Near East in History, op. cit.*, p. 332.

[34]Fisher, *op. cit.*, p. 235.

[35]*Ibid.*, pp. 241–245. The religious or thirty years Wars (1618–48) in Europe provided them with their last opportunity to conquer Europe as they had vowed. Their inaction during the period marks the end of the Ottoman threat.

[36]Europa Foundation, *loc. cit.*

[37]Fisher, *op. cit.*, p. 362.

[38]*Ibid.*

[39]George Lenczowski, *The Middle East in World Affairs* (New York: Cornell University Press, 1966), p. 60.

[40]*Ibid.*, pp. 71–72.

[41]Lenczowski, *op. cit.*, pp. 87–90.

[42]Fisher, *op. cit.*, p. 380.

[43]*Ibid.*, p. 417.

[44]*Ibid.*

[45]Stephen H. Longrigg, *'Iraq, 1900 to 1950: A Political, Social and Economic History* (London: Oxford University Press, 1953), p. 126.

[46]Lady Bell, D.B.E. (ed.), *The Letters of Gertrude Bell* (New York: Boni and Liveright, 1927), II, p. 528.

[47]*Ibid.*, p. 530.

[48]Brockelman, *op. cit.*, p. 496.

[49]Longrigg, *op. cit.*, p. 130.

[50]Bell, *op. cit.*, pp. 552–53.

[51]Brockelman, *op. cit.*, p. 497.

[52]Philip W. Ireland, *Iraq, A Study in Political Development* (London: Jonathan Cape, 1937), pp. 338–339.

[53]J.C. Hurewitz, *Diplomacy in the Near and Middle East* (Princeton: D. Van Nostrand Company, Inc., 1956), II, pp. 111–14. See Appendix A.

[54]*Ibid.*, p. 272. See Appendix B.

CHAPTER 5
THE STRUGGLE FOR POWER

Independence, and even admission to the League of Nations in 1932, did not mean for Iraq self-government free from difficulties. There were, however, grounds for optimism. King Faisal provided wise leadership at the outset and he inspired public spirit with his approach to a progressive, modern form of government. His unexpected death in 1933 interrupted whatever progress had been initiated. There followed "a period of disequilibrium . . .[in which] personal differences among the politicians became more acute, and there was no Faisal to effect a compromise."[1] Faisal was succeeded by his son, Ghazi I, then only twenty-one years of age. "During his short reign (1933-39) Iraq lacked the leadership which was necessary for stability and progress."[2]

The difficulties which faced the new nation during its first period of trial-and-error in self-government included the problem of age-old animosities between the *Sunni* Muslims and the *Shi'ite* tribes on the Euphrates; the persistent problem of relations with the Kurds in the northeast; the massacre of Assyrians in 1933 to suppress the Assyrian "peril;" and political intrigues which led to the first military *coup d'etat* of 1936.

A considerable amount of the difficulty was precipitated by an anti-British group formed in 1930 called the *Ikha al-Watani* (National Brotherhood) Party which had opposed the Anglo-Iraqi treaties. This group dominated Iraqi politics following King Faisal's death. They were opposed by those who favored continued cooperation with the British and were led by General Nuri es-Said. In addition to these two groups, some educated young men in Baghdad formed what was called the *Ahali,* or People's Group, which preached a mixture of socialism and democracy referred to by the founders as "populism." At the same time dissent and unrest became apparent in the army. Army officers looked upon the western-imposed division of the Arab world as artificial, and advocated instead some sort of Pan-Arab federation. The leader of the military group was General Bekr Sidki, the "hero" of the Assyrian massacre. On Bekr's initiative a coalition was formed with the *Ahali* group and a conspiracy was organized to overthrow the existing *Ikha* cabinet. A successful *coup de'etat* was executed on October 29, 1936.[3]

The new regime, however, based on cooperation between the army and the progressive *Ahali* group, failed to fulfill its assurances of reform. Behind the facade of what they called the Society for National Reform, serious tensions and conflicts developed which even extended to the armed forces. The only positive contribution of Bekr's rule was to conclude the Sa'dabad Pact on July 9, 1937. This treaty joined Iraq with Turkey, Iran and Afghanistan in an arrangement for consultation in all disputes that might affect the common interests of the four states. Bekr's arrogant behavior, his Kurdish background, and his several political assassinations led to his downfall. On August 11, 1937, he was assassinated in Mosul by rival army leaders.[4]

The British attitude during this period had been strangely noncommittal in that Bekr Sidki was outspokenly anti-British. The British even expressed a readiness to come to terms with the regime as evidenced by a loan of one million pounds granted the month before Bekr's assassination. However, no regrets were expressed when the dictator left the scene. As usual, British diplomacy adjusted to the situation.

A friend of Britain, General Nuri es-Said, the head of another army clique, was soon installed in power. The army now "having tasted power, constantly interfered with political developments."[5] The old pattern of personal rivalries and intrigue had added a new element to an already complex situation.

World War II

Relations with Great Britain deteriorated in spite of a strong pro-British faction in the Iraqi army. The death of King Ghazi in an automobile accident on April 4, 1939, was accompanied by angry demonstrations. The British consul in Mosul was assassinated by an angry mob and there appeared to be an inclination to blame any Iraqi misfortune on the British. British policy in Palestine at the time contributed greatly to this resentment. German and Italian propaganda was quick to take advantage of all adverse situations.

A series of coups by various army and political cliques marked the early years of World War II. The most dominant figure during the period was Rashid Ali al-Gailani, who, in conspiracy with a group of four colonels known as the "Golden Square," tended to favor a pro-axis position. Actually, Iraq's position changed as the fortune of war changed. "The prevailing opinion in Iraq was that, after the fall of France, England had no chance of survival. The Iraqi nationalists were seemingly no wiser than those French generals who advised their Prime Minister after their collapse that 'in three weeks England will have her neck wrung like a chicken!' To these nationalists the Anglo-Iraqi alliance had become a liability."[6] On the other hand, "if he had had his way, Nuri would have declared war on Germany."[7] To complicate matters, Ghazi was succeeded by his infant son, Faisal II, and a regency was established under Prince Abdul Ilah, a maternal uncle who was acceptable to the British.

Rashid Ali and his associates hoped to obtain military assistance from the Axis and liaison was established with German Ambassador Franz von Papen. Iraq became a center of Nazi and Italian intrigue. Secret negotiations were conducted with the Axis powers with aspirations to achieve freedom and independence from Great Britain and to obtain military assistance. In the latter area the results were disappointing because Germany was then busy in Greece and was preparing for the Russian invasion. In these efforts, the Rashid Ali government was strongly supported by the exiled mufti of Jerusalem, Haj Amin el-Husseini and a number of extremist Syrian politicians.[8]

While negotiations were going on between the Arab leaders and the Axis powers to outline the relationships between the countries concerned, Italy and Germany were carrying on discussions for dividing the Arab world into spheres of influence. Briefly, the German government recognized the Arab world as an "area of priority of Italian interests; but Germany reserved her rights in the economic interests in that area . . . [and] the Soviet Union's sphere 'would presumably be centered south of the territory of the Soviet Union in the direction of the Indian Ocean' . . . [Also] Molotov specifically demanded that 'the area south of Batum and Baku in the general direction of the Persian Gulf [should be] recognized as the center of aspirations of the Soviet Union.' ''[9] In other words, the Axis was proceeding to divide the French and British empires among themselves.

Although Rashid Ali paid lip-service to Anglo-Iraqi friendships, his actions revealed his true intent. Further, dissension within his cabinet caused considerable concern in Great Britain. This prompted a British request for the removal of Rashid Ali from the premiership. Subsequent coups by army leaders and the landing of British troops in Iraq from Palestine finally forced Rashid Ali out of power. The British forces landed at Basra on April 29, proceeded to relieve the beleagured British base at Habbaniya, and had entered Baghdad by the end of May. The so-called thirty-day war between Great Britain and Iraq was concluded with a negotiated armistice.[10] Rashid Ali and the mufti rapidly departed the country, moving from one place to another ahead of the allied advance. Rashid Ali eventually reached Saudi Arabia where he was given *dakhala* (asylum) by the late King Abd al-Aziz ibn Sa'ud. The mufti, denied residence in Switzerland, finally reached Cairo where he was received as the guest of King Farouk.

The collapse of the Rashid regime enabled the Regent, Amir Abd al-Ilah, to re-establish legitimate authority. On May 4, 1941, a proclamation was issued to the people of Iraq in which the Regent stated:

A group of military tyrants, aided and abetted by Rashid Ali and other ill-disposed persons bought by foreign gold, have by force thrust me from my sacred duties as guardian of my nephew, your beloved young King. Under their evil sway the noble land of Iraq has been poisoned by falsehood and lies and brought from the blessings of peace to the horrors of a venomous war.

My duty is plain. I am returning to restore the tarnished

honour of our native land and to lead it back again to peaceful prosperity under the lawfully constituted government.[11]

The Regent afterwards played a more prominent role in exercising an influence on the government. He helped to ensure continuity in a pro-ally government, kept internal peace, but allowed wide latitude to the press and played a leading part in the Arab unity movement. The British Tenth Army, assisted by Polish troops recruited in Russia, guarded the northern approaches to Iraq against a possible German attack in 1942–1943. The United States became directly involved for the first time in 1943 when an American military mission was established in Basra to facilitate the transportation of war supplies to the Soviet Union. As a consequence, Iraq became a recipient of lend-lease aid. Major political difficulties were minimized throughout the remainder of the war years. British dominance temporarily continued and American influence began to be felt.

Oil Concessions and Their Consequences in Iraq

Oil concessions in Iraq originated in the late nineteenth century with a contract awarded to Germany for control of interests to carry out preliminary surveys in the vilayats o: Mosul and Baghdad.[12] This concession never became fully operative and in 1912 a German-born English banker, Sir Ernest Cassel, formed a British joint stock company—the Turkish Petroleum Company—for the purpose of acquiring all claims to the oil fields in Iraq, in addition to prospecting rights in other parts of the Ottoman Empire. These rights were granted by the Ottoman government and by the terms of the agreement, all European interests were united in one concession, with absolute control in the hands of the British.

While the original concessions were of a limited nature, that granted by the Iraqi government in March 1925 to the Turkish Petroleum Company covered the whole country. Drilling operations were begun in 1927 and by 1932 twenty-six wells had been drilled. "The initial well at Baba Gurger was a gusher which flowed at a rate of 95,000 barrels per day, and it soon became apparent that the reservoir was of giant size. Reserves are estimated at 7.5 billion barrels, enough to last until the year 2000.''[13] Production was not effective, however, until 1934, upon completion of the construction of 12-inch pipelines to the Mediterranean terminals at Tripoli and Haifa. In the interim, the name of the Turkish Petroleum Company was changed to the Iraq Petroleum Company. World War II interrupted production, but by 1947 some eighty wells had been developed. The Palestine War of 1948 disrupted the pumping of oil to Haifa and an alternative pipeline was constructed to the north with a terminal at Banias in Syria. This 30–32 inch pipeline, completed in 1952, more than doubled the previous capacity. With the development of other major fields and the construction of additional pipelines and refineries, the production of oil in Iraq has risen rapidly. The production in 1935 averaged 71,000 barrels per day and in 1962 it reached 1.4 million barrels per day.[14]

The nationalization of oil in Iran in 1951 and the agreement concluded between Saudi Arabia and the Arabian American Oil Company (Aramco) in 1950 precipitated serious difficulties in Iraq. The latter agreement provided for a half-and-half division of profits between Aramco and the Saudi Arabian government. This set the pattern for other oil agreements in the Middle Eastern countries. In order to forestall any nationalization attempt in Iraq, the Iraq Petroleum Company (IPC) readily agreed to arbitrate a revision of royalties based on this new pattern with the Iraqi government. The final agreement was signed in February 1952 on the basis of the 50/50 profit formula, retroactive to January 1, 1951. Approval by the Iraqi Parliament was also effected at this time but not without strong opposition. This opposition took form in statements published in the press, and the Independence (*Istaqlal*) Party called for a strike. However, the public reacted favorably to the agreement. "General Nuri was deemed prudent in waiting to see what the outcome of the Persian nationalization would be before Iraq should embark on a similar experiment, and his steadfastness in carrying on the negotiations amidst his opponents' protests and opposition was fully appreciated by the entire nation."[15]

A major consequence of this oil settlement was the impetus given to the Iraqi government towards more constructive reform. A Development Board, charged with the responsibility of developing the country's productive resources to raise the standard of living, was created by an Act of Parliament in 1950. A large portion, 70 percent of the abundant funds made available through the new oil agreement, was entrusted to the Board. This autonomous body, which included the Prime Minister as chairman and the Minister of Finance as an *ex officio* member, proceeded to obtain the services of outstanding experts, foreign firms, and technical assistance in carrying out planning and administration of new projects. There was no reluctance to use foreigners in responsible positions. This, of course, led to the inevitable criticism that the Board was under the direction of foreign influences. Although the composition of the Board was originally intended to be free of political conflict, popular dissatisfaction, impatience, charges of corruption and favoritism—combined with political protest in the Parliament relative to its autonomous structure—led to the Board's reorganization and to a dilution of its efforts.[16]

The Board was unable to cope with many of the fundamental and social problems confronting the country and has focused its energy almost entirely upon large projects such as the Wadi Tharthar project, which was primarily for flood control. While the dams completed under the project do serve to halt floods, they have at the same time diminished the flow of water to the southern farm lands. Huge building projects have been completed in Baghdad, but little was accomplished in rural areas. The Development Board was reorganized in 1959 after the revolution and was reduced to a supervisory capacity rather than performing executive functions.

The resources available to the authorities in power in Iraq, if spent in a judicious manner, could provide sufficient basis for social and economic reconstruction to the ends of social order and security for the people of the country. However, dissident groups, such as wealthy absentee land-owners and opposition parties have, as will be seen, objectives other than a stable, orderly state.

The Anglo-American Issue

American interest in the petroleum resources of Iraq dates from the post-World War I peace conferences. It was the original position of American statesmen that there should be equal opportunity for United States nationals in all mandated territories based on a rather abstract Open Door Policy.[17] The disillusionment which followed the high idealism generated by President Wilson resulted in suspicion and distrust of British motives and actions, especially after the revelation of the secret agreements concluded during World War I with the French. Further, "the cry over the exhaustion of American oil resources, the attack on the British oil exploitation practices, and the demand for retaliatory action against British oil companies in the United States forced the American Government to try to obtain outside oil resources, especially those in territories under British control."[18]

In order to achieve the desired end—specifically outside oil resources for the United States to be controlled by American oil companies—the United States Department of State overcame the monopolistic control of the Turkish Petroleum Company by various plans to sub-lease. In other words, American companies gained an inroad to participation through negotiations with the Turkish Petroleum Company. This, in fact, involved "direct warning of the U. S. Secretary of State Frank Kellogg to the British Government that failure of the Turkish Petroleum Company to allow U. S. company participation would result in American efforts to secure 'a fair share in the development of oil resources of Mesopotamia through other means.' "[19]

The American group continued to negotiate, however, and what became known as the "red line agreement," was effected which limited the activities of all participants to certain specified areas, marked on a map attached to the agreement by a red line. The British, then, had acceded to American demands for a share in the development of Mesopotamian oil resources. However, the British, as usual, managed to come out rather well in the transaction. While they granted the American group 23 3/4 percent of the shares involved through the Anglo-Iranian Oil Company, the British collected a royalty on *all* oil produced. "The State Department's insistence on equal opportunity for American companies to exploit Iraq's oil fields was thus vitiated."[20]

American oil interests in Iraq became a fact by inclusion in the "red line agreement" of July 31, 1928. With the construction of additional pipelines, production increased and Iraq's interest in the world oil market became pronounced. A new agreement between the company and the Iraqi government was concluded on February 3, 1952 which gave the government a fifty-fifty share in the profits. The Iraqi government later decided to exploit such areas which were not covered by revised concessions and established a national petroleum industry, the Iraq National Oil Company (INOC) in

February 1964 for its own exploratory purposes.

Russian Interest

The U.S.S.R. did not become involved in any of the post-World War I competition for petroleum concessions. When the Bolsheviks came to power in November 1917, they were primarily occupied with problems in Europe and at home. Although Lenin was much more Asia-conscious than his socialist contemporaries, events outside of Europe were virtually ignored. Further, the theory of having "socialism in one country" fully developed came to dominate the thoughts of Lenin's successor, Stalin, with the result of a policy of isolationism for the time being. Soviet interest in Iraq was practically non-existent until the military *coup d'etat* of 1936 in which left-wing elements took part. The Bekr Sidki regime was viewed by Moscow as a progressive movement and as a "national front" in which radical left-wing forces were influential without being conspicuous. This was a gross miscalculation, however, since events soon demonstrated that the new regime was committed to self-interest in terms of power and had no inclination to oppose the current Fascist threat. The regime answered Soviet approaches by continuing to outlaw the Communist Party and, after a succession of coups, embraced the pro-axis regime of Rashid Ali.[21]

During the Second World War and as a result of it, conditions changed and subsequent to the invasion and occupation of Iran by the Red Army in the north and the British forces in the south the U.S.S.R. initiated a policy of penetration and influence similar if not identical with expansive policies of Imperial Russia. The Great Alliance with the West, the military realities of the time and the desperate need that existed for close cooperation limited the scope of this policy primarily to Iran, and to a lesser degree, Turkey. Iraq remained on the periphery and followed a policy of "neutrality" towards the U.S.S.R. which permitted the formation and activities of the pro-Communist National Union Party. In 1947, when the need for this pretention had disappeared, the Government of Iraq dissolved the party. As a matter of fact, during the period under discussion, a number of other Communist groups were fully active underground, with widespread and efficient organization, including cells in government offices. "Suleymania was their principal centre, where contact was easy with the trans-frontier Communists and the merging of Communism and Kurdish nationalism was an effective device."[22] Politicians of Communist sympathy were able effectively to organize a serious strike at Kirkuk among the workers of the Iraq Petroleum Company. Although the strike was settled by arbitration, an illegal meeting had to be suppressed by force. Significantly, propagandists were able to blame the tragic episode on the company. Consequently, and following further demonstrations, Prime Minister Nuri es-Said located hotbeds of Communist activity and suppressed them.[23]

During the early years of the 1950's Iraq's political forces were divided into two major groups who competed for power. The ruling conservative group, led by Nuri es-Said, derived most of its strength from the land-owning elements. The nationalist and socialist opposition relied primarily on support in the cities. The relatively peaceful period was not unmarked by violence as evidenced by an abortive coup in February 1950 attempted by the Baghdad chief of police, who was promptly arrested by the government.

Official circles in Iraq under the leadership of Nuri es-Said, while he was either in or out of office as Premier, were decidedly pro-West during the early 1950's. During 1953-54 Moscow's main efforts in Iraq were directed towards prevention of Iraqi involvement in U. S. Secretary of State John Foster Dulles' attempt to set up a Middle East defense organization. The Soviet *charge d'affaires* in Baghdad delivered a note to the Iraqi government in March 1954 in which the Western-sponsored organization was defined as a "hostile act toward the Soviet Union."[24] The Iraq Prime Minister of the moment, Fadhil Jamali, was well known for his pro-Western position and came in for a full blast of Soviet vituperation. Nuri es-Said, who followed Jamali as Prime Minister again was also not spared. The attack from Moscow, however, took the form of propaganda directed towards influencing the opposition. The Iraqi government's close relationship with Turkey at the time led the Muscovite propagandists to label Iraq as a "second Turkey" to be exploited as an American colony. Other objects of attack were the Western oil companies which, according to the Soviets, were exploiting the country at the expense of the Iraqi worker.

Actually, official relations between the two countries abruptly ended in November 1954 when Iraq closed its legation in Moscow. This was followed by the severance of diplomatic relations on

January 3, 1955. The Russians henceforth operated in Iraq under the cover of illegal and officially outlawed local Communist parties, various front organizations and political sympathizers.[25]

Communist activities concentrated on propaganda among secondary school and university students. The General Association of Iraqi Students, dominated by Communists, claimed membership of 85 percent of all their students. Increased effort was directed among the peasants also, under the general slogan of "land and freedom." The main Soviet objectives continued to be strong opposition to the Western-oriented collective security system which had by now become known as the Dulles' Northern Tier concept.

Between World Wars I and II there was an attempt to develop a meaningful Pan-Arabism based on a mixture of socialism and democracy which failed to gain any popular support. The events of World War II saw the British continue in playing their dominant role in the country's politics with little or no difficulties. They could not, however, maintain a monopoly of power in an area which had been the case after World War I. The emergence of the U.S.S.R. following World War II as a major world power, the dominant role played by the United States during and after the war, and the rise of revolutionary movements in the Middle East made the preservation of the pre-war conditions impossible. Consequently, despite the best efforts of the British Government to protect their imperial interests in Iraq, a complicated power struggle developed between the British and American economic interests on the one side and between the United States, England and the U.S.S.R. on the other. Thus, Iraq became involved not only in the oil diplomacy of the Western powers but also in the international struggle for power which is known as the Cold War.

The immediate aim of the Iraqi nationalists was, of course, the elimination of all foreign interests. To do so, they had first to decide which foreign interest provided the greatest threat to national sovereignty and in what way, if any, what interests could be relied upon to eliminate the threat and to maintain national integrity. The task was obviously a difficult one. In addition to differences of opinion, each of the three interested powers had ways and means to influence events. This resulted in an internal struggle for power which paved the way for the bloody events of 1958.

NOTES

[1]Majid Khadduri, *Independent Iraq 1932–58: A Study in Iraqi Politics* London: Oxford University Press, 1960), p. 30–31.

[2]*Ibid.*

[3]George Lenczowski, *The Middle East in World Affairs* (New York: Cornell University Press, 1966), pp. 273–74.

[4]Ibid., p. 275. See J. C. Hurewitz, *Diplomacy in the Near and Middle East* (Princeton: D. Van Nostrand Company, Inc., 1956), II, pp. 214–16 for text of Sa'adabad Pact.

[5]*Ibid.*, p. 276.

[6]Khadduri, *op. cit.*, p. 175.

[7]*Ibid.*

[8]Lenczowski, *op. cit.*, p. 277.

[9]Khadduri, *op. cit.*, pp. 190–91.

[10]*Ibid.*, p. 227.

[11]*Ibid.*, p. 244.

[12]Benjamin Schwadran, *The Middle East, Oil and the Great Powers 1959* (New York: Council for Middle Eastern Affairs Press, 1959), p. 193.

[13]George B. Cressey, *Crossroads: Land and Life in Southwest Asia* (New York: J. B. Lippincott Company, 1960), p. 213.

[14]*Ibid.*, p. 215.

[15]Khadduri, *op. cit.*, p. 355.

[16]George L. Harris, *Iraq* (New Haven: HRAF Press, 1958), pp. 163–65.

[17]See Maurice K. Dorion, "The Relationship Between the Department of State and the American Oil Companies Operating in the Middle East" (Unpublished Master's thesis, University of Utah, Salt Lake City, 1964), for full discussion of this policy.

[18]Schwadran, *op. cit.*, p. 242.

[19]*Ibid.*, p. 245.

[20]*Ibid.*, p. 263.

[21]Walter Z. Laquer, *The Soviet Union and The Middle East* (New York: Frederick A. Praeger, 1959), pp. 123–24.

[22]Stephen H. Longrigg, *Iraq, 1900 to 1950: A Political, Social and Economic History* (London: Oxford University Press, 1953), p. 336.

[23]*Ibid.*, p. 340.

[24]Laquer, *op. cit.*, p. 203.

[25]*Ibid.*

CHAPTER 6
PRELUDE TO REVOLUTION—
THE HASHEMITE ERA

The Middle East Defense Organization as suggested by U. S. Secretary of State John Foster Dulles was abandoned in late 1953 primarily because of Egyptian opposition. The so-called Northern Tier concept was then devised by Washington and London to work primarily with Turkey and Pakistan, who were more immediately conscious of the Soviet threat from the north. The initiative was taken by Turkey and a military assistance pact was concluded with Pakistan on April 2, 1954. The United States, although not directly involved in these arrangements, gave evidence of support by continuing and increasing its aid to Turkey and by concluding a mutual assistance agreement with Pakistan on May 19, 1954.[1]

The Government of Iraq in 1954 was confronted with two basic problems as a result of these arrangements: first, whether or not to join the Northern Tier defense pacts, and secondly, how to change her relationship with Great Britain, to whom she was still linked by the 1930 treaty.[2] Prime Minister Nuri es-Said made clear the Iraqi government's objectives in a press interview on November 1, 1954. According to the Baghdad press, Nuri stated: "We are not strong enough to be able to assist others, but we are trying to find a means to correlate our foreign policy with the provisions of the Turkish-Pakistani Pact. All that we can do at the present is organize the defense of Iraq through cooperation with neighboring states."[3]

This was to lead soon to the conclusion of the Baghdad Pact, which held tragic consequences for Iraq. Both Arab nationalism and the formation of the Arab League influenced this event.

"One Arab Nation with an eternal message."[4] This descriptive introductory remark to the Resolutions of the Sixth National Congress of the National Command of the Arab Ba'ath Socialist Party summed up the feeling or concept of Arab nationalism as then viewed by contemporary exponents of this idea. As the idea was more fully stated by King Hussein of Jordan to the First Ordinary Session of the 8th Jordanian Parliament on November 2, 1953, it means that: "We believe that what is good for any one Arab country is good for all the Arabs, and that any injury that may be inflicted on any Arab land is an injury to all Arabs. We call upon the Arabs to close their ranks and to consider only the common destiny of the entire Arab nation."[5]

The birth of the concept of Arab nationalism was discussed in Chapter 3, but it is clear that, "All that the Arabs wanted at first—the masses were still indifferent—was that the Arab provinces within the Ottoman Empire should have an autonomous Arab government."[6] Both the "promises" of the Allies during the course of World War I and President Wilson's ideas of self-determination and independence led to the Arab desire for political independence. Prince Faisal, the future ruler of Iraq, addressed a memorandum to the Paris Peace Conference on January 1, 1919, in which he wrote: "The country from a line Alexandretta-Persia, southward to Indian Ocean is inhabited by 'Arabs'—by which we mean people of closely related semitic stocks, all speaking the one language, Arabic. . . . The aim of the Arab nationalist movements . . . is to unite the Arabs eventually into one nation."[7] These desires, as we have seen, were temporarily frustrated by the secret wartime agreements and their consequent finalization in the form of mandates.

The actual presence, however, of the Mandatory Powers did much to intensify the struggle for independence, as well as increasing opposition to foreign intervention, and fostering local nationalism rather than Arab nationalism. In addition, Western political and economic competition in the entire area served to aggravate the situation. As a consequence, three related impulses seemed to have directed this national movement: first, and foremost, was a desire for emancipation from foreign domination;

secondly, independent socio-political development; and finally, some form of political unification.

These aspirations were pursued first by independent actions on the part of the various nation-states of the Middle East. For example, Egypt removed British influence and consequently nationalized the Suez Canal in 1956; oil was nationalized in non-Arab Iran in 1951; and the United Arab Republic was formed in 1958 through the unification of Syria and Egypt. "Arab nationalism . . . is the spontaneous expression of a natural longing for universally-cherished values, within the peculiarities of a concrete national context and in response to specific historical experiences and challenges. Its substance is universally human; its specific form, the timing of its actions, and the pattern of its evolution are peculiar to the Arab situation."[8]

Arab nationalism, however, as previously was pointed out, does not have a single creed; there is no unanimity as to its basic principles, nor is there agreement as to the manner in which these goals should be pursued. Such events as the disruption of the United Arab Republic in 1961 and the advent of "Nasserism" as a creed in itself which suggests that Arab nationalism can succeed only under Nasser's leadership exemplify this disparity. There is an underlying and unifying element, however, in the concept of Arab nationalism in the sense of belonging to the Arab nation, in having Arabic as a common tongue, in the fact of having been born an Arab in an Arab land, and in being a Muslim. Further the desire to attain the third of the aforementioned objectives of political unification, Arab unity, is strongly evident. Arab unity, although it is implicit in the feeling and awareness of Arabism, has generally been directed towards some practical approach to political unification, however unsuccessful. The formation of the United Arab Republic in 1958 and its dissolution in 1961 was one such attempt to translate Arab nationalism into Arab unity. Another such effort was the creation of the League of Arab States.[9]

The League of Arab States

Anxious to strengthen and consolidate the ties which bind all Arab countries and to direct them toward the welfare of the Arab world, to improve its conditions, insure its future, and realize its hopes and aspirations,

And in response to Arab public opinion in all Arab countries, . . . [it is agreed that]
A League will be formed of the independent Arab States which consent to join the League.[10]

In this document the hopes and desires of the Prime Ministers and other high level representatives of the existing seven independent Arab states was expressed on October 7, 1944. This introduction to a series of resolutions which later became known as the Protocol of Alexandria, defined the general purposes of the proposed League of Arab States and expressed the principles of inter-governmental Arab cooperation.

Significantly, it was the Iraqi Prime Minister, Nuri es-Said, who preceded these resolutions with a plan for a federation of Syria, Palestine, Lebanon and Jordan under the sponsorship of the United Nations. He outlined his plan for Arab unity in the so-called Blue Book or "The Fertile Crescent Plan" as a memorandum to Mr. R. G. Casey, the British Minister of State for the Middle East, in the spring of 1943. His proposal included the establishment of an "Arab League," to be formed initially by Iraq and Syria, with the proviso that "the other Arab States are permitted to adhere to it whenever they please."[11]

Nuri's plan for Arab unity was based on a practical approach and because he recognized the limitations of an all-inclusive Arab League, he suggested that historical Syria, (Iraq, Syria and Lebanon which is frequently called the Greater Syria) should be a focal point for further extension at a later date. Yet his long-range view of fundamental Arab nationalism was made evident in these words: "Many of our problems are the same; we are all part of one civilization; we generally think along the same lines and we are all animated by the same ideals of freedom of conscience, liberty of speech, equality before the law and the basic brotherhood of mankind."[12]

Nuri had been encouraged in his ideas by the British. Sir Anthony Eden, British Foreign Secretary, in response to a question in the House of Commons on February 24, 1943 as to Britain's position on greater cooperation among Arab states and the possibility of Arab federation, replied that "clearly the initiative . . . would have to come from the Arabs themselves." He went on to assert that the British would not obstruct Arab progress toward union.[13]

It is doubtful whether Nuri envisioned at this point anything more than a loose political confederation of Arab states that might possibly become a sovereign political entity in the future. Other Arab leaders, however, also took note of Eden's invitation, including the Egyptian premier, Nahhas Pasha. In an address to the Egyptian Chamber of Deputies on March 30, 1943, he referred to Eden's speech and stated that he had "come to the conclusion that the Egyptian government should take up the matter officially and should discover the opinion of the various Arab governments and at what they aim."[14] He proposed to serve as a mediator for conflicting proposals to work out a program for an Arab Union. He subsequently met with the leaders of each independent Arab state and a joint conference was convened on September 25, 1944 at Alexandria. Delegations from Lebanon, Egypt, Iraq, Syria and Trans-Jordan participated. Observers were sent from Saudi Arabia, Yemen, Libya, Morocco and Palestine. The resultant Alexandria Protocol was essentially a memorandum of understanding and provided for little more than a loose confederation based on coordination and cooperation on a voluntary basis. A "Council of the League of Arab States" was formed in which all participating states would be on an equal basis, yet the Resolutions of the Council would be binding only on those states which accepted them. "The idealistic drive toward some form of Arab unity subsided in the face of practical politics."[15]

The Protocol did provide that a General Arab Congress would be called to consider a constitution of an Arab League. Committees were formed to draft such a constitution, but the consequences of these preliminary arrangements were not foreseen by the delegates. Lively debate ensued in all Arab capitals and opposition was quick to form. Two days after the approval of the Protocol in Egypt, Nahhas Pasha was relieved as prime minister; the Syrian and Jordanian prime ministers were also dismissed; and reaction in Beirut was particularly violent, where the Christian Arab community denounced the Protocol as a threat to Lebanese sovereignty. The work of the drafting committees continued, however, and their preliminary work embodied the ideas of the Alexandria Protocol.

In spite of the opposition, the General Arab Congress convened in Cairo on March 17, 1945 and the draft pact was approved and signed by six of the seven founding members on March 22nd. The resulting covenant of the League of Arab States is an international treaty signed by the heads of states and has been duly ratified by its respective members. According to Article II of the Covenant:

> The object of the League shall be to strengthen the ties between the participant states, to co-ordinate their political programmes in such a way as to effect real collaboration between them, to preserve their independence and sovereignty, and to consider in general the affairs and interests of the Arab countries.[16]

Further areas for cooperation include economic and financial affairs, communications, cultural affairs, nationality, passports and visas, social questions and matters relating to public health. Cairo was designated as the permanent seat of the League of Arab States in Article X.

It is significant that the founders of the League of Arab States recognized the impracticality of Arab unity in 1945 and that they settled instead in favor of a regional organization with a view towards future ties under the auspices of the developing United Nations. The text of the Dumbarton Oaks proposals were available to drafters of the Covenant; Nahhas Pasha was known to have studied the organization of the Union of American Republics at this time; and finally the Covenant itself makes no allusion to eventual unity. It has functioned characteristically as a regional organization in a non-directive manner. This has obviously raised criticism from those who maintain that the League is an inadequate substitute for genuine Arab unity.

The League, then, is not a union, since it did not foresee the unification of Arab countries. It is an inter-governmental link between independent states which have lost none of their independence by joining the League; the members remain ultimate and supreme; and the League of Arab States is a symbol of relations existing between sovereign entities. "It was an association of real political beings, not a real political being in its own right; . . . not a state in itself; not a super-state; not a federation nor a confederation of states; and not a union of states—but merely a network of relationships among states."[17]

The Baghdad Pact

The League of Arab States and the United Arab Republic are two of the many unsuccessful attempts toward Arab unity over the past two decades. The first, a lone association of member-states, as stated above never intended nor achieved real unity. The second, while quite serious at first, proved both limited and temporary as the Union collapsed in 1961. In addition to these, there have been also concerted efforts on the part of the independent Arab nations to acquire defense arrangements against any threat from the outside.

Nuri es-Said, the perennial prime minister, was convinced that Iraq's best interest could be served by joining a Western-sponsored security system, but he was at the same time concerned with the necessity of ridding Iraq of the inequities imposed on her by the terms of the treaty of 1930 with Great Britain. Although Nuri was not prime minister during the time preceding the conclusion of the Baghdad Pact, he was minister of defense and foreign minister frequently when not occupying the "first among equals" position, and in such capacity he wielded considerable influence.

To this end, Nuri made concrete moves towards closer collaboration with Turkey. In January 1955 Turkish Premier Adnan Menderes and Nuri es-Said conferred in Baghdad and announced that a mutual assistance pact would soon be signed. Arab reaction was immediate, especially on the part of the Egyptian premier, Gamal Abdul Nasser, who called a conference of Arab premiers in Cairo to discuss the Arab League's relationships with the West and "insisted on a resolution which would not only declare any military pacts concluded by League members outside the League as inconsistent with the League's charter . . . but would also condemn Iraq with her expressed desire to sign a pact with Turkey."[18] The assembled premiers were not prepared to go this far, so no resolution or final communique was issued.

The Turkish-Iraqi Pact was signed in Baghdad on February 24, 1955 by the President of Turkey and the King of Iraq. It stipulated that the two countries would cooperate for mutual security and defense and would refrain from interference in each other's internal affairs. The treaty left open the possibility of future participation by other states. On April 4, 1955 Great Britain and Iraq concluded a Special Agreement in Baghdad whereby (1) Great Britain acceded to the February 24 Pact of Mutual Co-operation between Iraq and

Turkey; (2) the 1930 Treaty of Alliance between the two countries was terminated; and (3) Britain agreed to give Iraq military aid and "in the event of armed attack or the threat of armed attack [as seen by the two parties] endangers the security of Iraq, . . . make assistance available, including if necessary armed forces to help defend Iraq."[19]

The British participation was of considerable significance because it introduced a major power into an agreement which linked only medium or small states. However, the failure of the United States actively to participate, after having tacitly sponsored the concept, greatly weakened the alliance. The United States Ambassador to Iraq, Waldemar T. Gallman, believed that U. S. participation was in order. According to Ambassador Gallman:

> I urged our early adherence upon the State Department for the following reasons: We were the originators of the Northern Tier concept and gave the inspiration and encouragement which led to the Turkish-Iraqi Pact. . . . Our adherence, along with Britain's, would give the Middle East proof that we and the British were co-operating in the defense of the free world . . . [and]. . . . Nuri had shown great courage in aligning Iraq with Turkey and the West, risking not only much at home but also much in his relations with his Arab neighbors, and had earned our full support.[20]

In spite of repeated urgings on the part of Ambassador Gallman, as well as those expressed by American Ambassadors in Ankara, Tehran and Karachi, the United States refused to join the Baghdad Pact, nor did it join its successor, the Central Treaty Organization. Apparently, the United States State Department was reluctant to antagonize Egypt and feared Israeli protest, since Israel attacked the Pact as being hostile to her national interests.[21]

Pakistan joined the Pact five months after Britain and Iran followed in October 1955. The Northern Tier defense concept thus became a reality in a relatively short period of time—eight months—and the participating states could proceed to set up the required machinery for the operation of the Pact. A permanent secretariat was consequently established in Baghdad, and an Iraqi, Awni Khalidi, was selected as the first Secretary-General. This was a crowning achievement for Nuri es-Said, who had steadfastly maintained a pro-Western position in the face of serious opposition from Egypt.

American hesitation to participate had unfortunate effects. It encouraged Iraqi opposition to the Pact which was based on the criticism that the Pact was in reality nothing more than a British instrument of control, and that instead of linking Iraq with the West, it did little more than allow Britain to retain a foothold in Iraq. Further, the dramatic development in the Middle East during the period 1956–1958 exposed Iraq to further attacks from Arab States hostile to the Pact which were now rallying around Nasser as a result of the ill-fated invasion of Suez in 1956.

The Suez crisis of October-November, 1956, created the fear in Iraq that Egyptian-Israeli hostilities might expand beyond Sinai. This prompted Iraq to send troops to Jordan at the latter's request. In early November Baghdad broke off diplomatic relations with France and decided to boycott any Baghdad Pact meetings attended by British representatives. In the United Nations, Iraq's delegate, Dr. Fadhil Jamali, proclaimed Iraq's support of Egypt. The Suez crisis gave the leader of the opposition full opportunity to embarrass the government of Nuri es-Said internally and public indignation was aroused against Western imperialism. This led to protest demonstrations and serious riots in Mosul, Nejef and Kut. The government responded by arresting five of the principal opposition leaders and on December 1, it proclaimed martial law for all of Iraq.[22]

It is of interest that at the height of this explosive situation the United States issued an official statement supporting the Baghdad Pact. Noting the recent events which were seen as grave threats to the peace and security of the world, the United States statement concluded [that]:

The United States, from the inception of the Baghdad Pact, supported the pact and the principles and objectives of collective security on which it is based. . . . The United States reaffirms its support for the collective efforts of these nations to maintain their independence. A threat to the territorial integrity or political independence of the members would be viewed by the United States with utmost gravity.[23]

However, despite the stern measures taken by the government and despite tacit United States support, Nuri's opposition gained strength when President Nasser of Egypt turned military defeat into political victory. When he emerged as a potential, if not the actual, all-Arab leader and became a symbol of anti-Western imperialism, opposition forces in Iraq found considerable support. The Iraqi government had no choice but to combat this Cairo-inspired Arabism, and Allies were sought in this struggle from among the monarchical regimes remaining in the Arab world. In February 1957, Iraq's crown prince, Abdul Ilah, journeyed to Washington the same time that King Saud of Saudi Arabia was visiting President Eisenhower. Abdul Ilah and King Saud met, discussed the situation in the Middle East, and laid the foundation for a "Kings' alliance" which was later expanded to include the Hashemite Jordan. In a series of joint visits in the various capitals, the relationships were cemented and joint communiques were issued condemning communism, imperialism and Zionism.

This first reaction to the spread of Nasserism was followed by a confederation of Iraq and Jordan on February 14, 1958.[24] The King of Iraq became the head of the federation, known as "The Arab Federation," and its capital alternated every six months between Baghdad and Amman. During this entire period, Nuri es-Said remained in power, whether or not he was officially premier. In fact, he was appointed premier of the federation on March 3, 1958, not many months before the tragedy of July 14, 1958.

The 1958 Coup d'Etat

Young King Faisal came of age in 1953 and had been duly crowned in an elaborate coronation ceremony. He had been less than active in politics and had frequently absented himself from the country along with the crown prince and former regent, Abdul Ilah. This led to considerable criticism even with allowances made for the King's youth and inexperience. The U. S. Ambassador observed that "Soon after my arrival in Iraq, I came to feel that the King should begin to assert himself. He had admirable qualities, an alert mind and a warm, appealing personality."[25] He went on to relate, however, the severe handicap of the presence of the Crown Prince who was unpopular, undiscerning and "had gained a reputation for petty political maneuvering and intriguing."[26] Nuri es-Said, on the other hand, was respected and was considered the "strong man" of the regime. As in all Arab politics, it is essential that power be firmly asserted in terms of army control and police surveillance as well as by skillful political maneuvering.

Nuri es-Said was a professional soldier[27] and had the interests of the army at heart. He was careful to keep the army well equipped with the latest and best equipment he could obtain and did not indiscriminately commit them to impossible tasks. Until 1958 the army leadership refrained from political maneuvering and was considered a strong supporter of the crown. However, the intensive emotional involvements concerning Arab nationalism, which showed anti-Israel and anti-British feelings were not isolated from its officers since they shared the opinions and emotions of the civilian population from which the sentiments originated.

"Nuri was passionately devoted to public order. He knew that nothing permanent could be built without peace and security."[28] To this end he never hesitated to call out the police to suppress disturbances and, as we have seen, to declare martial law. Communists and students received special police attention. Strikes were immediately contained and eternal police vigilance was the order of the day.

On close examination, the above observations became no more than an understatement of the situation which then existed in Iraq. The majority of the cited observations have been made by those closely in sympathy with the existing regime. A more realistic evaluation clearly demonstrates that Western statesmen grossly misread the conditions existing in that country during the pre-revolutionary period. They failed, for example, to report the effective methods employed by the Iraqi government in preventing information seekers from entering the country and generally in keeping the world ignorant of events in the country. According to Professor Shwadran:

> The truth . . . was that Iraq, of all the countries of the Middle East, was the closest to a police state. Parliaments and other outer manifestations of democratic institutions notwithstanding, the regime was one of absolutism.
>
> Nuri es-Said, the perennial premier, and Amir Abd al-Illah, the real royal power, were the most hated men in the country because of their methods of tyrannizing and terrorizing all opposition, actual or potential, including the families of

suspected persons. The police, but even more decisively the army, maintained the rulers in power.[29]

As events developed, the latter view seems the more accurate because the new group of army officers who had not taken part in earlier Arab liberation movements had neither personal nor emotional attachment to the ruling house and were deeply impressed by the currents of Arab nationalism as well as by the developing influence of a socialist-communist ideology. In their opinion, two great crimes—Western style imperialism and feudalism—hindered progress in Iraq. Nuri and his conservative, *status quo*, regime was blamed for both of these crimes. In their judgment, Nuri was only a tool of the Great Western Powers, whose governments used him and his counterparts in former colonies and protectorates for their own political and economic advantage, to the detriment of the controlled country. "Indeed, every ill that befell Iraq was ascribed to imperialism, including the Arab regime itself."[30]

This is further substantiated by others:

[Nuri] ruled through an alliance of top military commanders (placated by large-scale donations of modern British tanks, artillery and jets) and the feudal land owners, who dominated Iraq's rigged Parliament. All political parties were banned, the press censored, and there were 10,000 political prisoners, torture was regularly employed and Nuri spent three times as much on the police as on public education.[31]

In spite of Nuri's precautions, there was in Iraq no real deterrence for the strong impulses of revolutionary movement which reacted against oppression. The actual events proceeded rapidly. The 20th Army Brigade which was considered safe, had been ordered to move because of events in Jordan and Lebanon. However, under the command of Brigadier-General Abdul Karim Kassem, it moved to Baghdad during the early morning hours of July 14, 1958 and took control of the city. Within a short period of time all members of the royal family in Baghdad, including King Faisal and the Crown Prince, were put to death. Cabinet ministers and key government officials were all apprehended and arrested, with the exception of Nuri, who fled into hiding, "but was discovered a few days later disguised as a woman and killed."[32]

New revolutionary authority was then established by a Council of Sovereignty, which had three members and a cabinet headed by General Kassem, who also retained supreme command of the armed forces. On the day following the coup, General Kassem issued a public statement in which he:

(1) Proclaimed the liberation of the "country from the domination of a corrupt group which was installed by imperialism."

(2) Announced the formation of "an Iraqi republic which will preserve Iraqi unity" and,

(3) [called for] "brotherly ties with the other Arab countries."[33]

Nuri es-Said, the foremost statesman of modern Iraq, died wretchedly in the streets of Baghdad, wrapped like a woman in black cloth, his face made up and covered with a veil that native harlots usually wear. Only one woman stayed in heroic fidelity at his side to die with him. Not one friendly door offered sanctuary; for hours he and his companion wandered through streets crowded with people who hated him and all he stood for. At most there is to be found in Baghdad some pity in the manner of his death; and that is rare.[34]

This sequence of events gives rise to the question of whether the new regime could have changed the pattern of politics in Iraq. The following chapter will consider this imporant question through an examination of developments which followed the violent events of the summer of 1958.

NOTES

[1]See J. C. Hurewitz, *Diplomacy in the Near and Middle East* (Princeton: D. Van Nostrand Company, Inc., 1956), for text of agreements.

[2]See Appendix B.

[3]As quoted in Waldemar J. Gallman, *Iraq Under General Nuri: My Recollections of Nuri al-Said, 1954–1958* (Baltimore: The Johns Hopkins Press, 1964), p. 25.

[4]Walid Khalidi and Yusuf Ibish (eds.), *Arab Political Documents, 1963* (Beirut: American University of Beirut, 1963), p. 438.

[5]*Ibid.*, pp. 64–65.

[6]Zeine N. Zeine, *The Emergence of Arab Nationalism* (Beirut: Khayats, 1966), p. 149.

[7]*Ibid.*, p. 151.

[8]Fayez A. Sayegh, *Arab Unity* (New York: The Devin-Adair Company, 1958), p. 7.

[9]It is of considerable interest that the original plan for an "Arab League" came from Nuri es-Said of Iraq, who was opposed by the then Egyptian Premier, Nahhas Pasha. See Robert W. Macdonald, *The League of Arab States* (Princeton: University Press, 1965), p. 34ff. and Appendix C.

[10]Muhammad Khalil, *The Arab States and the Arab League: A Documentary Record* (Beirut: Khayats, 1962), Vol. II, p. 54.

[11]*Ibid.*, p. 10. See Appendix C for the primary portions of Nuri's Fertile Crescent Project, officially entitled "Arab Independence and Unity: Memorandum on the Arab Cause," printed by the Government Press, Baghdad, 1943.

[12]As quoted in Gallman, *op. cit.*, pp. 134–35.

[13]House of Commons, *Parliamentary Debates* (London: H. M. Stationery Office, 1944), Vol. 398, p. 142.

[14]Macdonald, *op. cit.*, p. 36.

[15]*Ibid.*, p. 39.

[16]Khalil, *op. cit.*, p. 58.

[17]Sayegh, *op. cit.*, p. 121.

[18]George Lenczowski, *The Middle East in World Affairs* (New York: Cornell University Press, 1966), p. 292.

[19]Khalil, *op. cit.*, pp. 368–76. See Appendix D for full text of the Baghdad Pact.

[20]Gallman, *op. cit.*, pp. 58–59.

[21]Lenczowski, *op. cit.*, p. 293.

[22]*Ibid.*, p. 295.

[23]Khalil, *op. cit.*, p. 376.

[24]This was, in part, in response to the Egyptian-Syrian union as the United Arab Republic two weeks earlier. See Khalil, *op. cit.*, pp. 79–80 for text of agreement between Iraq and Jordan. The text of the Proclamation of the United Arab Republic, February 1, 1958 has also been translated from the original (Arabic) by Khalil, *op. cit.*, pp. 601–2.

[25]Gallman, *op. cit.*, p. 90.

[26]*Ibid.*

[27]He served admirably in the desert campaigns of World War I and was a member of the groups of British and Arabs who took part in the Arab revolt. See Thomas E. Lawrence, *Revolt in the Desert* (New York: Doran, 1927).

[28]Gallman, *op. cit.*, p. 92.

[29]Benjamin Shwadran, *The Power Struggle in Iraq* (New York: Council for Middle Eastern Affairs press, 1960), p. 12. See also D. F. Fleming, *The Cold War and Its Origins* (London: George Allen and Univin Ltd., 1961), pp. 921ff.

[30]*Ibid.*, p. 13.

[31]"Politics of Iraq," *New Statesman*, July 19, 1958, p. 74.

[32]Lenczowski, *op. cit.*, p. 298.

[33]"Announcement of Coup d'Etat in Iraq," *Middle Eastern Affairs*, IX (August-September 1958). See Appendix E.

[34]"Iraq's New Regime," *Economist*, August 2, 1958. p. 380.

CHAPTER 7
MILITARY DICTATORSHIP—
THE KASSEM ERA

One author described the Middle Eastern events of the summer of 1958 as "Midsummer Madness."[1] In June there was growing tension in Lebanon; in July there was upheaval in Iraq; in the same month the United States landed troops in Lebanon and Great Britain did the same in Jordan; and in August a frustrated United Nations attempted to cope with the problems raised by the positioning of Western military forces in the Middle East.

"The Lebanese scene presented a maze of local conflicts and rivalries of clans and families, chieftains and politicians, feuding localities and denominations, their younger branches equipped with the modernized paraphernalia of party and ideology."[2] It could well be added that these groups were torn by internal strifes. When the Arab League proved unable to resolve the problems of violent opposition against President Camille Chamoun, the case was put before the U.N. Security Council. The Council, aided by a U.S.S.R. abstention, was able to send a force of observers to Lebanon. The Middle East members of the Baghdad Pact, Iraq, Pakistan, Iran, Turkey, announced their support of the regime in power. Yet, the Lebanese government saw great threat of foreign United Arab Republic subversion, which they interpreted as being

Soviet-supported. President Chamoun asked "of what use [was] the Eisenhower Doctrine . . . if Lebanon could not be helped against the evident danger."[3] The reply was that the Doctrine did apply in case of direct aggression from Communist-ruled countries, and U.S. marines were landed.

King Hussein of Jordan saw himself likewise threatened primarily from the United Arab Republic-based incitement and subversion. With the collapse of his cousin's regime in Iraq, he, too, appealed for help from the British, who responded with military forces. American troops in Lebanon numbered about 15,000, while the British sent about 4,000 troops to Jordan.

Activity in the United Nations Security Council centered around conflict between the U.S.S.R. and the U.S. The U.S.S.R. felt that the whole Western involvement "reeked with the smell of oil" and that American policy was dictated by the oil interests in the Middle East. The Soviets vetoed a U.S. bid for a U.N. police force in the Middle East on July 18, 1958 and spoke of a British-American plan of aggression intended to suppress national liberation movements in the Middle East area. To their mind, the landings in Lebanon and Jordan were aimed at the suppression of the popular revolution in Iraq. Discussion in the Security Council proved inconclusive and a special emergency session of the General Assembly was called on August 8. After considerable debate and behind-the-scenes talks, the Secretary-General, Dag Hammarskjold, left for the Middle East to make "practical arrangements" to uphold the U.N. Charter and to effect early withdrawal of foreign troops from Lebanon and Jordan.[4]

The subversive influence of the United Arab Republic and President Nasser's new brand of Arab nationalism were repeatedly pointed to as the underlying causes of the events of the summer, especially as applied to Iraq. The United Arab Republic at this point was merely an oil-transit power, strengthened by the Suez Canal nationalization in 1956. The union with Syria provided additional control of the oil flow (via pipeline) through that country. Successful *coup d'etat* by Nasser-controlled forces would add Lebanon and Iraq to the fold, and with the addition of Iraq, oil producing revenue would supposedly then be available to Nasser. Although it was believed at the time that the *coup* in Iraq was designed to bring Iraq into Nasser's camp, this proved to be an erroneous assumption on the part of Western statesmen.

Two questions for Iraq were apparent: Could the new regime change the pattern from the traditional, Western-oriented alignment and if so, could the change be dictated from outside sources?

What, in fact, happened was that General Kassem's military *coup d'etat* in 1958 "opened a veritable Pandora's box of long-suppressed forces. Of these the most militant were the Communists, the *Ba'athists,* and the less well organized but intensely committed Nasserites."[5] In addition, two long-standing internal opposition groups re-emerged: the nationalist and conservative *Istiqlal* Party and the National-Democratic Party, the socialist heir to the *Ahali* movement of the 1930's. The first general impression, especially in the United States, was that the *coup* had been engineered by President Nasser of the United Arab Republic, indirectly assisted by the Soviet Union. Lebanon and Jordan were considered merely stepping stones toward the major objective: Iraq and her oil resources.[6] It was assumed that General Kassem and his "Free Officers Revolutionary Movement" would come forth in the Egyptian pattern and embrace the new hero of Arab nationalism, President Nasser of the United Arab Republic. In this respect, it was also believed that General Kassem was merely a "front man" of the General Naguib type in Egypt (1952) who would soon give way to the supposed power behind the *coup,* Colonel Abdul Salem Aref, who represented a strong unionist tendency with the United Arab Republic.[7]

These assumptions proved to be erroneous. General Kassem proved to be the foremost personality in the entire drama. He was not only the leader of the revolution, but he was also the head of the revolutionary regime. Abd al-Karim Kassem, born into a lower middle class family, spent practically his entire life in the army. A rather quiet, secretive person, he apparently believed he was destined by fate to fulfill a great mission assigned to him by Allah; his dedication finally reached the martyr-complex stage. On August 5, 1958 he declared: "People, I am the son of the people. I pledge before God that I will sacrifice myself for your sake. I shall offer my life in defense of the Iraqi people."[8] It soon became evident that the motivating force of Kassem was Iraqi nationalism rather than Arab nationalism and local symbolic attachments prevailed over regional loyalties based on outside interests.

Further, the ever-present theme in all his speeches, regardless of what group he was addressing, was that of Iraqi unity and cooperation. He apparently recognized the divisive forces in operation and was conscious of the fact that Iraq was not a solid, nationally aware unit which would relegate individual or group interests for the sake of so-called national interests. He was also a practical Middle East politician who realistically recognized that his basis of strength was the army. It was Kassem's aim to establish a modern state based on the sovereignty and independence of Iraq. He did not want his state to be dependent on Western support; nor did he want it to be in political union with President Nasser's United Arab Republic despite the lip service paid by him and his colleagues to the cause of Arab nationalism. The pressure of popular demand, however, could not be overlooked. Consequently, on July 19, 1958 the United Arab Republic and the Republic of Iraq issued a joint communique in which the two Republics pledged themselves to the support of the Arab League, to mutual aid against foreign aggression and to closer cooperation in the future. By the first week in August, General Kassem's government had been recognized by most states and statements had been issued regarding the resumption of diplomatic relations with the Soviet Union, Yugoslavia and the People's Republic of China.[9]

Kassem had established himself as Premier and Minister of Defense and in the two weeks following the *coup*, he proclaimed a provisional constitution.[10] Under which terms Iraq was to be an independent, Islamic Arab state in which executive authority was placed in the Council of Ministers. A three-man Council of Sovereignty had the authority to approve or reject laws passed by the Council of Ministers. Previous legislation passed under the Hashemite Monarchy would remain in effect until changed or abolished. Although personal and religious freedom and the independence of the judiciary were guaranteed, there was no reference to political parties in the provisional constitution. Further Kassem declared that certain basic reforms should be undertaken before holding a plebiscite on the provisional constitution.[11]

While all of this has the appearance of progressive posture and promised reform,[12] signs of conflict and repression were evident. It was not long before the idea that revolutions rarely produce a stable order overnight was confirmed. The establishment of a modern state was not an easy task.

The first major rift occurred between Premier Kassem and his Deputy Premier, Colonel Abdul Salem Aref, the Minister of the

Interior in the *coup d'etat* cabinet. Aref, who was closely associated
with the *Ba'ath* or Renaissance Party, was an outstanding
spokesman for union with the United Arab Republic. Whereas
Kassem's public pronouncements significantly omitted any reference of the Egyptian ruler. Colonel Aref paid tribute to "Big
Brother Gamel Abdel Nasser" in nearly every public statement he
made after July 14th, 1950.[13] It should be noted here also that Aref
was instrumental during the weeks following the *coup* in generating
frenzied street scenes with the assistance of Communist and
pro-Nasser agitators, first in Baghdad, then in other cities and
towns. To say the least, Kassem was disturbed by his Deputy's
behavior.[14] In September, Premier Kassem decided to relieve him
of his post as Deputy Prime Minister and as compensation appointed
him Ambassador to the German Federal Republic. "The first
intimation the German Embassy or the Bonn government had of the
appointment was when it was announced in the Baghdad
press. . . . Aref went through the motions of setting out for Bonn.
He never got there."[15] A month later he was arrested in Baghdad
for plotting to overthrow and assassinate Premier Kassem. He was
sentenced to death by a secret trial with an option to commute his
sentence to life imprisonment. Others, however, who had
committed "crimes" against the Kassem regime were dealt with in
a less civilized manner, often involving shocking spectacles.

The law of trying officials of the old regime stated that "a
criminal court shall be formed and be called the Special Supreme
Military Court to try the crimes committed under this law or other
penal laws referred to it by the Commander-in-Chief of the armed
forces. This court shall consist of a president not lower than a
colonel, and four members not lower than majors, to be appointed
by a republican decree upon recommendation of the Defense
Minister."[16] There were no provisions for appeal and the decisions
of the court were to be final.

Colonel Fadil Abbas al-Mahdawi, Kassem's cousin, was named
President of the Court. "A person with a good education but
somewhat naive in his assessment of the value and importance of
knowledge, and lacking in wisdom, al-Mahdawi exploited the
possibilities for popularity which the court afforded; he did not feel
the awesomeness and sacredness of a court of law."[17] This appears
to be a gross understatement on actual proceedings as revealed by
reports of the court's activities. The proceedings were broadcast and

televised live and receiver sets were installed in all public places. Since seating was limited in the court's chamber, tickets were carefully distributed to known supporters of the regime, whose function it was to display enthusiasm for the performance of the Court's President. "With a steady flow of unbridled and inciting words he [al-Mahdawi] carried on a dual role of judge and prosecutor. He repeatedly interrupted the defendants . . . with accusations and tauntings and he encouraged the spectators to do the same."[18] Although many Iraqis sickened of this travesty of justice and were shocked by the death sentences meted out to once prominent public figures, it was to Kassem's credit, and also a source of his downfall, that he commuted many of them to prison terms and even rescinded some. However, the Court was allowed to continue well into 1959.

The Court came to serve as a national platform as well as an instrumentality for al-Mahdawi's own promotion. Foreign dignitaries were often invited to attend proceedings and then were subjected to long welcoming speeches which glorified the Iraqi revolution and its leadership. In addition, the United Arab Republic, President Nasser, the Israelis, the British, the Americans, and anyone who dared criticize the Court were attacked unmercifully.

A Political Maze

A member of the British Parliament visited Premier Kassem in late October 1958 and described the general atmosphere of the regime.

At every turn on the way in [to Kassem's office] there were armed, heel-clicking sentries. The Prime Minister's small anteroom was full of colonels and majors. His staff, as far as I could see, was exclusively military. His own room was almost equally small and unimpressively furnished. His desk was untidy and looked . . . as though he had been continuously at it for several days and nights. The general atmosphere was more that of the field headquarters of a military commander . . . than of the office of a Prime Minister.[19]

Premier Kassem had attempted to form a coalition cabinet

representing a compromise of all political factions. He invited outstanding leaders of former opposition parties to join the government. Mohammad Hadid of the National-Democratic Party was named Minister of Finance; Siddiq Shanshal of the Istiqlal (Independence) Party was designated as Minister of Guidance; Fuad Rikabi of the Arab Socialist Renaissance (Ba'ath) Party was named head of the Ministry of Development; and Ibrahim Kubbah, a Marxist, was selected as Minister of National Economy.[20] However, the early dismissal of Colonel Aref, the Deputy Premier, and the activities of al-Mahdawi's Court gave clear indication that all was not well and that opposition to the revolutionary regime existed within the country itself. Kassem, although aware of this threat, as evidenced by his constant guard, did not share his predecessors' nor Nasser's belief that political parties were corruptible and mere tools of imperialistic forces against Arab nationalism. "He believed that different political parties would all work for the overall good and welfare of the country."[21] Consequently, on January 6, 1960, parties were licensed and permitted to function. This fact is rather misleading, however, since the revolution did not in reality bring the expected freedom. Rather, the Kassem era became more authoritarian, more arbitrary, less predictable and more intolerant of the opposition than was the Nuri regime.

The major political groupings were:

(1) The *Istiqlal* (Independence) Party, which was the major opposition to Nuri es-Said's rule. It became the chief protagonist of the new Iraqi nationalism, opposing closer association with the United Arab Republic and advocating a moderate neutralism with a pro-Western slant.

(2) The National-Democratic Party, the "socialists" of Iraq, closely aligned with the *Istiqlal* Party, with the exception of a few leaders such as the Minister of National Economy, Ibrahim Kubbah, who were extremely pro-Soviet.

(3) The *Ba'ath* (Arab Socialist Renaissance) Party, an off-shoot of and closely related to the Syrian *Ba'ath* Party which largely brought about Syria's merger with Egypt. Its birthplace was Damascus, and its tight organization preached freedom, socialism, and Arab unity.

(4) The Communist Party of Iraq, which once was the strongest party in the Middle East until Nuri es-Said decimated its ranks,

enjoyed an incomparable resurgence. Kassem released almost all political prisoners after the *coup* and the Communists benefitted the most. "In 'Soviet Friendship,' the Iraqi CP's purpose was obvious, and it found fertile ground. The average Baghdadi in the street is still very unlikely today to include Khrushchev as one of his 'friends.' The sudden mushrooming of new Communist-bloc diplomatic missions, information offices, delegations, etc., following on the adoption of a neutralist policy by the republic, found the CP well placed to benefit."[22]

(5) The Kurdish Rebels should be included here as a separate grouping although they represented a pro-Soviet element in Iraq. A number of these rebels were permitted by the Kassem government to return from prison and exile. The most prominent of these was Mullah Mustafa Barzani, who had spent fifteen years behind the Iron Curtain. "This benevolent attitude of the Baghdad government towards Kurdish rebels is inexplicable, for the slogan of Free Kurdistan must be anathema to Kassem's nationalists no less than to the old regime. Iraqi politics seem to have a logic of their own."[23]

Kassem's cabinet, at first, represented a genuine national coalition, including all shades of political opinion, except the Communists; it represented an equilibrium of sorts. Since there was a tendency towards the political left, and because they were allowed freedom to publish and organize, the Communists voiced no objection. They even refrained from criticizing Kassem's tolerance of the Iraq Petroleum Company, a feature of Kassem's prudence.[24] This was not to last, however, as the upsurge of Communist activity encountered resistance. This resistance saw the resignation of six cabinet members on February 7, 1959. These included Fuad Rikabi, Minister of Development, and Siddiq Shansal, Minister of National Guidance, whose replacement, Hussein Jamal, stayed in office only five days. This passive expression of resistance to the Communists failed at the high-government level, but other activities took a more drastic turn.

The Mosul Revolt and the Kirkuk Massacres

On March 8, 1959, a revolt against Kassem's regime took place in Mosul. Ostensibly it was a revolt against Kassem. A dissident group of army officers led by Colonel Abdul Wahab el-Shawaf, the commander of the Mosul garrison, chose the occasion of a meeting of thousands of Peace Partisans (a Communist-front organization) who had been brought to Mosul for a major rally in trains provided by the government. The new group described Kassem's rule as a mob dictatorship and called for him to resign. In addition, Kassem was charged with dangerous hostility towards the United Arab Republic and he was called an anti-Arab-nationalist who had abandoned the principle of positive neutrality. These charges were broadcast from the Mosul radio and citizens of Iraq were called to join in the new revolt. It is highly significant that these charges coincided with similar outbursts carried by the United Arab Republic press and radio.

The military operation, however, was poorly planned and provided no air cover. The rebels had further counted on the support of Staff Brigadier Nazim al-Tabaqchali, commander of the 2nd Division based at Kirkuk. When this failed to develop, the revolt was doomed. Loyal government troops supported by the air force and armed Kurdish tribesmen easily suppressed it. Colonel al-Shawaf, wounded in a bombing of his headquarters, was later shot to death in the hospital by a male nurse. The uprising was a dismal failure. The aftermath, however, "could be likened to Dantean horror scenes. Communist liquidation squads went on a rampage, attacking homes of the Mosul bourgeoisie and perpetrating all sorts of atrocities."[25] Nasser was publicly accused of complicity in the revolt and was hung in effigy. Nasser retaliated in a speech from Damascus in which he asserted that the Communists had taken over Iraq with the aid of unscrupulous opportunities, including Premier Kassem. Cairo's official Middle East News Agency reported on March 13 that: "Members of the Communist Party rush into the houses of Arab nationalists and kill them. If they fail to find the master of the house, they kill the women and children.[26] A self-appointed proletarian court sitting in a public square meted out summary justice and executions were carried out on the spot. Cairo press accounts of the terror in Iraq were undoubtedly exaggerated, but there remained sufficient grains of truth to serve as a shocking reminder to the people of Iraq of what might lay in store for them should the Communists effectively seize power. From that time onward, opposition to the Communists increased among the nationalist elements.

On the other hand, Communists sought to strengthen their

position by bolder advances. They pressed Kassem for two specific concessions: first, the immediate execution of those who had been condemned to death by al-Mahdawi's People's Court; and, second, Communist participation in Premier Kassem's cabinet. They were unsuccessful in the first instance, but constant pressure forced Kassem to reshuffle his cabinet and on July 14, 1959—the first anniversary of the revolution—he appointed four new ministers, two of whom were generally believed to be Communist Party members. The Communists, however, were not satisfied and resorted to violence and terror in order to seize power in provincial centers in the country.

The most notable instance of evidence was a bloody massacre in Kirkuk from July 14 to 19, 1959. Communist agitation took advantage of ethnic antagonisms between Arabs and Turkomans and incited the various segments of the population into action. Communists, aided by local Kurds, attacked private homes and business establishments, most of them Turkomans. "First reports gave the dead as over one hundred, including women and children, and large numbers seriously wounded. Unsuspecting victims had been invited to come out of their houses and had been murdered and their mutilated bodies carried through the streets of the city.''[27]

Premier Kassem saw in the disturbances a systematic plan which was to be repeated in other places, including Baghdad. He saw in this "anarchist plan" a conspiracy against the leaders and the government against which he promised retaliation. On August 6 he announced over the radio: "We have adopted measures and made preparations to destroy every anarchist in the future, regardless of his ideology or race.''[28]

The Kirkuk incident dramatized the confused picture of politics in Iraq, especially as regards Communism itself. At the time it was universally believed that the Kirkuk massacre was the product of Communist tactics. In fact, the central Committee of the Iraqi Communist Party drew up a lengthy report in mid-July in which it freely indulged in self-criticism not heard previously. It practically admitted responsibility. The Committee acknowledged that it had made "a wrong assessment, which exaggerated our own forces and minimized the role of the patriotic government and the other national forces in safeguarding the Republic." It admitted to taking a wrong stand on the "excesses of the masses.''[29]

In any event, this position served Kassem well because it placed the Communists on the defensive, their strength decreased, and he was able more readily to balance forces against each other for his own advantage, at least temporarily.

The demonstrations of Communist strength apparently impressed the Premier deeply and caused him to reorient his position toward the party. The change was gradual and he refrained from open attack, but he did use government influence to eliminate Communists from control of trade unions, professional and mass associations, and applied various repressive measures against the Communist press. However, there were still other pressures to be reckoned with and there was constant effort on the part of the Pan-Arab and pro-Nasser elements to undermine his position. This was vividly demonstrated when, on October 7, 1959, a group of Ba'ath Party members shot and wounded him in the shoulder while he was driving a station wagon on the main street of Baghdad. His martyr complex became more evident and he was then even more convinced that he was destined to become Iraq's savior. And who was to blame for this latest attack? He made it clear whom he believed to have been responsible for it in a recorded broadcast from his hospital bed: "We will triumph against imperialism and destroy any power which covets our country."[30] There was no question in anyone's mind that he was referring to the United Arab Republic.

Kassem-Nasser Controversy

The antagonism between the two leaders apparently began to take shape when Kassem refused to unite Iraq with the United Arab Republic. If the first year of Kassem's regime is seen as a series of moves to play Nasserites and the Communists against each other, the second was surely a period of alienation from both. The Communist conflict has briefly been noted above. What, then, of the Nasser controversy?

Six months ago a hero, the most unpopular man in Iraq today is President Gamal Abdul Nasser. The streets of Baghdad are plastered with obscene pictures of him, mostly pastiches made of Nasser's head pasted on the bathing-beauty bodies of American film starlets or on the body of a donkey or pig.[31]

Nasser was no longer the hero or the revolutionary movement.

> Arabists with long experience in Iraq, working in the
> country until the last hour before the revolution, have
> confessed their astonishment at the pattern of loyalties in 1959.
> The revolution itself they could either guess or predict with
> varying emphasis. But I have yet to meet the Englishman who
> foresaw that eight months after the death of Nuri es-Said, Iraq
> and the United Arab Republic would be conducting a war of
> mutual recrimination as bitter as anything in the previous 40
> years; . . .[32]

It would seem again that national interests came first. Despite
attachments to the historical legacy of an Arab-Islamic past the
immediate problems as translated into the struggle for power take
precedence over a commitment to regional loyalties. Also, whatever
contributed to the old struggle between regions of the Middle East
seems to be active again. And, of course, oil adds to it.

The struggle between the Nile and Mesopotamia began with the
dawn of history. Separate and distinct civilizations gave rise to
different cultural and social traditions, but today the stakes are
higher. The prize in reality is oil, wealth and the power it generates,
politically and otherwise in the marketplaces of the world.

President Nasser set the early keynote immediately after Iraqi
coup in a speech delivered in Damascus on July 19, 1958:

> I told you . . . that Arab Nationalism which every one of
> you represents is almost manifest in every Arab country, that
> Arab Nationalism which is resolutely determined to start on
> the Sacred March . . . has countless armies everywhere. I
> also spoke about the vanguard of the Sacred March in Iraq, and
> about the revolution of Iraq and told you that that was Arab
> Nationalism and that those were the armies of Arab
> Nationalism and that we, every one of us, shall consider
> ourselves its men and armies.[33]

The question is, of course, what changed this spirit of unity?

The controversy between the two leaders apparently had its
origins in the arrest, the trial and the conviction of Colonel Abdul

Salem Aref in February 1959. Colonel Aref had visited President
Nasser in Damascus shortly after the *coup* and it was apparent that
the two men were in accord. During Aref's trial, testimony was
given which clearly indicated that rapprochement between Iraq and
the United Arab Republic would be forthcoming if Aref assumed
Iraqi leadership. When the death sentence for Aref was announced
by the Court, new and more vicious attacks were directed by the
United Arab Republic against the Kassem regime. While Kassem
himself refused to enter into the debate, reply was made by
al-Mahdawi from his position as President of the "People's" Court.
The antagonism became even more open and pronounced after the
Mosul revolt. A couple of examples of these exchanges will suffice
to illustrate the vehemence of these verbal attacks on both sides.

In March, 1959, in a series of speeches in Damascus, President
Nasser accused Kassem of working with international communism
in order to sabotage Arab unity; Nasser claimed credit for arming
the Kassem revolt of July 14, having "issued instructions to Cairo
to give the Iraqi revolution everything it desired and requested."
and accused Kassem of "being a tool of British imperialism and the
Communists."[34]

An Iraqi newspaper reacted in the following manner:

What lies behind the abuses and vilification of the plotter
whose black froth sprays the air? What does this failure
Pharaoh want now that, as of yesterday, he has obtained the
unity which he so deserved when rolled in the U.A.R. flag the
corpse of a traitor plotter [one of the victims of the Mosul
revolt]? Does the failure Hulagu of modern times want to build
a pyramid of his unity on the skulls of the millions of the Arab
peoples, as Egypt's Pharaoh did when he raised his pyramid on
the skulls of millions of Egyptians?[35]

Nasser took especial aim at Kassem for not withdrawing from the
Baghdad Pact. He interpreted this as proof of Kassem's intent to
continue working with British imperialists. When Iraq formally
withdrew from the Pact on March 24, 1959, al-Mahdawi remarked
sarcastically, "Comrade Khrushchev agreed with MacMillan to
withdraw from the Baghdad Pact."[36]

A major attack upon Premier Kassem's regime came from
President Nasser during a speech at Deir ez-Zeir, Syria, on February

16, 1960. Nasser declared that "the UAR has no ambitions for Iraqi oil or dates," and maintained that the Iraqi had "fallen into the claws of Communist agents," and that the Iraqi people should not be "terrorized by Kassem's tyranny and Communist terror and filling Iraq's prisons with freedom fighters."[37]

In spite of the "propaganda war" and the mounting tension between the United Arab Republic and Iraq, the burning issue was apparently Syria and not an interpretation of Arab unity. The major outlet for Iraq's oil was a pipeline which passed through and was controlled by Syria. Iraq has long schemed for the annexation of Syria as illustrated by Nuri es-Said's "Fertile Crescent" plan. Syria is of basic economic importance to Iraq, but each time an attempt has been made to consummate some sort of union, Egypt has managed to disrupt it. It is significant that when the United Arab Republic was first formed, Iraq refused to recognize it. President Nasser continuously pointed to Iraq's desire to annex Syria as one of his major reasons for opposing the Kassem regime. Kassem left little doubt about his intentions in a November 1959 interview with the Baghdad newspaper, *Al-Thawrah*, where he was quoted as saying: "Syria and Iraq are neighbors and should eventually be merged."[38] This was probably precipitated by the growing dissatisfaction in Syria with the merger with Egypt.

The Kurdish Rebellion

Another major development during the period under discussion was the Kurdish rebellion of 1961 which will be briefly discussed here.

Kurdish independence movements and demands for Kurdish autonomy were not new. The Kurds, who present a bitter claim both to "racial purity" and to ethnic unity, have a longer cultural history than any western European can claim; albeit this culture pattern is of the nomad-herdsman type, it has at least been consistent. "Since about 2400 B.C. . . . they are known to have lived in the central part of the area over which they are now scattered . . . on both sides of the Zagros mountain range . . . "[39] The basis of their language was adopted from the Medes and Persians in the twelfth century B.C., and their social and political organization has continued to be tribalism. Unsuccessful attempts to attain an autonomous Kurdistan were made in 1919, 1937-38, and again in 1946 to no avail. However, the leader of the 1946 rebellion in Iraq, Mustafa Barzani, was allowed to return from exile in 1958 by the Kassem government.

The new government included a Kurd, Shayk Baba 'Ali, as a member of the cabinet. Further, the Provisional Constitution made specific mention of the Kurds as co-partners within the framework of Iraqi unity. The return of Mustafa Barzani was a notable occasion. "On October 6 he was met at Baghdad airport by ministers, officers and a vast concourse of the public, and conducted in triumph, under banners . . . to his hotel."[40]

In January 1960, under the new authorization for the formation of political parties, Mustafa Barzani and his supporters presented a program to form a party, the Kurdistan Democratic Party; the program was accepted by the Ministry of the Interior and the party was legalized. During the summer of 1960, Barzani demanded full autonomy for the Kurds in Kurdistan. Premier Kassem replied by supplying anti-Barzani Kurdish tribes with arms and money. In retaliation, Barzani went to Moscow to obtain Soviet support for his position. Upon his return early in 1961 his position became firm.

> After persuading most of the Kurdish tribes to demand full autonomy, Barzani raised the flag of mutiny. In September 1961 the Barzani rebels clashed with police forces. Kassem . . . sent army and air force units against them. The revolt was crushed after two months of continuous air attacks, though not completely. Barzani, wanted by the authorities, could not be apprehended, but the party was outlawed by the Military Governor-General.[41]

During the course of tne military operations, several small towns in the mountainous territory along the Iraqi-Turkish frontiers were damaged and about 270 villages destroyed. This did not, however, end the insurrection. During the summer months of 1962 it was estimated that some 20,000 Kurdish insurgents continued guerrilla warfare in northern Iraq. One result of the hostilities during July and August 1962 on the Turkish-Iraqi border was a series of charges and counter-charges by the respective governments and the recall of the Turkish Ambassador from Daghdad in August 1962.

The combined consequences of the events reviewed above

directly affected the struggle for power in Iraq by developing deeper divisions within the country and by greatly aggravating political unrest. The conflict did not end at this time but continued on in spite of a change of regimes, for on February 8, 1963, a military *coup* carried out in Baghdad overthrew the Kassem regime and a new military junta assumed power.

NOTES

[1]M. Perlman, "Midsummer Madness," *Middle Eastern Affairs*, IX (August-September 1958), 246–61.

[2]*Ibid.*

[3]*Ibid.*, p. 248. It should be noted that Lebanon's President Camille Chamoun and Foreign Minister Charles Malik were essentially pro-Western and desired closer cooperation with the West, the United States in particular. In order to accomplish this it was considered desirable to have Chamoun succeed himself. This would require a constitutional amendment which was proposed. This precipitated the events noted here. Foreign Minister Malik accused the United Arab Republic of massive intervention, a charge refuted by U.N. observers, after which Chamoun appealed to the United States for direct military aid which was provided as noted. See George Lenczowski, *The Middle East in World Affairs* (New York: Cornell University Press, 1962), pp. 339ff.

[4]See United Nations, *Security Council Official Records*, S/PV. 830, 16 July 1958; S/PV. 838, 7 August 1958; S/PV. 840, 25 November 1958.

[5]George Lenczowski, "Iraq: Seven Years of Revolution," *Current History*, XLVIII (May, 1965), 283.

[6]Benjamin Shwadran, *The Power Struggle in Iraq* (New York: Council for Middle Eastern Affairs Press, 1960), p. 11.

[7]In every incident of this kind, the people involved are usually the last to be considered responsible and the social-political-economic internal forces motivating them are disregarded and it is assumed that an outside power should have accomplished the act. This so-called "vacuum theory" is a left-over from by-gone ages and is, of course, absurd.

[8]As quoted in *ibid.*, p. 16.

[9]Muhammad Khalil, *The Arab State and the Arab League: A Documentary Record* (Beirut: Khayats, 1962), II, 376–77.

[10]See Appendix F.

[11]Maurice Harari, *Government and Politics of the Middle East* (Englewood Cliffs: Prentice-Hall, Inc., 1962), p. 100.

[12]An agrarian law was actually proclaimed on September 30, 1958 which limited individual holdings to about 250 acres of irrigated land or 500 acres of unirrigated land.

[13]News analysis in the *Near East Report*, November 17, 1958, p. 146.

[14]Waldemar J. Gallman, *Iraq Under General Nuri: My Recollections of Nuri al-Said, 1954–1958* (Baltimore: The Johns Hopkins Press, 1964), p. 206.

[15]*Ibid.*, p. 207.

[16]As quoted in Shwadran, *op. cit.*, pp. 60–61.

[17]*Ibid.*, pp. 18–19.

[18]Gallman, *op. cit.*, p. 208.

[19]Roy Jenkins, MP, "Kassim and Pan-Arabism," *The Spectator*, November 14, ?°58, pp. 527–39.

[20]Lenczowski, *op. cit.*, p. 298.

[21]Shwadran, *op. cit.*, p. 31.

[22]Erskine B. Childers, "Iraq After Aref," *New Statesman*, December 13, 1958, pp. 839–40.

[23]*Near East Report* November 17, 1958, p. 146.

[24]Desmond Stewart, "Iraq's Political Maze," *The Spectator*, October 24, 1958, pp. 537–38.

[25]Lenczowski, *op. cit.*, p. 303.

[26]As quoted in Walter Z. Laqueur, "As Iraq Goes Communist: Days of Decision in Baghdad," *Commentary*, XXVII (May 1959), 369-75.

[27]Shwadran, *op. cit.*, p. 45.

[28]*Ibid.*, p. 46.

[29]Lenczowski, *op. cit.*, p. 305.

[30]Shwadran, *op. cit.*, p. 47.

[31]"The Iraqi Tragedy," *Economist*, April 4, 1959, p. 47.

[32]Lord Birdwood, ' Nuri, Nasser and the Middle East," *Contemporary Review* (June 1959), pp. 335–37.

[33]See text of speech in Khalil, *op. cit.*, p. 289.

[34]*Near East Report*, April 15, 1959, p. 186.

[35]*Al-Thawrah*, March 14, 1959.

[36]Shwadran, *op. cit.*, p. 56.

[37]*Midcast Mirror*, February 21, 1960, p. 6.

[38]As quoted in *Near East Report*, November 16, 1959.

[39]William L. Westermann, "Kurdish Independence and Russian Expansion," *Foreign Affairs*. XXIV (July 1946), 675–86.

[40]C.J. Edmonds, "The Kurds and the Revolution in Iraq," *The Middle East Journal*, XIII (Winter 1959), pp. 1–10.

[41]Vito Priestly, "The Political Situation in Iraq," *Middle Eastern Affairs*, XIII (May 1962), pp. 139–145.

CHAPTER 8
THE FALL OF KASSEM AND
NEW REVOLUTIONARY MOVEMENTS

Sons of the valiant people, units of our valiant army, listen to this good news.

After our heroes, the eagles of the air force, destroyed the den of the criminal traitor, and after all our military units moved forward proclaiming the revolution and determined to destroy the den of the tyrant and to erase all his tyranny and acts of treason, our brothers, the officers and troops of the Defense Ministry, rose up and killed the criminal traitor who fell dead as the price of his crimes against this people.[1]

The National Council of the Revolution Command issued the above communique, quoted in part, to announce the fall of Abdul Karim Kassem, head of the Iraqi government and chief author of the 1958 revolution. The National Council further announced that "the revolution has been staged to restore the July [1958] revolution to the sons of July and the people of July."[2]

There are many explanations as to why Kassem fell. First of all, he failed on the domestic political front. He promised, but did not produce, a permanent constitution and an electoral system. In a speech celebrating Iraq's Army Day on January 6, 1963, General Kassem referred to a promise made the previous July to grant Iraq a permanent constitution. He announced that committees would be set up at the latest by the next month (February) to write a new constitution whereby the president would be elected directly by the people.[3] He never did so. Further, Kassem failed to acquire a political constituency of his own, but continually played one party or group off against the other. "He rejected the extremists, snubbing Communists and purging Nasserites, playing them off against each other."[4]

Secondly, he quarreled with and agitated his neighbors. This involved the aforementioned Kassem-Nasser controversy but extended even to peace-seeking Kuwait. In June, 1961, Kassem laid claim to Kuwait on the grounds that Kuwait has been in the past a part of the Ottoman province of Basra, a fact which was ostensibly accepted by the British in the Pact of 1899 by which Kuwait was placed under British protection. Iraqi troop movements in the region of Basra induced Kuwait to seek British military assistance. Great Britain provided navy and army support to the small kingdom. This precipitated protests on the part of Iraq and Kuwait to the Security Council of the United Nations and the Arab League. The admission of Kuwait to the Arab League on July 20, 1961, was opposed by Iraq, which now withdrew from the League. Tension subsided temporarily but a reaffirmation by Kassem to "liberate" Kuwait later in the year gave rise to additional protests to the United Nations Security Council.[5]

Iraq's curious claim to sovereignty over Kuwait led to much speculation.[6] There was no question that the claim had validity only under international law, for . . . Kuwait had recently passed from the status of a British Protectorate to one of independence tied to Great Britain by a treaty of alliance in June 1961. This treaty provided for British military aid if Kuwait should request it. Kassem must have known that the British would have relished the opportunity to intervene in Kuwait, yet he proceeded in the face of this possibility. Kassem declared his preference for absorption of Kuwait, not union with it, which aroused suspicion of his real motives. In addition to Kuwait's enormous oil reserves, that country's natural bay is an ideal terminus and port for a railroad out of Iraq. One author, in discussing the problem, sees the sudden move as Kassem's personal action, without the knowledge or assent of his Foreign Minister, who reportedly tried to resign in protest. Kassem was observed, from personal interviews, as being:

. . . a man with an unstable mind, like quick silver—erratic, fitfully shrewd, but psychologically insecure. He openly claims to be "The Sole Leader" and "above party." His tactic of knocking nationalist and Communist heads together below him has cost him most of his early popularity in Iraq, and I believe it has also cost him what little personal sense of security he ever had: he does not know where to turn for support.[7]

Protests to the Security Council and Arab League were again submitted in March, 1962. During the interim, Kuwait had gained her independence and Iraq had broken off diplomatic relations with those states which officially recognized Kuwait. The Iraqi government severed diplomatic relations with Jordan in January, 1962, with Japan and Iran in March, 1962, with Lebanon in May, 1962, with United States in June, 1962, and with Tunisia in August, 1962. Unquestionably, Kassem was at odds not only with his neighbors, but also with a good portion of the world.

Curiously enough the Iraqi Premier saw it differently. In a statement to a Lebanese journalist on February 5, 1963, it was reported that:

His excellency [Kassem] denied accusations made against Iraqi policy towards Kuwait. He said that this policy did not lead to the isolation of Iraq from the Arab world. . . . Iraq withdrew its ambassadors only from the countries that recognized Kuwait, as a way of protesting against their stand. He added that all the Arab countries have a high esteem for Iraq because it had not got involved in the abusive battles going on between the Arab countries. Iraq had not insulted anyone.[8]

It should be noted that British forces were subsequently withdrawn from Kuwait and that Arab League forces, for a time, replaced the British "in safeguarding the independence and sovereignty of Kuwait."[9]

A third reason for his fall is that in foreign relations outside the immediate realm of Arab politics, Kassem succeeded in alienating and confusing the Great Powers. Iraq's withdrawal from the

Baghdad Pact and its plea to the Soviet Union for armaments did little to enhance Kassem in the eyes of Washington diplomats. On the other hand, he surely incurred Soviet displeasure with his bloody onslaught against Iraqi Communists.

Fourth, Kassem seemed endlessly bogged down in a hopeless war to suppress the Kurds. Here again, he did little to encourage strong Soviet support.

Finally, and perhaps most importantly, Kassem managed to antagonize a large segment of the army. His attempts to keep the army pacified with a large supply of the latest arms from the Soviet Union were insufficient to ameliorate counter-military ambitions. One of the principal objectives of the military intervention in the 1958 *coup d'etat* had been the establishment of a modern state. Abdul Karim Kassem had failed miserably. Would the new revolutionary regime be any more successful?

Ba'ath Rule

The military *coup d'etat* which overthrew the regime of General Kassem was accomplished the *Ba'ath* party[10] in alliance with the Pan-Arab faction of the Iraqi army. The group of army officers was led by Colonel Abdul Karim Mustafa, a 35-year-old paratrooper, who used planes and tanks to destroy Premier Kassem's regime. The affair was a bloody repetition of the 1958 *coup* which elevated Kassem to power. According to one report, Kassem held out for nearly eleven hours until his ammunition ran out. He was executed, along with his cousin, al-Mahdawi, President of the People's Court, and others, by a firing squad at 1:30 p.m., February 9,1963.[11]

Abdul Salem Aref, Kassem's former Deputy Premier, was named transitional president of Iraq by the National Council of Revolutionary Command (headed by Colonel Mustafa). Colonel Ahmed Hassan Bakr was named Premier. It is significant that both Mustafa and Bakr were among army officers who had previously been discharged by Kassem for intrigue. In its first official statement the Council announced that: "This revolution of the people and the armed forces must achieve two goals: first, realize the people's national unity, second, to achieve the participation of the masses in guiding and organizing the regime."[12]

Reaction from Iraq's neighbors and from countries abroad was immediate.

Cairo jubilantly hailed Kassim's overthrow. President Nasser was the first head of state to recognize the new regime. . . . Yesterday [February 11, 1963], the United States swiftly recognized the new regime, in a move to improve relations. So did the Soviet Union and the United Kingdom. . . . Kuwait quickly recognized the new regime, apparently hopeful that Iraq's pressures against its independent existence might cease. . . . [and] Significantly, the new regime promised to respect the rights of minorities and there is now a possibility of autonomy for the Kurds and an end to the struggle which weakened the Iraq army and which was a principal cause of the uprising.[13]

At first glance it appeared that the Revolutionary Council was determined to repair as much as possible the damage done by Kassem's four year military rule. For example, the New Foreign Minister, Taleb Shahib, promised restoration of the traditional bonds between Kurds and Arabs and, replying to the question of relations between the United Arab Republic and Iraq, he said: "We believe that all free Arab countries are of the same rank and destiny. They are all working for the realization of Arab unity. Accordingly, we . . . will exert all-out efforts and will will work for concerting those of free Arab countries in a bid to realize Pan-Arab unity."[14]

It was well known that the *Ba'ath* Party, with its roots in Syria, was dedicated to the principles of Arab unity and socialism. The new Iraqi leaders who were now in power were seeking rapprochement with the United Arab Republic in order to strengthen their hold on the basis of Arab unity before they introduced socialist measures. President Nasser responded on February 21, when he told a large gathering in Cairo that Egypt and Iraq were "one nation having one aim" and that "the U.A.R. people were wholeheartedly with the Iraqi people."[15]

Consequently, negotiations for a federation between Iraq, Syria and Egypt were initiated in order to form a new United Arab Republic. Meetings were held in Cairo, Baghdad and Damascus during February and March. Out of these and other consultations came an agreement, signed at Cairo on April 17, 1963, for the federation of these states.

Throughout their talks, the delegations were inspired by their belief that Arab unity is an inevitable objective which derives from a common language which is the carrier of culture and thought, a common history which is the maker of sentiment and conscience, a common popular struggle which determines and shapes destiny, common spiritual and human values and emanating from divine revelation, and common social and economic concepts based on freedom and socialism.[16]

A referendum was to be held in five months to elect a President of the Federation; a transitional council and cabinet were provided for, with provision for an eventual Legislative Assembly and Senate, Regional Parliaments and a federal government which would control foreign affairs, defense and national security, finance, economic planning, justice, education and communications. However, the Syrian and Iraqi Ba'athists clashed with Nasser. Three major issues dominated the conflict: (1) equality versus inequality of the three parties, (2) collective versus personal leadership, and (3) the monopoly of Syrian Ba'athists across a broader front which included pro-Nasserites. Interpretation of the agreements following its conclusion began to vary between Cairo and the other two capitals with the consequence that the provisions of the agreement were *never* implemented. "Instead, a campaign of mutual recrimination began between the Ba'athists and Cairo, a campaign punctuated by a few abortive attempts of the Nasserites, in both Syria and Iraq, to seize power."[17]

It was later revealed, however, that the federation proposal was essentially a propaganda move at least on the part of the Egyptians. Publication by Cairo of the secret minutes of the March 14 to April 17 "unity" talks among Syria, Iraq and Egypt revealed that "Nasser wanted unity; he would accept Ba'athist Iraq but not Ba'athist Syria. Syria wanted unity but intended to maintain Ba'athist supremacy. Iraq wanted unity for the sake of public relations and had no objections to unity with the Syrian Ba'athists."[18] It was quite clear, then, that the proposed federation was nothing more than a propaganda mirage.

The outcome was to drive the Iraqi Ba'athists into closer cooperation with their Syrian counterparts. On September 2, 1963, the two countries announced their agreement to establish closer cooperation with a view to achieve the ultimate objectives of "Unity, Freedom and Socialism."[19]

Having failed to re-establish solid relationships with the United Arab Republic, the Ba'athist regime in Iraq was also having difficulties with attempts to restore harmony and good will between the Kurdish and Arab segments of the population. On June 10, 1963, the government announced resumption of the war against the Kurds, committing 45,000 troops to the attack. The primary objective was to clear the northern area of Barzani elements.[20] In an official statement issued on the same day, the Iraqi government claimed that the enemy was not the Kurds, but the "Barzanists [who] were one of the groups who strongly supported Kassem's dictatorial regime and helped him to carry out the appalling massacres in Mosul and Kirkuk."[21] Iraqi forces were initially successful yet attempts to negotiate a settlement by offering the Kurds limited self-rule and indemnities were rejected by Barzani. The conflict was to continue unresolved during the Ba'athist regime.

In addition to the difficulties with the United Arab Republic and with the Kurdish element, internal dissension appeared within the Iraqi Ba'athist regime and this led to its ultimate downfall late in 1963. A leftwing group led by Ali Saleh al-Saadi, the Deputy Premier, advocated ruthless destruction of the Kurds, promoted a specific anti-Nasser party line, and urged immediate, complete socialization. Al-Saadi was supported by the Iraqi National Guard Forces which had been created by the Ba'ath Party as an independent command from the army to control internal security.[22]

The rival faction was a group of moderates led by the Premier, Hassan Bakr and the Foreign Minister Taleb Shahib. They had little sympathy for the extremes advocated by Saadi. They also feared the power structure which Saadi had developed on the basis of National Guard Forces. The very existence of this militia enraged the regular army whose leadership sided with the moderates. The conflict culminated in the deportation to Spain of Saadi and his few followers.[23]

Iraq Under Aref

On November 18, 1963, a new and successful coup d'etat

overthrew the *Ba'athist* regime after only eight months in power, from February to November, 1963. During this time it had contributed virtually nothing constructive to the country. Staff Marshal Abdul Salem Aref dissolved the National Guard and assumed full control of the country.[24] The mood of the times was aptly described by a British correspondent.

> Exasperation is perhaps the key to the latest change in Iraq. The army was exasperated by a fledgling SS [the National Guard], insolently opposing the authority of thugs to that of soldiers. The politically minded were exasperated by the mystical claims of a party [the Ba'ath] with a minority backing to total power. The intelligent were exasperated by a political group whose actions veered from the unscrupulous massacre of Communists in February to the aging of their policies in October. This contradiction also exasperated the moderate Ba'athist who believed the liberal passages in an ambiguous party constitution. Iraqi merchants, taxi drivers and housewives were exasperated by an economy which had gone back since 1958.[25]

Aref's military regime abandoned the idea of collective leadership in favor of the new president's personal rule based on support of the army. The Aref regime from its inception until his death in a helicopter crash in April, 1966 was a continuation of revolutionary turmoil. The period was marked by (1) the creation of a one-party system dedicated to the concept of Arab socialism; (2) attempted rapprochement with the United Arab Republic; (3) formulation of an Iraqi Republic with a new constitution; and (4) development of plans for economic reform.

There are at least three versions of Arab socialism: *Ba'athist*, Nasserism, and post-*Ba'ath* Iraqi socialism. The original version was without doubt that of the *Ba'ath* Party as developed by its chief advocate and Secretary-General of the party, Michel Aflak. In his writings Aflak defined Arab socialism as an indigenous movement based on an Arab heritage which rejected both the Communist and Western socialist philosophies. The Communist ideology was found unacceptable because, among other things, it negated nationalism, preached a mechanical economic theory and presented a threat to individualism. Western socialism, according to him, not only turns against capitalism but against its allies, nationalism and religion. Arab socialism is closely linked with both. Insistence on the national character of Arab socialism is equally characteristic of the Nasser and Iraqi versions. However, interpretation in the Aref regime departs from the Cairo formulation because Aref asserted that Arab socialism derived its inspiration from Islam, whereas Nasser stressed the secular aspects of the concept. The essential point here is that Arab socialism was inseparably tied to nationalism and as the interpretation of Arab socialism varied, so did interpretations of nationalism.[26]

Mr. Aflak in a congratulatory telegram to President Aref on February 12, 1963, made clear the aims of the Arab revolution as he saw them:

These aims combine the causes of the masses, expressed through socialism and popular democracy, with the nationalist concepts which accompany them, exemplified in the plan to unite all the Arab countries, in order to correct national deviation, to abolish reaction, to recover from the lapse of secession and to realize all other national goals.[27]

The aims of which Mr. Aflak spoke were unity, freedom and socialism. The goal of unification of all Arab countries is as far from realization today as it was in 1963.

In a speech by President Nasser at Port Said on December 23, 1961, he vowed that: "In our revolution we aim at creating the new society—without classes, capital dictatorship, feudal dictatorship, exploitation, and monopoly, but with social justice and equality."[28]

Nasser succeeded to a greater degree than the *Ba'athists* in achieving the same socialist goals. A gradual extension of state control through nationalization procedures converted a private enterprise economy into a predominantly state-owned economy. The road to achievement of the goals of social justice, unity and freedom lies in the use of the power of the state with a further goal of achieving unity with all other Arab states on a state-to-state basis. The state, then, was the sole institution that Nasser could have used to achieve the ultimate aim of Arab unity and Arab nationalism. Past efforts for the achievement of this goal, however, have produced no results.

President Aref of Iraq attempted, in part, to imitate Nasser's program by the establishment of the Arab Socialist Union in Iraq. This led to rivalry between Egypt and Iraq, in which both countries have claimed leadership. He further developed a governmental program with the following objectives:

> It [the Government] will stress in particular the unity of the national ranks, the sovereignty of laws, the realization of social justice in accordance with Arab socialism, and the ensuring of the basic freedoms which will guarantee the citizen his dignity, protect him from tyranny and help him to advance towards progress and prosperity.[29]

For Aref, however, the state was not the sole instrument of control and direction. As he expressed it, "we have in our Arab legacy and Islamic *Shari'a* all that is needed to give our system meaning and content, without recourse to imported principles."[30] Aref thus brought socialism into the fold of Islam.

The above action was formalized in a Provisional Constitution, April 29, 1964, in the following terms:

> The Iraqi Republic is a democratic socialist state deriving the rudiments of its democracy and socialism from the Arab heritage and the spirit of Islam. The people are a part of the Arab nation and its aim is total Arab unity. The government binds itself to achieve this unity as soon as possible, starting with unity with the UAR.[31]

President Aref continued in the Egyptian pattern when, on July 14, 1964, celebrating the sixth anniversary of the 1958 revolt, he announced the merger of all political parties into a new organization known as the Iraqi Arab Socialist Union. At the same time it was revealed that all banks and insurance companies and thirty-two leading industrial companies would be nationalized. Workers of the nationalized companies would henceforth share in the profits earned by these enterprises. Former owners were compensated with an allotment of government bonds equal to the value of their share holdings. One notable exception in the Nationalization Program was the oil industry.[32]

A further move was made in the direction of unification with the United Arab Republic on October 16, 1964, when it was made known that President Aref and President Nasser had resolved to create a unified political command which was to act as the highest authority in Iraq and Egypt. The joint communique which was broadcast simultaneously by Cairo radio and Baghdad radio announced that the command would be composed of the two Presidents, and at least six other members from each state. The command was to have supervision over the foreign policy, defense, economic planning, national security, national guidance and affairs of a cultural and educational nature for both countries. The unification was to be accomplished in two years and it was maintained that a

Genuine national effort was the only way to realize this aspiration and was, in itself, a consolidation of honour and sacrifices, which had been made in this direction. It had been established, from experience, that a sound basis for the establishment of union between the two countries was through unification of political action and the establishment of a unified political command, to work for the creation of a constitution . . . and to study various problems.[33]

Although repeated assurances were made by Aref that the union with Egypt was progressing and merely lacked the formalities of a constitution, events proved this to be another abortive attempt at Arab unity. The constant reshuffling of cabinet members at the direction of President Aref saw pro-Nasser ministers either voluntarily resigning or removed from office by presidential order. Aref continued to stress internal affairs as having primary importance; this presumably meant that internal problems of Iraq should be solved before further steps were taken towards Arab socialism and unification with Egypt. A letter from Aref to a new Prime Minister asking him to form a new cabinet in the fall of 1964 stressed that the following points should be considered:

(1) return of constitutional and parliamentary life within a period of not more than a year;
(2) a speed-up in the reconstruction of northern Iraq and solution to all outstanding problems there whilst preserving

national unity;

(3) the setting up of a consultative council within a month which will share the responsibilities of the Government;

(4) a display of interest in building up the armed forces and keeping them away from politics.[34]

Once more it was national unity, rather than Arab unity, which was occupying the minds and actions of the Iraqi leaders. Plans for Arab unification received a similar setback in July, 1965, when a number of pro-Nasser ministers again handed in their resignations.[35] Again, in November, 1965, re-examination of governmental policy insofar as it concerned unification was advocated, and in an official policy statement by the government private enterprise was to be encouraged! In addition, Iraq's Minister of Culture and Guidance, discussing the Arab Socialist Union's future, said his government was "now considering dissolution of the organization in Iraq with a view to re-organizing it on the basis of new concepts."[36]

The development of plans for economic reform did not fare much better. In fact, if anything, the country regressed from the pre-1958 *coup d'etat.* "In the turmoil which Iraq has experienced since 1958, both its human and its economic resources have suffered inevitable depletion."[37] Economic growth cannot be entirely determined because of the fact that successive dictatorships have manipulated figures to the extent that the distinction between fact and propaganda is extremely difficult. As one commentator has said, "Since 1958 an unending stage of transitional paralysis has prevailed."[38] On the occasion of the second anniversary of the revolution which toppled the *Ba'ath* Party, President Aref forecast a new prosperity for the country to result from a huge industrialization which was to be financed by revenue from oil and agriculture. There is no question that these revenues make Iraq's potential for economic development considerable. However, their utilization for this purpose could produce the desired results only under a stable government. Ironically, these same revenues make Iraq a center of international intrigue which contributes to her internal problems.

Internal problems, of course, included the Kurdish questions with which President Aref was quite concerned until his sudden death in 1966. In the spring of 1965, nearly 50,000 Iraqi troops prepared for battle with the Kurds. The official Baghdad press denounced the

Kurdish leader, Mustafa Barzani, as a madman who had lost his senses and called him a traitor because of his demands for Kurdish autonomy.[39] However, Aref recognized the national rights of the Kurds by the fall of the year and demanded new legislation which would pave the way "for democratic life, [which] would emphasize the national identity of the Kurds and would enable 'our citizens in the north to safeguard their language and cultural heritage.' "[40] He further gave them concessions by granting the Kurds local authority, but at the same time he asserted the necessity for the maintenance of the *Iraqi unity.*

Before his death in April 1966, Aref entrusted the premiership to a civilian politician presumably in an attempt to take the army out of politics. This incited some of the army officers to rebellion which was quickly suppressed by the army chief of staff, who was the president's brother and his subsequent successor. The army continued, however, to be a force in the struggle for power in Iraq. This became apparent in the early months of 1966 as conflict developed between Iraq and its neighbor to the east—Iran.[41] The tension between the two countries revolved around the Kurdish problem and it erupted into armed clashes in northern Iraq. The army became dissatisfied with the civilian Premier, Abdul Rahman al-Bazzaz, and continued to press for his resignation until President Aref's death.

President Abdul-Salem Muhammaa Aref died on April 13, 1966, when a helicopter flying him from a village in southern Iraq to Basra crashed in a violent sandstorm. Seven high ranking government officials and the helicopter crew of three died in the crash.

An inevitable early reaction was world-wide speculation regarding the identity of Aref's successor. The *Washington Post*, speculating on the possibilities of a new power struggle, said, "What now seems probable in the absence of a new political order is competition in the army for succession to Aref. The able civilian premier, a nationalist with more realism than many of the ideologists, may well be squeezed out in the process."[42] The *London Times* said: "Whatever President Aref's limitations may have been, his sudden disappearance from the scene could have far-reaching consequences."[43] The *Economist* said it was Aref who for three years had kept Iraq more or less in one piece through a period of turmoil and that "His death will encourage Iraqis to think hard about the new opportunities opening up. . . . But since

. . . ambitions conflict with one another the result will be a perilous maze.''[44]

It would seem the understatement of the decade to conclude that the struggle for power will continue. This is a fact of Iraqi life, past, present and future. It is a struggle which has been and will continue to be primarily based on national interest and, of course, nationalism as seen by the leaders of the moment. Under these circumstances, it is reasonable to state that despite the lip service paid by the Iraqi leaders to the cause of Arab nationalism as the foundation of Arab unity, the cause does not play a significant role in the struggle for power in Iraq and for that matter, in any Arab country with the possible exception of Egypt which is aspiring to the leadership of a United Arab World.

NOTES

[1]"Coup d'Etat in Iraq," *Middle Eastern Affairs*, XIV (March 1963), 78-80.

[2]*Ibid.*

[3]"Iraq Celebrates Army Day," *Mideast Mirror*, January 12, 1963, p. 8.

[4]"Needed: Laws for Peaceful Change," *Near East Report* (February 12, 1963), p. 13.

[5]United Nations, *Security Council Official Records*, S/PV, 957, July 2, 1961 (S/4845, S/4844).

[6]"A Question of Motive," *New Statesman*, June 30, 1961, p. 1032.

[7]Erskine B. Childers, "Kassem and Kuwait," *The Spectator*, July 7, 1961, p. 7.

[8]Walid Khalidi and Yusuf Ibish (eds.), *Arab Political Documents* 1963 (Beirut: American University of Beirut, 1963), p. 19. See Appendix G.

[9]*Everyman's United Nations* (New York: United Nations, 1964), p. 94.

[10]The *Ba'ath* Party (The Arab Renaissance Socialist Party) was started on a modest scale by a group of Syrian intellectuals in 1940. The basic principles of the Party comprise unity, freedom and harmony. The constitutional means which the *Ba'ath* commends for implementation of these principles are a secular parliamentary democracy, a decentralized administration and an independent judiciary. See Mohammed Shafi Agwani, "The *Ba'ath*: A Study in Contemporary Arab Politics," *The Contemporary Middle East*, Benjamin Rivlin, ed. (New York: Random House, 1965), pp. 452-60. Also see Sami A. Hanna, "Socialism and the *Ahali* Movement in Iraq," published in *The Middle East Journal*, XXII (Summer 1968). This article develops the interesting thesis that the modern *Ba'ath* movement has its foundations in the *Ahali* movement of the 1930's.

[11]Communique of the Military Governor-General in Iraq Announcing the Execution of General Abdul Karim Kassem," Walid and Ibish, *op. cit.*, p. 21. See Appendices I and J.

[12]*Ibid.*, p. 20. See Appendix H.

[13]"New Regime in Iraq," *Near East Report*, February 12, 1963, pp. 14–15.

[14]As reported in *Mideast Mirror*, February 16, 1963. p. 4.

[15]As quoted in *Mideast Mirror*, February 23, 1963, p. 3.

[16]"Declaration of the Tripartite Union: Announcement of the Creation of the Federal State of the United Arab Republic," Khalidi, *op. cit.*, pp. 227–46

[17]George Lenczowski, "Iraq: Seven Years of Revolution," *Current History*, XLVIII (May 1965), 281–289.

[18]"The Secret Minutes Talk," *Near East Report*, July 2, 1963, p. 58.

[19]"Joint Syrian-Iraqi Communique Issued on Visit of President Aref to Syria," Khalidi, *op. cit.*, pp. 370–71.

[20]"Iraq Renews War Against Kurds," *Mideast Mirror*, June 15, 1963, p. 2. The government offered a reward of 100,000 I.D. for the capture of Mustafa Barzani dead or alive.

[21]"Statement of the Iraqi National Revolution Council on the Barzani Movement," Khalidi, *op. cit.*, pp. 285–88.

[22]"The Iraqi National Guard Law, May 18, 1963," Khalidi, *op. cit.*, pp. 273–74. See Appendix K.

[23]Lenczowski, "Iraq: Seven Years of Revolution," *op. cit.*, p. 287.

[24]See Appendices L, M and N.

[25]Desmond Stewart, "The Mood in Iraq," *The Spectator*, December 6, 1963, p.

[26]George Lenczowski, "Radical Regimes in Egypt, Syria and Iraq," *The Journal of Politics*, XXVIII (February 1966), p. 31.

[27]As quoted in Khalidi, *op. cit.*, p. 24

[28]As quoted in Gordon H. Torrey and John F. Devlin, "Arab Socialism," *Journal of International Affairs*, XIX (January 1965), p. 47.

[29]"Ministerial Programme of the Iraqi Government, December 24, 1963," Khalidi, *op. cit.*, pp. 506–7. See Appendix D.

[30]*Ibid.*, p. 509.

[31]As quoted in Sharabi, *op. cit.*, p. 168.

[32]"Iraq Begins to Nationalize," *Near East Report*, July 28, 1964, p. 61.

[33]As quoted in "Unified Political Command for UAR and Iraq," *Mideast Mirror*, October 17, 1964, p. 6.

[34]As quoted in "Iraqi Government Reshuffles," *Mideast Mirror*, November 21, 1964, p. 3.

[35]Europa Publications, *The Middle East and North Africa* (London: Europa Publications, Ltd., 1965), p. 232.

[36]"Iraq Government's Policy Statements," *Mideast Mirror*, November 13, 1965, p. 4.

[37]Lenczowski, "Iraq: Seven Years of Revolution," *op. cit.*, p. 289.

[38]Kathleen M. Langley, "Iraq: Some Aspects of the Economic Scene," *Middle East Journal*, XVIII (Spring 1964), pp. 180–88.

[39]"Need for a Reappraisal," *Near East Report*, April 6, 1965, p. 28.

[40]"Iraq Government's Policy Statement," p. 7.

[41]The accusation was that Iran gave financial and military aid to the Kurds. These charges were not without grounds. The Kurds are often called "True Iranians" and the fear of union between Egypt and Iraq was great in Tehran. See Israel T. Naamani, "The Kurdish Drive for Self-Determination," *The Middle East Journal*, XX (Summer 1966), pp. 279–95.

[42]Editorial in *Washington Post*, April 15, 1966.

[43]Editorial in *Times* (London), April 15, 1966.

[44]Editorial comment in *Economist*, April 15, 1966.

CHAPTER 9
THE IRAQI REVOLUTION CONTINUES

The tragic death of President Abdul-Salem Aref on April 13, 1966, was mourned by the public throughout Iraq. "He had always been popular among the masses . . . because he spoke the language of the common man and possessed a fluent tongue."[1] Thirty days of official mourning were observed and genuine grief was displayed throughout the country.

Premier Abdul al-Rahman al Bazzaz assumed the power of the President on a temporary basis according to the Provisional Constitution of 1964 and arranged for an immediate election of a new President. Article 55 provided that:

> If the office of the President becomes vacant for any reason, the National Council of the Revolutionary Command, the Cabinet, and the National Defense Council shall hold a joint session under the Prime Minister's chairmanship to elect a President of the Republic with a majority of two-thirds of the total number of members, within a period of not longer than one week from the date of the post's vacancy. The new President shall be elected from among the members of the National Council of the Revolutionary Command.[2]

This particular provision of the Constitution provided some

difficulty since the National Council of the Revolutionary Command had previously been abolished. The Cabinet and the National Defense Council, to which the task fell, were dominated by the military, and after a series of preliminary meetings the outcome was clear. That is, an internal conflict first took place between the civilian and military factions and then between various military proposals. The military could not agree upon a single candidate, and, therefore, nominated two candidates. The civilian faction nominated one candidate. The civilian faction nominated Bazzaz, but with the understanding that he would not press his candidacy against a military leader. None of the three candidates obtained the required majority on the first ballot, and on a second ballot the civilian group supported Major-General Abdul-Rahman Aref, the elder brother of the late President. The announcement of his election was made over Baghdad Radio with the qualification that the election would be "for the duration of the transitional period and until the election of a President in accordance with the proposed permanent constitution provided the period does not exceed one year."[3] As will be seen, this was not to be.

The new President was a professional soldier who had graduated from the Iraq Military Academy in 1937. He had served as a battalion commander, brigade commander, division commander, and as commander of the Iraq field force. He took part in the anti-British army revolt in 1941, the July 14, 1958, February 8, 1963, and the November 18, 1963 Revolutions and was considered well enough qualified to be named as Chief of Staff of the Iraqi Army in 1964.[4] Aref, the elder, had a reputation as a political moderate, and he had developed close relationships with the Pan-Arab officers who favored Arab union primarily with the U.A.R. His opponent in the election, Brigadier Abd al-Azziz al-Uqayli, favored Iraqi unity in preference to Arab union. Uqayli was highly respected and appeared to be the favorite candidate of the army. The combination of the Pan-Arab military officers and the civilian faction was too much to overcome at this particular point, and as one commentator reported:

Had he [Uqayli] wished to impose his candidacy by force, as he once intimated to me, he could have rallied enough officers to seize power by a military coup; but he wanted to reach the Presidency through the proper constitutional channels. What prompted the joint meeting of the Cabinet and the National Defense Council to choose Abdul al-Rahman Aref in the final analysis, according to Uqayli, was the pressure brought to bear on his civil and military colleagues by the Cairo authorities, because Uqayli was opposed to Arab union and stressed Iraq's independence in domestic and foreign affairs.[5]

According to the Provisional Constitution, the previous cabinet resigned and the new President formed a new government. Dr. Bazzaz was re-appointed as Prime Minister and accepted the additional portfolio as Interior Minister. Uqayli and the three members of the former government preferred to remain out of the new government; otherwise it remained the same with only five new appointments. Premier Bazzaz held a significant press conference on April 23, 1966, which revealed to the Iraqi people for the first time the strong differences in viewpoint over the method of selection of the new President and the direction in which the nation should be governed. Among other things, he stated that Major-General Aref was elected "without any pressure"; that former ministers not appointed in the new Government had not accepted posts in the new cabinet "for private reasons"; and "that Iraq and the U.A.R. were advancing towards the same aim and working for the same goals."[6] These sample statements are indicative of contradictory positions, but even more importantly, they revealed an independence on the part of the Prime Minister not previously evident to *Pan-Arabists.* Rather than a cooperative program with the *pan-arab* faction, i.e., the Nasserites, Dr. Bazzaz antagonized Cairo's political circles through his efforts to establish friendly relations with Iraq's non-Arab neighbors, Turkey and Iran, and adopted a conciliatory attitude toward the Western powers. This led to an abortive *coup* on the part of pro-Nasser Iraqi military officers led by a former Premier, Air-Brigadier Aref Abdul-Razzak in late June, 1966. Military planes were sent to attack Baghdad, tanks moved towards the capital city, various radio stations were temporarily captured, and the usual announcements proclaiming success were broadcast to the people. However, within an hour Government counter-broadcasts were made, and "President Aref announced that the rebellion had been suppressed and that the rebels had surrendered."[7] This attempt to overthrow the ruling regime came at a time when some semblance of internal stability was anticipated. Just the night before Premier Bazzaz had announced the government's optimistic plan to end the bitter war with the Kurds in the North.

The unsuccessful coup marked the beginning of the end of the Bazzaz Government. President Aref, now fully supported by the military—at least temporarily—began to assert his own power, and on August 6, 1966, Dr. Bazzaz tendered his resignation. The military's desire and capability to assume full power became apparent. Ironically, Bazzaz had restored a civilian regime under the direction of Aref with the objective of settling Iraq's immediate national security interest, i.e., the resolution of the Kurdish question at the expense of *pan-Arab* nationalist objectives.

In the ensuing struggle for power between the *pan-Arab* and Iraqi nationalist factions, a military candidate emerged successfully. Major-General Naji Taleb was invited to form a new Government on the same day (August 6). The new cabinet included eleven new ministers, including three Kurdish ministers. Prime Minister Taleb also became acting Minister of Oil, positions which he held until May, 1967.

The regime of President Aref lasted until July 17, 1968, when it, too, became the victim of a bloodless *coup d'etat* which really did not surprise many observers. Many difficulties faced the Government during this period, such as the continuing Kurdish question, oil disputes with Syria, conflicts with Iran over navigation rights and the collection of tolls in the *Shatt al-Arab* with its attendant complications; and relationships with the U.S. and U.S.S.R. The Arab-Israeli War of June, 1967, and its consequences for Iraq, deserve special attention at this point, as it diverted the attention of the country from its objective of the establishment of a modern nation state with political stability.

Iraq and the Palestine Question

The 1967 Arab-Israeli War created shock waves throughout the world which have yet to subside. Iraq became more deeply involved than ever before in the conflict between Jews and Arabs with the June War.

Iraq's involvement, of course, in the Palestine problem has been directly related to and complicated by its relationships with her neighbors and the major powers. The development of Iraq's military capability was a major consequence of this involvement. Theoretically, internal security was the exclusive responsibility of Iraq since independence was nominally granted in 1932, while external defense was the joint responsibility of Iraq and Great Britain. The British, however, dominated both internal and external security in actual practice. As the Hashemite rulers, with British support, attempted to achieve Arab unity, at least within the Fertile Crescent Plan, Iraq's military forces gained new strength and stature in order to support the political moves necessary to achieve this goal. This led to a rather brief and abortive role in the Palestine war of 1948, and on several occasions thereafter the military was placed on alert to intervene, if necessary, in the neighboring states of Syria, Jordan and Lebanon as their political vagaries erupted. Iraq's involvement as a founding member of the Baghdad Pact in 1954–55 resulted in military assistance and political support from other members of Baghdad Pact (Britain, Turkey, Iran and Pakistan) and the United States. This condition was of short duration, which ended with the July 14, 1958, Revolution and "subsequent withdrawal from the Baghdad Pact significantly altered the general strategy and conditions of Iraq's armed forces."[8]

As has been observed and will be discussed further, the Kurdish problem aggravated internal security problems, and the demand for a stronger military capability became persistent. In addition, the nature of the new regimes (Kassem and the Aref brothers) was militaristic, and on-again-off-again quarrels with other Middle East countries, e.g., the U.A.R. (Egypt and Syria), Iran and Turkey, even Jordan and Saudi Arabia over Kuwait, added to the requirement for new, modern military weaponry. Since the Iraqi leadership had alienated themselves from Britain and most of the Western world after July, 1958, they turned to the Soviets to meet this growing demand. "From 1958 to 1963, the Soviet Union essentially replaced Britain in providing arms and technical assistance, and the Iraqi forces converted to Soviet military patterns while receiving enormous amounts of Soviet equipment."[9] This aid (allegedly worth $370 million) was temporarily suspended in 1963 with the overthrow of Kassem, but was resumed by mid-1965. The military strength by then was estimated to include an army of 70,000 troops organized into five divisions; an air force of 10,000 men with 200 planes (only half of which were combat-type); and a navy of about 2,000 men who manned a variety of ships, including three ex-Soviet sub-chasers, ex-Soviet armed gunboats, and small patrol boats for operation in the *Shatt al-Arab* and the Persian Gulf.

The strength and capability of this force was hardly formidable, but it was essentially these units which were available for the growing crisis of mid-1967.

President Aref was sufficiently confident in his military forces to declare in a special message to the army on the occasion of Army Day, January 6, 1967, that "despite past difficulties the present unity of the Army has never been stronger. It was . . . a true successor of the Arab Muslim armies whose achievements history had recorded in its great chapters."[10] Events, however, did not support his evaluation. Early in this fateful year there were renewed attempts to achieve Arab unity, at least on the military level. In February, 1967, President Aref paid a five-day visit to Cairo accompanied by senior officials and army officers. Upon his return the President spoke publicly of a "complete understanding between him and President Nasser on all issues, and that the U.A.R. would always give unlimited support to Iraq."[11] Symbolic of this unity was the establishment of new insignia and badges of rank for Iraqi armed forces in which the Egyptian eagle replaced the Iraqi Republican emblem. Also, a forty-man delegation from the Iraqi military academy spent a two-week tour of duty in Egypt during the same month.

To further strengthen his military base of power, Aref began showing an interest in acquiring more sophisticated aircraft from France. An Iraqi Air Force team visited France in March 1967, and viewed demonstrations of the French Super-Majester jet trainer aircraft, visited French Air Force training centers in Southern France, and toured French aircraft manufacturing plants at Toulouse.[12] Military and economic (oil) relationships between Iraq and France developed steadily from this point on.

The President was most active on the diplomatic front at the same time, making state visits to Turkey (six days in February), engaging in border talks with a Kuwaiti delegation, dispatching his Foreign Minister to India on a five-day official visit to discuss expansion of trade between the two countries, and completing a six-day official visit to Iran on March 19. This was the first visit of an Iraqi president to Iran since the establishment of a Republican regime in

Iraq. A joint communique issued by the two heads of state said that they had reviewed the Palestine question "not only as a problem of the Arab countries, but as a problem of interest to all Islamic countries, a problem directly linked with the security and the stability of the region" and expressed support for the struggle of the Palestinians "to vindicate their rights and their rightful demands in accordance with United Nations resolutions."[13] President Aref, in an interview with a newspaper correspondent, said, "I found full response from the Shah and good feelings toward us. He wishes peace and stability to Iraq. . . . It was a successful visit and its good results will not only be good for Iraq, but for the two neighboring countries [Iran and Turkey] and all the Arabs."[14]

By early April Aref was able to express satisfaction with Iraq's foreign relations based on much of the diplomatic successes noted above. Even internally he had temporarily ameliorated the Kurdish problem by receiving a statement of willingness of Kurdish elements to enter the cabinet under the current Prime Minister, Naji Taleb. A Baghdad daily newspaper marked this move as important "in the efforts to achieve the unity of the Iraqi people when some foreign newspapers and radio stations have alleged that the Kurds are ready to resume fighting."[15]

This consolidation of power and the apparent resolution of major problems gave the Government sufficient confidence to extend the one-year restriction on Aref's tenure of the presidency, which was to expire on April 16. Baghdad Radio announced that on April 3, 1967, a unanimous decision had been reached by a joint session of the Iraqi Cabinet and the Defense Council that President Abdel-Rahman Aref's term of office had been extended. The announcement did not say how long the extension would be, but it was assumed that this would be until a new, permanent constitution could be promulgated.[16] This objective has yet to be realized. (In fact, the Cabinet on May 3, 1967, extended the Provisional Constitution for a fourth year and the practice has continued.)

This, then, was the position of Iraq as events began to accelerate towards the six-day war. Almost immediately after the extension of the President's term of office, several high ranking officers met in the Ministry of Defense to discuss the Syrian-Israeli border situation and "the implications of the Israeli aggression" against Syria. The Iraqi Chief of Staff, Major-General Hammoudi al-Mahdi, announced that the Iraqi Army was "alerted to help the Syrian Army if need arises."[17]

The military dominance of the Government became near complete with the formation of a new cabinet on May 10, 1967. Prime Minister Taleb was removed and President Aref assumed that position. This was the first time an Iraqi cabinet was to be headed by a President of the Republic. Four Vice-Premiers (all military men) were named, one of them was Taleb, but more importantly, a Kurd, Major-General Fuad Aref, was included and put in charge of the development of the formerly rebellious northern Kurdish provinces. Nine military men were included in the cabinet of twenty members, and, of course, occupied such key positions as Premier, Vice-Premiers, Defense, Interior, Communications, and Agrarian Reform. After the oath-taking ceremony, President Aref stressed that the aim of the government "would be a return to normal parliamentary rule* [but that] necessity had forced him to take the premiership, but did not elaborate."[18]

On the eve of the war, mid-May, 1967, a state of emergency had already been declared throughout Egypt. Syria's armed forces had been alerted, tanks and artillery were moving into "defensive positions" on the frontier with Israel, and Jordanian forces had been mobilized. Israel was in a constant state of readiness for any eventuality.[19] The U.A.R. asked for the withdrawal of the United Nations Emergency Force from its positions on the UAR-Israeli armistice lines and at *Sharm al-Sheikh*, which guarded the entrance to the Gulf of Aqaba. UNEF was withdrawn by the end of May upon orders from the United Nations Secretary-General, Mr. U. Thant.** In Baghdad it was announced by the army that an Iraqi team would be going to Syria to discuss military coordination and that the Iraqi army and air force had been alerted. On May 24 it was disclosed that Jordan had given permission for Iraqi (and Saudi Arabian) forces to enter Jordan to complete defensive deployment of all available troops in the confrontation with Israel. On May 30 King Hussein of Jordan made public this fact when he visited Cairo and signed with Egypt a treaty of common defense which placed Jordan's armed forces and, presumably, Iraq's military forces in Jordan under Egyptian command in case of war.[20] Iraq then took the initiative to call for a conference of eleven oil-producing countries to consider the prohibition of the sale of oil to any country that

*Parliamentary rule was *not* provided for in the Provisional Constitution of 1964.

supported Israel. On the same day, June 4, Iraq formally adhered to the Jordanian-Egyptian defense agreement.[21]

On June 5, 1967, hostilities began early in the morning with Israeli air strikes on all fronts. "From about 7:30 a.m. onwards, and non-stop throughout the day, the Israel Air Force struck repeatedly at Egyptian, Jordanian, and Syrian airfields, and as far east as the Iraqi air base of Habbaniyah, with the result that a large part of the Arab air forces were destroyed on the ground within a few hours and absolute command of the air gained for Israel from Sinai to Galilee."[22] The military outcome was apparent within these first few hours. The war lasted six days. In the air war the Israeli air force destroyed "somewhat over 450 Egyptian, Jordanian, Syrian, and Iraqi planes during the entire war: 410 were destroyed on the first day, 19 on the second, 14 on the third, and 9 on the fourth."[23] However, on June 6 there was at least one serious air penetration over Israel:

> An Iraqi Tu-16 bomber dropped three of its six bombs on the town of Natanya; the pilot, a colonel and one of the commanders of the Iraqi air force, apparently thought it was Tel Aviv. With his three remaining bombs, he then headed home, but was downed by AA fire in the Afula area.[24]

Iraqi land forces were engaged on the Jordanian frontier with brigades integrated into the Jordanian defense plans on the West Bank of the Jordan River and at Latrun. However, the Israeli offensive on this front late in the afternoon and night of June 5 saw the defenses crumble. Stiff resistance was met on brief occasions, but Jordanian-Iraqi counter-attacks were neutralized by Israeli air superiority. The Israeli forces captured the city of Nablus on June 7, but this proved to be anti-climactic for the land warfare, as Jordanian land forces were near exhaustion and confusion abounded. In fact, "The people of Nablus [a city of 80,000 inhabitants] mistook the enemy coming unexpectedly from the east for an Iraqi brigade, which was expected to arrive from an assembly point near the Jordan River. Little did they suspect that the brigade,

---

**The United Nations Emergency Force was organized under a U.N. General Assembly Resolution of November, 1956, first proposed by Canada. Brazil, Canada, Denmark, India, Norway, Sweden, and Yugoslavia contributed units to UNEF.

which had come a long way from Iraq, would be entirely paralyzed by frequent visits of the Israeli air force alone.''[25] By this time the Israeli's had advanced across Sinai, captured *Sharm al-Sheikh* without a shot, had won full control of the old City of Jerusalem, and had launched a powerful attack on the Syrian frontier in the hills overlooking Galilee. A United Nations call for a cease-fire, strongly backed by the major powers, was accepted by all parties during the period 8–10 June, 1967. The aftermath of the war has seen no settlement of the fundamental issues created by the decades-long conflict. There has been no official recognition of the State of Israel by Arab States; there has been no settlement of frontier problems created by the war; the status of Jerusalem remains in dispute; and, even more significantly, and deeply related to the other issues, there has been *no* settlement of the acute problem of hundreds of thousands of refugees created by the succession of wars in the Middle East area. The causes for the almost complete defeat of the Arab forces and the reasons for Israeli success are considerable and will be the subject for historians for years to come, but the bitter consequences and reaction in Iraq were immediate and reflected the political instability prevalent since the Revolution of 1958 and demonstrated the intense struggle for power in that nation.

The Politics of Oil After the Revolution

Even before the July 1958 Revolution, the Free Officers were concerned about the oil policy of the future regime. They rejected nationalization as impractical, yet they desired and worked for an increase in Iraq's share of the profits. This also led to Kassem's abortive claim to Kuwait discussed in Chapter 8. Oil royalties were the country's major source of revenue, and the Revolutionary regimes could not afford to disrupt for any length of time the production of this vital commodity.

Immediately after the Revolution, the oil companies were given an assurance that the new regime would honor the oil agreements, and . . . declared it would respect all obligations under international agreements. The I.P.C. and its associates also declared that there would be no interception in the flow of oil from Iraq.[26]

In fact, for a brief period the Kassem regime continued the agreements developed under Hashemite rule with its attendant difficulties. As could be expected, however, the differences began to develop over the interpretation of these agreements, and they stemmed primarily from "elaborate retrospective calculations of the division of profits."[27] The agreements provided for arbitration of disputes, but attempts for negotiation between the Government and the oil companies proved fruitless. Kassem became adamant and declared publicly that "the Iraqi Government . . . would undertake ail possible measures to protect Iraqi rights, since the companies failed to accept its demands."[28]

Kassem then proceeded to issue the 11 December Law 80 (1961) which "was designed to dispossess the oil companies [I.P.C. and its affiliates] of all land not yet used for oil production, and its enforcement amounted to the dispossession of 99.5 percent of the area over which the companies held prospecting rights under the oil agreement."[29] Although the law provided for enforcement, it was not in the interest of either party to press the issue at this time. There was no firm resolution of this, and the problem of Iraq's share of the profits continued during the remainder of Kassem's rule. One obvious consequence of the Law 80 was a curtailment of the oil companies' investment in exploration in the areas in question, and there was a limitation to any rise in oil production which the Government might have anticipated.

Subsequent negotiations were resumed after the fall of Kassem, primarily during the period May 1964, and June 1965. All issues were thoroughly reviewed and attempts were made to reach a satisfactory settlement without repudiating Law 80. The Iraqi government was fearful in this respect in that the Aref regime was committed to the principals of the July 14 Revolution and did not want to appear too conciliatory to the foreign oil companies, which might arouse visions of the rule of the Monarchy. Agreements were reached, however, which increased very moderately the exploration and production areas of the oil companies with an additional area assigned, but to be developed in a joint venture with the newly formed and government-controlled Iraqi National Oil Company (I.N.O.C.). This new relationship between I.N.O.C. and the "member countries" of I.P.C. provided for specific shareholdings for each company, and the principle of profit-sharing on a fifty-fifty basis was established. A separate agreement with the Basra Petroleum Company, a subsidiary of I.P.C., dealt with problems of cargo dues, port dues, and previous claims. These agreements, only briefly noted here, greatly improved conditions over previous arrangements.

For Iraq, they promised to bring substantial benefits as well as removing hard feelings and resentments. The oil companies virtually retained for themselves production rights in the areas which they were exploiting at the time of Law 80, and in conjunction with the Iraqi National Oil Company, exploration rights, in some of the more promising areas in the country, although not in all of them.[30]

The economic and political difficulties concerning oil production in Iraq were not by any means settled with the aforementioned. Conflict between a "good neighbor," Syria, and the I.P.C. served to complicate the situation. As has been pointed out, Iraq was heavily dependent upon oil production for a major portion of its revenue. The production of oil for a "profit" relied upon a 1955 agreement between Syria and I.P.C. for the conveyance of the oil produced in Iraq by pipeline to the Mediterranean through Syria rather than by shipping from the Persian Gulf area. On 8 December, 1966, the flow of oil through the Syrian pipeline systems was stopped because of a dispute between the Syrians and the I.P.C. over transit dues. This dispute had been under negotiation since September. The Syrian government seized all I.P.C. installations in that country. The immediate effect of the seizure was the cessation of oil loading at the Syrian port of Banias, which became of immediate concern to Iraq for revenue. "With the stoppage of the oil outlet from Kirkuk to the Mediterranean, Iraq faced the stark possibility of bankruptcy. Its oil revenues from I.P.C. made up over 70 percent of the national income. Worse, I.P.C. pays Iraq its quarterly revenue installments in advance."[31] The Iraqi government, however, sided with Syria in the dispute and blamed I.P.C. for the stoppage because of alleged failure on the part of the oil company to pay back dues to Syria for the first nine months of 1966. President Aref went so far as to issue an ultimatum to I.P.C. on January 21, 1967, to resume pumping oil through her pipelines across Syria. He failed to say how this could be accomplished with pumping installations in Syrian hands and what would happen if they failed to comply. The ultimatum expired January 28 without action. The loss in royalties and taxes payable to Iraq was estimated at 20 million by mid-February, 1967. Also, "production by I.P.C. was down to a mere quarter of a million tons in January, little more than 5 percent of a normal month's production! . . . "[32]

The major issue, however, has proved to be much more than what was seen as a temporary loss of royalties and taxes and is fundamental in understanding the complexities of Middle East politics in the current era. This was quite clear in a speech made by the then Syrian Head of State, Dr. Noureddin al-Atassi, on February 8, 1967. He stated that Syria intended to continue the "petroleum battle" even after I.P.C. agreed to transit royalty terms as "The battle which we started against the monopolistic oil companies to attain a specific objective and will not end when that specific objective is reached, . . . It is a long, cruel and bitter battle. When we declared it, we knew its dimensions, and from the beginning we knew its significance . . . [The oil battle] will continue until the slogan 'Arab petroleum belongs to the Arabs' becomes a reality. . . . We are in a delicate geographical position, and 60 percent of the world's petroleum reserve is in the Arab homeland."[33] It was in this context that not only President Aref of Iraq, but President Nasser of the U.A.R. supported Syria in her oil-transit royalties dispute with the Western-owned I.P.C. This represented, or at least "sought to demonstrate" a Pan-Arab outlook with a semblance of Arab unity in a firm stand against a Western imperialist company. It was not likely that the current Iraqi government under Premier Naji Taleb had any choice but to accept the Syrian stand even though this meant substantial financial loss to Iraq, which was not believed to be recoverable. Realization of this prompted Premier Taleb to try to get Syria to accept arbitration as a method of resolving the conflict. I.P.C. was also insisting upon arbitration, but to no avail. The Syrian Government re-emphasized that there would be no change in their demands "that I.P.C. accept claims for ten years of back royalties, allegedly due under the fifty-fifty profit-sharing oil-transit agreement of 1955, and pay about £3,700,000 in increased royalties for the first nine months of last year [1966]."[34]

Negotiations between Syria and I.P.C. finally produced agreement on March 2, 1967, and on the same date Syrian police forces, which had occupied the company's pumping stations and offices, moved out. This was received as a great victory for Syria and Arab unity. The Syrian Prime Minister, Dr. Youssef Zeayen, appeared on television and made a speech over Damascus radio paying tribute to the support Syria had received from Iraq, the United Arab Republic, and other Arab nations in her oil "battle" against I.P.C. He claimed that the company "had been forced, thanks to the unity of Arab peoples, to accept the rates decided by [the Syrians]."[35] Iraq, however, had lost some £23 million during the dispute. President Aref and Prime Minister Taleb, though, expressed great satisfaction with the resumption of the pumping of oil from Kirkuk to the terminals in Banias, Syria, and Tripoli, Lebanon. A Baghdad newspaper said that President Aref "through his patience and unyielding position had contributed greatly towards the solution of the crisis . . . [and that] the wise and balanced policy coupled with far-sightedness adopted by Premier Naji Taleb has made the solution possible."[36] The underlying Iraqi bitterness over the rigid Syrian position to compromise with the I.P.C. was apparent through the pressures exerted by President Aref and the fact that the Syrian demand for retroactive royalties and compensation for the past ten years ended in an agreement "to study the matter." Syrian-Iraqi relationships were, in fact, strained by the crisis. This was apparent in President Aref's remark to the opening session of the Sixth Arab Petroleum Congress on March 7 when he said that "I hope that the [oil] companies will take note of growing national consciousness and not involve the oil-exporting countries in problems which do not concern them. They must assume the responsibility of their own mistakes."[37] Iraqi nationalism, that is, Iraq's national interest, was paramount. Iraq pressed for and obtained eventually from I.P.C. a negotiated settlement for losses incurred during the oil stoppage period.

The Syrian oil crisis overshadowed temporarily an internal conflict in Iraq concerning oil policy. Professor Khadduri has characterized this conflict in terms of two schools of thought concerning Iraq's position with regard to oil resources. The first became known as the school of "negotiations," which called for an accommodation or understanding with I.P.C., and the other, called the school of "confrontation," which advocated a strong nationalist policy requiring increasing pressure on I.P.C. to meet Iraq's demands. The nationalists pressed for enactment of a law which would prohibit the granting of a concession to any foreign country. This became Law 97, and its enactment caused the fall of the Taleb government which had advocated a compromise position with I.P.C [38]

The Arab-Israeli War of June, 1967, strengthened the position of the nationalists, and demands for nationalization of the entire oil industry in retaliation against Western support of Israel were pronounced daily. Even before hostilities began, Iraq took the initiative by calling on May 29, 1967, for a ministerial-level meeting in Baghdad on June 4 to discuss the adoption of a unified position towards the powers taking part or supporting Israel in any attack against any Arab state. Countries which participated in this conference were Iraq, Algeria, U.A.R., Saudi Arabia, Lebanon, Kuwait, Bahrein, Libya, Abu-Dhabi, and Qatar. The following resolution by the Arab oil ministers attending was passed unanimously:

(1) To suspend the flow of Arab oil to prevent it from reaching directly or indirectly any state which aggresses or supports an aggression against the sovereignty, territory or territorial waters of any Arab state, especially the Gulf of Aqaba. The conference defines aggression which can lead to the suspension of oil flow as (a) direct armed aggression by any state in support of Israel, (b) any form of military assistance to the enemy, and (c) any attempt to force merchant ships through the Gulf of Aqaba using any form of military support.

(2) If any state enters into any direct or indirect aggression against the Arab states, this will mean that the properties of its companies and nationals in the Arab countries will be subject to war regulations. This includes the properties of the oil companies.

(3) The conference recommends that all the Arab states hold an emergency meeting to apply these regulations against all other investments belonging to the companies and nationals of the aggressor states. The conference warns all the foreign oil companies operating in the Arab world against supplying oil to the Zionist gangsters operating in Palestine no matter from what source and no matter whether this takes place directly or indirectly or with the cooperation of other companies. The conference emphasizes that companies doing

so will be subject to the provisions of the standard boycott law.

The conference appeals to all oil-producing Islamic and friendly states, especially Iran, to take adequate measures to prevent oil from reaching the Zionist gangsters in occupied Palestine.[39]

By the morning of June 6, the resolution was accepted by most Arab countries. Cairo and Damascus radio broadcasts alleging Anglo-American military involvement in the June War led to major demonstrations in major Arab cities and the suspension of oil supplies to the United States and Great Britain by all Arab oil-producing states. Several major producers ceased all production. This was followed by the severance of diplomatic relations between the countries involved in the war. (An exception was Lebanon, which only recalled its ambassadors from Washington and London.) The U.A.R. closed the Suez Canal to all shipping. On June 15, Iraq placed a boycott on all goods from the United States, Great Britain and West Germany. The Iraqi Finance Minister further announced on June 22 "that Iraq had withdrawn all government deposits and current balances in British and United States banks, and that these would be transferred to banks in other countries."[40] However, very shortly thereafter (June 27) the Iraq Government agreed with Lebanon to export I.P.C. crude oil through the Tripoli terminal for destinations in France and Turkey. The ban on the flow of oil was only partial and temporary, yet the dominant school of oil policy—that of "confrontation" had gained ground and proceeded to develop its advantages.

The new Law 97 was approved on August 6, 1967, in its final form, which provided that the state-owned Iraq National Oil Company (I.N.O.C.) had the right to exploit all resources throughout Iraq except in the small areas already operated by I.P.C. and its associates. This, in effect, deprived I.P.C. of more than 99 percent of its concession areas. "Another law, known as Law 123, provided for the reorganization of I.N.O.C. and authorized it to begin at once to exploit the 'relinquished area.' The door was now thrown open for foreign companies to compete with the I.P.C., and negotiations began early in 1968."[41] Realization of the world-wide significance of Middle Eastern oil resources led to what can be called "positive oil diplomacy" on the part of the Arab states in

particular. This attitude was expressed in Resolution No. 4 of the
Khartoum Summit Resolutions which were passed by Arab Heads
of State who participated in the conference from August 29 to
September 1, 1967. Resolution No. 4 states:

> The conference of Arab Ministers of Finance, Economy and
> Oil recommend that suspension of oil pumping be used as a
> weapon in battle. However, after thoroughly studying the
> matter, the summit conference has come to the conclusion that
> the pumping of oil can itself be used as a positive weapon,
> since oil is an Arab resource which can be used to strengthen
> the economy of the Arab States directly affected by the
> aggression, so that these states will be able to stand firm in the
> battle. The conference has, therefore, decided to resume the
> pumping of oil, since oil is a positive Arab resource that can be
> used in the service of Arab goals . . .
>
> The oil-producing states have, in fact, participated in the
> efforts to enable the states affected by the aggression to stand
> firm in the face of any economic pressure.[42]

For Iraq, a new pattern of relationships took positive form with
the aforementioned reorganization of the Iraq National Oil
Company (I.N.O.C.). The reorganization became law on September 22, 1967. Under the provisions of the new law, I.N.O.C. was
given the right to exploit in all areas not under direct control of
I.P.C., and included off-shore concession areas. I.N.O.C. then
proceeded to conclude its first agreement with the French
state-owned group of companies, *Entreprise de Recherches et
d'Activites Petrolieres* (E.R.A.P.) on November 24, 1967. Under
this new pattern of agreements I.N.O.C. was to be the owner of the
oil industry and the foreign companies would act as controllers of
I.N.O.C. For example, E.R.A.P. was given prospect rights in areas
where oil had not yet been discovered (3,088 sq. miles of land area
and 1,080 sq. miles off-shore). Major provisions in the agreement,
as announced by the Iraqi Minister of Oil, were:

(1) The French companies will act as a contractor within the
framework of Laws Nos. 97 and 123 of 1967.

(2) The oil and installations will at all times be the property

of I.N.O.C.

(3) The duration of the contract is six years for prospect and drilling and twenty years for production.

(4) At the end of the first six years, the French companies will confine their activities to the producing fields only and will give up the rest of the land covered by the contract.

(5) Five years after production and export has started, I.N.O.C. will take over administration of the project and carry out all operations in cooperation with the French companies.

(6) When oil is discovered in commercial quantities, it will be divided into two equal shares. The French companies will take half the discovered oil to process on I.N.O.C.'s behalf. The other half will be left for I.N.O.C. as a national reserve to dispose of at its own discretion according to national interests.

"Positive oil diplomacy" continued with the announcement on November 27 that a Soviet delegation of sixteen members had arrived in Baghdad for talks with I.N.O.C. about oil prospecting and exploitation and with an announcement two days later that Iraq would export petroleum products worth about £1.6 million to Turkey under an agreement signed the day before. It was even reported that I.P.C. had offered to cooperate with the I.N.O.C. in exploiting areas taken from I.P.C.[44] The latter proposal, however, was rejected by I.N.O.C. With the Turkish agreement concluded, I.N.O.C. continued discussions with the Soviets, and a preliminary agreement was signed on December 24. The Soviet Union pledged to extend the necessary aid and equipment to I.N.O.C. to help develop its oil industry, drill wells in Southern Iraq, and to facilitate transportation and marketing of its products. The agreement provided for further talks to decide upon the exact location of wells to be drilled in Southern Iraq, which included the unexploited oil rich Rumaila Field. At the same time, President Aref attacked I.P.C. in a speech on December 26 and accused the Western-owned company of carrying out "subversive activities" to prevent Iraq from exploiting her oil resources, and that monopolistic companies "like the I.P.C. are blood suckers. We have already broken the ring imposed on us by these companies. Subversive attempts will be of no avail."[45]

Although it can be speculated that Iraq might have been using French, Turkish and Russian contracts as leverage to obtain better terms from the Western oil powers, it is more likely that the long-range objective of Aref in Iraq was subsequent nationalization of the oil industry. Significantly, in April 1968, I.N.O.C. decided to "go it alone" to exploit the areas of the North Rumaila oil field. This was a rejection of both French and Soviet offers to assist in this area. Baghdad Radio announced that "all exploitation rights had been granted to the Iraq National Oil Company (I.N.O.C.) because Iraq could make more by operating the field than from royalties from foreign firms."[46]

Iraqi nationalists greeted these developments as bold steps which would enable Iraq "to establish a public oil sector in addition to the private sector [I.P.C. continues to operate in its limited area], in accordance with Arab socialist doctrine. . . . Iraq would no longer remain dependent on royalties from one foreign country. It . . . demonstrated a triumph for the 'confrontation' school of thought when its views were put to the test."[47] The objective of Iraq, as well as the other major Middle East oil-producing countries, has been to maximize their revenue out of their oil resources and further to increase their control over the operational aspects of the oil industry in their respective countries. This has been achieved in Iraq to some extent, but to further their interests the various Iraqi Governments have also joined and supported the Organization of the Petroleum Exporting Countries (O.P.E.C.) since 1960. This combination of oil-producing countries has resulted in economic and political power in the hands of member countries* which constitutes a clear challenge to the historical structure of the internationally integrated oil industry. This is of major significance when the demand for oil has increased so rapidly. For example, "oil consumption in the non-Communist world increased from 10 million barrels daily in 1950 to 39 million in 1970, and will reach 67 million in 1980; U.S. oil consumption shot up from only 1.2 million barrels daily in 1950 to 12 million in 1970, . . . and will reach 23 million in 1980; while Japan's consumption zoomed from 100,000 barrels daily in 1950 to 3.7 million in 1970 and will triple to 10 million in 1980. . . . [although world production parallels consumption] on the basis of present date, U.S. reserves have a life span of perhaps 12 years; that of the combined reserves of the Middle East and North Africa at least 60 to 70 years. The output of O.P.E.C. members was 22 million barrels daily in 1970 and their exports accounted for nearly 90 percent of total free world oil trade.''[48] Recent rounds of oil agreements between O.P.E.C. members will result in total increased revenues from $7 billion in 1970 to around $18.5 billion in 1975. (Settlements involving Iraq had not been completed at the time of this writing, but it is clear that the advantages of such agreements are not being ignored by the current government of Iraq.) On the other hand, consuming countries must consider the major importance of this challenge and respond accordingly. In the short run, accommodation and compromise would be the realistic course of action. The U.S. position in the Arab-Israeli dispute, for example, at least from the Arab point of view—pro-Israel—could be counter-productive in terms of future oil resources. It would be hoped on the part of the affected Western countries that political stability in Middle East countries such as Iraq could be realized and that a community of shared interests will develop.

Unfortunately, political stability has proved to continue to be an elusive state of affairs in Iraq, for on July 17, 1968, in a pre-dawn military take-over, the government of President Aref was replaced by a new regime under the direction of Ahmad Hassan al-Bakr. Before analyzing this latest *coup,* it is necessary to review developments concerning the Kurdish problem since the death of the first Aref in April, 1966.

The Kurds and the Revolution

The Kurdish War or rebellion of 1961 as briefly discussed in Chapter 7 was not resolved during the Kassem regime. This large minority group, which constitutes about one-fifth of the total population of Iraq, has continued to present a major problem for the various revolutionary regimes from the inception of the Republic in July 1958. Ironically, under the Hashemite Monarchy, it appeared that a concerted armed revolt as occurred in 1961 and thereafter was highly improbable. The uprising of 1961, however, developed into a national uprising which continued sporadically throughout the decade of the sixties. The war has been interrupted by periods of

*O.P.E.C. has eight members: five Arab states—Iraq, Kuwait, Libya, Saudi Arabia and Qatar—and Iran, Indonesia and Venezuela. In 1967 the five Arab states organized themselves as the Organization of Arab Petroleum Exporting Countries (O.A.P.E.C.) but continued to operate through O.P.E.C.

uneasy armistice and prolonged negotiation.

The first attempt at a "cease-fire" took place during the *Ba'ath* rule of February-November, 1963. In March, the military junta ruling Iraq issued a proclamation which recognized the natural rights of the Kurdish people based upon the concept of decentralization. This was consistent with the Kassem "Temporary Constitution" which specifically related to the Kurds as co-partners with the Arabs within the framework of Arab unity and guaranteed them communal rights. A Kurdish delegation to Baghdad was unsuccessful in an attempt to negotiate the details, and on June 10 the Government, with General Ahmad Hassan al-Bakr as Premier, "arrested the Kurdish representatives, issued an ultimatum demanding the surrender of Mulla Mustafa [Barzani] and his forces within twenty-four hours, and launched an offensive with savagery. The Kurdish quarter of Kirkuk . . . was bulldozed out of existence."[49]

The second cease-fire took place in February, 1964, when President Aref and Barzani attempted negotiations without concrete results. The 1964 Constitution, in fact, was less satisfactory than Kassem's "Temporary Constitution." The Kurds were not even mentioned. The armistice lasted until April 1965, when full-scale fighting resumed when the Iraqi Government committed even larger forces to combat. However, when Dr. Bazzaz assumed the Premiership in September of that year, an amendment to Article 19 of the 1964 Constitution was promulgated and provided that "this Constitution confirms the national rights of Kurds within the framework of the fraternal national unity of the Iraqi people."[50] The death of President Aref in April, 1966, and the succession of his brother, Abdul al-Rahman Aref, to the Presidency brought no immediate change of policy. In early May a new offensive by the army was launched against the "Kurdish insurgents" in Northern Iraq. News reports said that 24,000 regular soldiers, supported by 2,000 Kurdish irregulars of the Salaheddin Cavalry drove into the northern province of Erbil.* Reports on the results of this offensive varied considerably. On May 16 the Iraqi Minister of Defense announced "that the army was in full control of all strategic positions in the north and that only remnants of the Kurdish insurgents remain. . . . The insurgents' lines of communications had been severed and heavy losses inflicted upon them. . . . While *Baghdad News* reported that more than a thousand insurgents had been killed . . . , a *British United Press* report from Beirut quoted a Kurdish communique as saying that more than a thousand bodies littered the battlefield."[51] It was also reported that three sons of Mustafa Barzani were killed in the action. Although the Iraqi Government claimed complete success and denied heavy casualties, foreign correspondents reported heavy casualties on both sides, and one report described the Iraqi offensive had "proved a humiliating failure."[52] Edmonds characterizes this offensive as the "most serious defeat [of the Iraqis] of the whole war . . . "[53] In any event, retaliatory bombing was carried out by the Iraq Air Force and subsequently a third formal cease-fire was agreed to in the middle of June. On June 29, 1966, Premier Bazzaz announced a twelve-point peace plan to end what he termed the civil war in northern Iraq to give recognition to Kurdish sentiments. This peace plan was a result of negotiations with a delegation representing Barzani, and it was announced by Baghdad Radio that Barzani had cabled the Premier his acceptance of the proposals. Officially known as the Declaration (or Agreement) of June 29, 1966, it is summarized as follows:

(1) the recognition of 'Kurdish nationality' to be confirmed in the Permanent Constitution;

(2) enactment of a Provincial Administration Law providing for decentralization and the transfer of wide powers to locally elected councils;

(3) use of Kurdish [language] for administration and public instruction;

(4 and 5) early parliamentary elections and representation of the Kurds in the National Assembly and all branches of the public service in proportion to their members in the total population;

(6) generous grants for study abroad, establishment of a faculty of Kurdish studies in Baghdad University . . .

(7) appointment of Kurdish officials to Kurdish districts;

(8) permission for political association and for literary and political publications;

(9 and 10) a general amnesty 'when violence ends' . . .;

(11) formation of a special ministry to supervise reconstruc-

---

*The Salaheddin Cavalry was composed of Kurdish tribes who had ancient feuds with the Barzanis and who were attracted by the high pay.

tion and compensation for sufferers 'in the north,' and to
coordinate administration in the various Kurdish districts;

(12) resettlement of persons evicted from their homes, or
compensation in lieu.[54]

Supplementary "unpublished articles" allegedly provided for
release of all political prisoners and permission for the free function
of the Democratic Party of Kurdistan. All in all, the terms of the
Declaration seemed to favor the Kurds and surely indicates that they
negotiated from a position of strength following the May conflict,
and strongly suggests that the Kurds displayed superior military
capability, which, at the very least, surprised the Iraqi army and
quite likely defeated the engaged battalions decisively. One
newspaper (Sawt al-Arab) in an editorial expressed the hope of the
day by saying that "Having heard the good news, people can now
dream of prosperity and stability when they go to sleep." Such
optimism was hardly justified.

For the immediate aftermath, however, and until the coup of July
1968, which brought Ahmad Hassan al-Bakr to power, neither side
seemed very anxious to resume hostilities. Yet both sides "used"
the provisions of the Declaration to their own ends, and there never
was full implementation of its terms. For example, Kurdish political
prisoners were released, but on bail of $300 each; it was proposed
that if the Kurdish army (a force believed to number 10,000) were
disbanded, the government would promise to dissolve the
Salaheddin Cavalry—never completed. (It was reported by Sawt
al-Arab on January 23, 1967, that Colonel Sabir al-Zaybar,
commander of the Cavalry, was assassinated while traveling near
Kirkuk); and Mustafa Barzani, still apprehensive, wrote a letter to
President Charles de Gaulle of France, urging him "not to sell arms
to Iraq pending settlement of the Kurdish question."[55]

Following the extension of Aref's tenure as President in April
1967, and the announcement in May 1967, that the 1964
Provisional Constitution was to remain in effect for another year,
President Aref was asked about a definite plan for an end to the
transition towards a parliamentary system. He replied that "the
present disintegration in the country does not encourage the carrying
out of general elections properly. The rank of loyal citizens must
first be organized so that we can elect real representatives of the
people."[56] He went on to say that the Declaration of June 29, 1966,

would be faithfully implemented. Barzani took exception to this and maintained that a larger part of the program should have already been carried out. He said initial steps must include "releasing democratic freedoms, ending the extraordinary situation [the Provisional Constitution] and holding free democratic elections." He appealed particularly for general amnesty for political prisoners and detainees who had not yet been released. The Iraqi Government was granting amnesty, but on a limited basis, first for four months, then for one year. These views of Barzani were made public in the newly authorized Kurdish newspaper, al-Taakhi, which was issued April 29, 1967 for the first time. Although secessionist demands are often expressed by various Kurdish factions, it seems certain that the predominant demand here is for an Iraqi unity which holds that "the Republic is a Partnership, the integrity of which can be safeguarded only if it spells out and guarantees full equality for and the existence of the Kurds as another distinct nationality in that Republic."[57] It is significant that the expressions and feelings of the Kurds were toward the safety and preservation of Iraq as a nation-state, including the Kurdish population, as an enduring entity as opposed to a larger concept of a Pan-Arab nation-state based upon the concept of an Arab homeland or Arab nationalism.

The various cabinets under the second Aref regime continued to issue statements of policy promising a just and peaceful settlement of the question of the North. Kurdish ministers were included in cabinet positions, often without their previous knowledge, yet there was little, if any, progress towards promised decentralization or meeting satisfactorily other provisions of the Declaration. "The army . . . continued to garrison the towns and some of the larger villages."[58] Violence soon recurred, and on April 14, 1968, Baghdad Radio reported "that in two incidents in Northern Iraq in the two previous days 'rebels' [Kurds] had killed six civilians and four soldiers and wounded two civilians and nine soldiers."[59] This was reportedly the first major incident in the area since the cease-fire was proclaimed in 1966. In May, publication of the Kurdish daily, al-Taakhi was suspended for 30 days by the Minister of Guidance on the grounds that it had published statements "prejudicial to national unity." The newspaper had criticized the Government for continued postponement of general elections. This action precipitated the resignation of two Kurdish ministers from the Cabinet, on May 17, which were finally accepted by the Government on June

23. The situation was becoming more tense daily as it became clear to the Kurds that the Aref Government had no intention of abiding by the proposals contained in the Declaration of June 29, 1966. The Kurdish War continued.

The Ba'ath Party Coup of July 1968

As the Kurdish War began to "re-activate," the Government of President Aref was overthrown in the bloodless coup of July 17, 1968. "At 3:00 a.m. (Baghdad time) . . . the presidential palace was surrounded by commandos and retired soldiers, and artillery was trained on its fortifications. After two telephone calls, Aref agreed to surrender.''[60] President Aref was placed on a special Iraqi Airways flight to London the same day. The only shots fired were said to have been "fired . . . in celebration of the victory.''[61]

This coup represented a return to power of the Arab *Ba'ath* Socialist Party, which had been ousted five years before by President Abdel-Salem Aref and which had been banned from political activity by the ousted President. After a brief internal power struggle, Ahmad Hassan al-Bakr became the acknowledged leader of the coup and the Government. A new Revolutionary Command Council was formed, and Bakr was designated President of the Republic. On July 31, a new cabinet was announced in which Bakr himself assumed the Premiership. General Hardan al-Tikriti was named Deputy Premier and Minister of Defense. He had already been appointed Chief of Staff and Commander of the Air Force. The 26-man government then formed was dominated by the military.

President Ahmad Hassan al-Bakr is a *Sunni* Muslim who was born in 1912 in a village north of Baghdad. He attended a teachers' training institute and the Iraqi Military Academy. It is believed that he became affiliated with the Ba'ath Party while a student at the Military Academy. He was one of the "Free Officers" who took part in the July 14, 1958 Revolution, but soon fell into disfavor with Kassem and was forced to retire from the army in 1959. After the overthrow of Kassem in February, 1963, Bakr was appointed Premier and held that position until the November 1963 coup by Aref. His moderate views, at least at that time, enabled him to survive the November purges of the *Ba'athists,* and for a brief period he held one of the Vice-President positions under Aref. Internal conflicts and fundamental differences between Bakr and the Premier forced his resignation in 1964, and he was again retired from the army. Bakr, along with various other retired officers, became politically active under the regime of President al-Rahman Aref, and is said to have "decided upon a course of active opposition to the . . . government in January 1968, ... On April 21, 1968, Bakr and twelve other retired army officers petitioned President Aref to establish an interim legislature and form a coalition government."[62] This failing, the group proceeded with their plans to overthrow the Aref government. It is of interest that many Middle Eastern countries viewed the coup merely as a palace revolt and did not necessitate recognition.

In the first communique issued by the new leadership they stated that "the professed aim of the coup was 'to restore the clear socialist progressive line' of July 14, 1958, Revolution . . . [and] accused President Aref's regime of having neglected the army, failing to take a single step to settle the Kurdish question, and sharing in the June 1967, setback [in the Arab-Israeli War]. It branded the ousted regime as a group of 'thieves, spies, agents and ignorant people.' "[63]

The major policy of the Bakr regime was then put in official form as Proclamation No. 1, which states:

SOCIAL POLICY: The Revolution is determined to achieve national unity, ensure the supremacy of the law and equal opportunities to the citizen, review the laws and regulations which were promulgated under extraordinary circumstances and which do not conform to the wishes of the people . . . shore up Iraqi and Arab national security, end the problems in the North [the Kurds] . . . and establish a society of fraternity, love and domestic friendship. . . .

Revolution affirms its faith in and
s interests. . . . therefore the
lertake):
rarian reform law to realize an
guarantee the interests of the

oil policy, independent of the

world monopolies . . . and the strengthening of the National Oil Company to enable it to set up an independent oil sector and start production as soon as possible.

the strengthening of the public sector establishments . . . and the giving of special attention to the private sector to reactivate it.

ARAB POLICY: The Revolution announces that it will adhere to the Arab League . . . and affirms its determination to work seriously for political, economic and military unity in the Arab homeland. It declares that it will . . . work determinedly for the strengthening of the unity of the Arab struggle against imperialism and Zionism . . . [and] that it will mercilessly go ahead with the battle against the Zionist-imperialist aggression until the aggression is wiped out. . . . It also declares that it fully and positively supports the *fida'i* (commando) action in our occupied territory.

FOREIGN POLICY: The Revolution bases itself on the resolutions of the non-aligned conferences and on the national Arab interests. The Revolution will reconsider its stand toward world states according to their attitude toward Arab issues—particularly the Palestine issue.

The Revolution declares that it will abide by the principles of international justice and human rights, and that it will adhere to the United Nations Charter. . . . The Revolution also affirms its respect for all agreements and treaties concluded between Iraq and other states. The Revolution announces its determination to proceed with establishing the closest brotherly relations with all fraternal Arab and Muslim countries and all friendly countries.[64]

How well and to what extent has the Bakr regime achieved these objectives? The ambiguities and conflicts of objectives in the Proclamation are obvious, e.g., Iraqi unity versus Arab homeland, yet specific evaluations can be made within certain areas already discussed in this chapter, i.e., Iraq and Palestine; the politics of oil, the Kurdish question, and internal political structure—the politics of retaining power.

First, the Iraqi commitment against what is above termed

"Zionist-imperialist aggression" became even more determined than had previously existed. President Bakr was quoted as saying that "we shall never accept the existence of the State of Israel on Arab soil . . . [and that he was convinced that] the imperialist states want Israel to expand so as to give them a broad base in the Middle East. Their aim is to create an Israel stretching from the Euphrates to the Nile."[65] He blamed division and dissension along with dispersal of Arab resources and a lack of a sense of responsibility as the causes for defeat in the June War. The theme that war with Israel was still inevitable was repeatedly reflected in authorized newspaper editorials. One such statement concluded that "we must mobilize all our forces for a battle of destiny because all the voices which proclaimed themselves in favor of a political settlement have ceased."[66] Further, President Bakr in early December 1968 refused to withdraw Iraqi troops from Jordan and "the Iraqi Ambassador to the United Nations said in the General Assembly's Special Political Committee on 9 December that Iraqi troops (estimated at 15,000 in number) would stay in Jordan as long as that country is threatened by attack and the expansionist policies of Israel."[67]

Jews living in Iraq were declared to be second-class citizens, and the purge of Iraqi-Jews continued under the new regime.

> The number of Jews living in Iraq has declined from about 12,000 in 1948 to an estimated 2,500. Considerable legislation has been directed against them, . . . Law No. 1542 of 3 March 1968, . . . prohibits Jews from disposing of their property without government permission. Payment received from the sale of property must be deposited in an approved bank and cannot be withdrawn without special authorization.[68]

Jews living in Iraq were periodically included in the numbers of persons accused of participation in various spy rings, and were summarily executed. One of the most savage of these events occurred in January 1969. Fourteen men were accused of spying for Israel (the United States' C.I.A. was also often accused of spying activities in Iraq) and a three-man Revolutionary Tribunal found them guilty and sentenced them to death by public hanging. Nine of the fourteen were Jewish, four Muslim, and one was a Christian. The trial was a farce. The defense counsel apologized to the court for assuming his assignment and said he believed all his clients were guilty. "At dawn on January 27, the men were hanged, one by one, from tall wooden gallows in a macabre celebration at Liberation Square. They were dressed in red prison garb. . . . Baghdad Radio summoned the mob to 'come and enjoy the feast.' Some 500,000 men, women, and children paraded and danced past the scaffolds and through the city to rhythmic chants of 'Death to Israel' and 'Death to All Traitors.' "[69]

There was world-wide revulsion over the savagery of the executions. United Nations Secretary General U. Thant expressed his "regret and concern" and formally condemned the acts as "particularly abhorrent and dangerous when they are carried out in such a way as to inflame the emotions of the populace."[70]

United States Secretary of State William P. Rogers forwarded a letter to the U.S. Representative to the United Nations for delivery to the President of the Security Council. The letter stated in part:

> We have had no United States representative in Baghdad since the Government of Iraq broke relations in 1967. We are not, therefore, in a position to comment on the facts surrounding the trial, on humanitarian grounds [however] these executions are a matter of deep concern to us. The spectacle of mass public executions is repugnant to the conscience of the world. . . . [71]

Baghdad Radio described the hangings as "a courageous first step towards the liberation of Palestine." The Iraqi Ministry of Information declared: "We hanged spies, but the Jews crucified Christ." The Government announced and carried out the prosecution of a considerable number of additional "spies" throughout 1969. The reaction of Cairo was rather mild, as editorially expressed in *al Ahram:* "The hanging of fourteen people in the public square is certainly not a heart-warming sight, nor is it the occasion for organizing a festival."[72] However, Moscow Radio fully supported Iraq and called the hangings "fully justified." President de Gaulle of France, while refraining from criticizing Iraq, maintained that the hangings were an "inexorable" part of the Arab-Israeli crisis.

The growing list of accused spies and traitors extended during the year to even include the former premier, Abdul Bazzaz, a former

Mayor of Baghdad, and various Ministers of Defense, Finance, and Interior who opposed the rule of Hassan al-Bakr. The witch-hunt included Muslims as well as Jews, and appeals for leniency from world dignitaries, including U. Thant and Pope Paul, fell on deaf ears. The Iraqi press merely replied that the government is "unshakably bent on cleansing the world of traitors."[73] A more likely explanation is that Bakr was determined to consolidate his power and strengthen a weak regime. Unquestionably, he was adhering to his policy of "struggle against imperialism and Zionism [and he would] mercilessly go ahead with the battle against the Zionist-imperialist aggressions until the aggression is wiped out." (See ARAB POLICY quoted above).

Iraq's posture *vis a vis* the Palestine question remained firm and unyielding during 1970 and the early part of 1971. Iraqi army strength was increased in both Jordan and Syria and the Iraqis argued for centralized command of *all* Arab military forces for the continuation of the war of liberation. Disunity was believed to be the greatest obstacle "to the Palestine revolution in fulfilling its role. . . . The Iraqi people attached great hope in this advance [a National Council in Cairo]. Since the Palestine Arab Revolution . . . best typifies the contemporary Arab struggle, unity of its fighters in the field . . . must take precedence over all peripheral differences."[74] In an anniversary speech broadcast on July 17 commemorating the 1968 Revolution, President Bakr said that "the urgent tasks" before his government included "strengthening national defense, purging the country of agents, spies, and bribery, . . . [and] continuing its cause of devoting its resources to the Palestinian cause, [with] increased defense allocations for 1970 to ID 212 million ($140 million)—an increase of ID 24 million ($29 million) over the previous year."[75]

The Iraqi "hard-line" attitude, however, came into conflict with what appeared to be a moderation of the U.A.R. position resulting in tension between the two countries. This conflict began to develop in July 1970, after President Nasser's announced acceptance of American peace proposals concerning the Arab-Israeli imbroglio. President Nasser defended his acceptance of the American proposals in a letter to President Bakr which was broadcast over Cairo Radio on August 2. Nasser condemned the Iraqi attitude and wondered about the effectiveness of the Iraqi army on the Eastern Front (Jordan and Syria). He declared that he had sometimes asked himself "why Iraqi front line forces had never been ordered to attack, why no Iraqi aircraft had raided enemy positions, or why Iraqi forces had not come under enemy attack."[76] The ancient feud between the Nile and the Tigris-Euphrates had not been laid to rest in the name of Arab unity.

Retaliation was quick to come. Egyptian leaders were attacked in the Iraqi press for casting doubt on the role of Iraq and its "brave army." The "advocates of liquidation" were attacked, and it was stated that "Nasser's propaganda media have spat . . . at the July Revolution which has rightly represented . . . the Arab masses for full liberation. Those who adopted the slogan 'what is taken by force can only be regained by force' are now trying to persuade the masses that the new slogan is 'what is taken by force can only be recovered by negotiation with the Zionists.' "[77] Relations between the two countries continued to deteriorate, and the verbal campaign became even more heated. Iraqi and Egyptian authorities eventually took restrictive measures, including arrests, against nationals of the other country. Plans for implementing an economic unity pact between the two countries were shelved and the war of words continued throughout the year. The death of President Nasser in September 1970 only temporarily suspended the bitter charges and counter-charges. The symptoms of Arab disunity extended finally to include tension and conflict between Iraq and Jordan and Syria. In December 1970, the Syrian Supreme State Security Court "passed out sentences which included life imprisonment in the 'case of armed gangs formed in Iraq to carry out sabotage in Syria.' "[78] By January, 1971, most of the Iraqi troops which had been stationed in Jordan had been withdrawn to the Iraqi side of the Iraqi-Jordanian border. Iraqi troop withdrawals were simultaneously carried out in Syria. The Iraqi press then began a strong attack on Jordan, holding that the Jordanian peace proposals were merely setting the stage for full *pan-Arab* recognition of Israel. President Bakr repeatedly rejected all peaceful solutions to the Middle East crisis. This was seen, of course, by most other Middle East Arab countries as a determined effort on his part to take the lead in an armed struggle for liberation of occupied Arab territory and a bid for Iraq to replace Egypt in the struggle for power in the Middle East.

In an interview granted to a Beirut daily newspaper on April 9, 1971, President Bakr, when asked about the projected federation of the four Tripoli Charter States—the United Arab Republic, Sudan,

Libya and Syria, replied: "This union, which has been imposed from above and is isolated from the working masses, gives the enemies of unity an opportunity to strike at the concept of true and comprehensive unity which our people want to achieve on a democratic, socialist, and revolutionary base. . . . "[79] He went on to say that there was no way to restore Arab rights "except by force, blood and sacrifice." Concerning troop withdrawals from Jordan and Syria, he said: "Our brave army went to the front to carry out a sacred national duty. When certain Arab regimes abandoned the pan-Arabism of the battle, and further indulged in surrender and capitulation . . . , the stationing of our forces outside Iraq was no longer justified."[80]

President Ahmad Hassan Bakr pursued a policy which has effectively isolated himself from his Arab neighbors. Insofar as the Palestine question is concerned, Iraq has rejected the United Nations Security Council Resolution No. 242, the Rogers Plan, the artificial Palestine State formula, "and the rest of the proposed solutions insulting and humiliating to Arabism."[81]

A second area of major concern—the politics of oil—to the Bakr regime continued much in the same pattern as had developed throughout the Aref regime. Conflict continued with the London-based Iraq Petroleum Company (I.P.C.) and efforts were made to speed up development of Iraq's oil resources through the operation of the Iraq National Oil Company (I.N.O.C.) independently and with the cooperation of other foreign countries. Iraq's oil policy was stated to be "based on direct oil exploitation of petroleum resources free from oil monopolies. . . . " (See ECONOMIC POLICY above). In September 1968 the Revolutionary Command Council dissolved the Board of I.N.O.C., and the Minister of Oil was empowered to act as a provisional chairman with the announced objective of establishing a national oil industry in accordance with the above stated policy.

Although Iraq acknowledged receipt of more than $47 million in second quarter royalites (1968) from the I.P.C. oil companies and their affiliates—about $22 million more than was received during the same period in 1967—President Bakr, in a speech opening the 17th conference of the Organization of Petroleum Exporting Companies (O.P.E.C.), accused oil companies operating in Iraq of "procrastination and maneuvers." He said that "international oil monopolies were still obtaining the greatest benefit from the various stages of oil industry and trade operations . . . at the expense of the peoples of the producer countries.''[82] During the year 1969, economic aid was received from the Soviet Union for help in oil exploitation, work was started in the North Rumaila fields, and plans were announced that a new refinery would be constructed near Basra with Czechoslovakian aid—all of which was consistent with Bakr's program of "breaking the foreign (I.P.C.) oil monopoly. Oil production in Iraq by the I.P.C. and its affiliates increased, nevertheless, in 1969 over that of 1968 from 72.6 million long tons to 77.3 million long tons. Payments to the Iraqi Government by the group in 1969 totalled $469.4 million. A major issue with the I.P.C. remained in terms of increased production by the oil companies, that is, as stated by an Iraqi spokesman in July 1970, "Iraq's yearly increase in production [by the I.P.C.] was less than 6 percent compared with increase of 10 percent in the production of most of the Gulf States, and perhaps 14 percent in the case of Iran. The short fall of production . . . hampered the economy and impeded Iraq from fulfilling its duty to the Palestine cause."[83] From the start of the Bakr regime it was evident that his Government had decided, wherever possible, on direct national exploitation of mineral resources, to pressure the I.P.C. for increased production and royalties—with the threat of nationalization always omnipresent.

A major portion of the oil program was to strengthen the Iraqi National Oil Company by additional financing and the development of independent agreements with various "other" foreign nations. For example, the French oil group, E.R.A.P., under agreement with I.N.O.C., began drilling in Southern Iraq in October 1968, and it was reported that oil was discovered in January 1970, "in commercial quantities"; an oil barter agreement under which I.N.O.C. would supply crude oil to the Spanish state-owned *Compania Financrea de Exportaciones Industrides* in return for capital goods projects, including a steel mill, was concluded early in 1970; I.N.O.C. agreed to supply crude oil to the Ceylon Petroleum Company (1970); plans were made for a new 750-mile oil pipeline from the North Rumaila fields to the Mediterranean (through Turkey rather than Syria because of the "volatility" of Syria which had closed the I.P.C. pipeline to Banias four times in 14 years); arrangements were made to supply crude oil to Poland; the Czechs were contracted with to construct the new oil refinery at Basra for I.N.O.C.; a contract was concluded with a Spanish shipbuilding company to construct oil tankers for Iraq; oil agreements with the Soviet Union were completed in June, 1970; Hungary became involved in the exploitation of the North Rumaila fields along with the Russians; and it was announced in October, 1970, that I.N.O.C. had signed a ten-year agreement with Bulgaria for a $5 million loan from Bulgaria in terms of services and technical assistance in the petroleum industry to be repaid at 2.5 percent interest with shipments of I.N.O.C. crude oil starting in 1972-73.

The above represent some of the major steps taken (there were others) by the Iraqi Government to attain its objectives as stated above. Pressure and threats continued against I.P.C., and the Bakr regime warned international oil companies "that collective measures would be taken against them if they rejected the just demands of the oil-exporting companies."[84] In this, Iraq fully supported the O.P.E.C. Resolutions (December 1970) calling for increased oil prices and taxes on oil. It is significant that following a Tehran conference (February 1971) between major Western oil companies and six of the Gulf's oil-producing companies, the posted price for Basra crude oil (an affiliate of I.P.C.) was raised from 172 cents to 215.5 cents a barrel, to be increased at an annual rate of 2.5 percent over a five-year period. Iraq's oil revenues are on the increase, and it is quite likely that more demands will be made in the future—oil is Iraq's major economic mainstay. Production by I.N.O.C., however, is still considered "negligible" by the Iraqi Government, and difficulties are foreseen. In order to alleviate these difficulties, Iraq plans the following measures:

1. Increase the exploitation of oil to the amount of 18 m. tons a year to enable the Iraqi National Oil Company to honour its long-term commitments and agreements with other countries. This is to be achieved by the mid-seventies.

2. Building . . . pipeline from the Rumaila Field (the first in operation to the Mediterranean, in addition to the pipeline to the Basra Gulf.)

3. [More] purchase of oil tankers.

4. The participation of Iraq in the cost of building pipeline that connects some socialist countries to a port in Yugoslavia on the Mediterranean, a project under study . . . in East Europe.

5. Entering into Barter agreements with friendly countries

to increase the volume of trade with them and to encourage the participation into joint ventures with such countries not only in matters of oil, but also in other vital projects. . . . ''[85]

While the "oil-front" seems to have progressed peacefully and with some advantage to the Bakr rule, the same cannot be said for the "Kurdish-front."

The Revolutionary Command Council under the control of President Bakr pledged to bring about a peaceful settlement of the Kurdish problem in Northern Iraq. On August 3, 1968, Baghdad Radio announced that the Council had decided to adopt the June 29, 1966, 12-point program summarized in Chapter 9 as the basis for settlement of the problem. Fighting in Northern Iraq ceased after the Council's position was made public by the radio broadcast. The peace, again, was not to last for any significant length of time. By the Fall of the same year, hostilities were reported to have begun again. A Beirut news digest reported that during November 1968 "the heaviest fighting since 1961 had broken out in the north between Kurdish forces led by Mulla Mustafa Barzani and Iraqi regulars."[87] Sources were quoted claiming that 51 government soldiers had been killed and 86 taken prisoner. It was also reported by Kurdish leaders that all Kurds between the ages of 14 and 50 would be mobilized. The internal struggle for control of the North was "on again." President Bakr's new regime had done practically nothing to implement the 12 point program, and it was well-remembered by the Kurds that during Bakr's tenure as Premier in 1963 there occurred one of the bitterest campaigns against the Kurds of the war, and as a consequence there was little trust placed in the new Iraqi Government. The battles were limited to begin with, but by the spring of 1969 a major offensive against the Kurds was launched with "large Iraqi forces estimated by the Kurds and the correspondent of the London Daily Telegraph . . . in the area at about 60,000 soldiers, aided by air force, armor and artillery . . . attacking the Kurdish rebels and even civilian targets."[88] This development came as no surprise to the informed observer. It was almost expected that the Bakr regime would attempt to impose a military solution. Bakr undoubtedly at this stage of the game saw the Kurds rather than the Zionists as the greatest threat to the future of his rule.

The Kurdish rebels on the other hand seemed "to be quite good, both materially and morally." They had managed to obtain considerable material assistance from neighboring Iran, and acquitted themselves quite well in battle. Barzani also warned that oil installations in Northern Iraq, which meant the I.P.C., were not immune from attack, and, in fact, such a guerrilla strike against Kirkuk installations took place in March 1969, with considerable damage inflicted. Although a spokesman for the Kurdish Revolution—as Barzani's followers refer to themselves—declared that the shelling at Kirkuk was a local operation, the attitude of the Kurds is best expressed in a statement in one of their own publications:

> Perhaps the shelling [at Kirkuk] even indicates a definite change in Kurdish policy. If so, it may very well be the beginning of the end of a period during which the Kurds in Iraq, and particularly the Kurdish Revolution, have practiced an unusual degree of self-restraint at a high cost to Kurdish life and property. . . . This was done in the hope that the legitimacy and moderation of Kurdish demands and attitudes will finally and without resort to more military tactics be interpreted in their true meaning. . . . The tragedy of it all is that self-restraint was taken for impotence and moderation for fear. It is this self-delusion by the Iraqi Governments and the indifference on the part of others that has finally compelled the Kurds to resort to the one thing which more than anything else seems to attract attention and draw headlines, something which in addition is a most effective weapon against a viciously hostile Iraqi regime.[89]

The war continued throughout 1969 with major Iraqi army offensives conducted in an effort to regain strategic areas held by the Kurdish guerrillas. Kurdish sources estimated that they were outnumbered 20 to 1 and accused the Iraqi army of numerous atrocities. One major Iraqi attack was made on the village of Dakan in the Mosul Province. Here, on August 8, 1969, according to Kurdish sources:

> The children and the women of the village escaped to one of the caves in the vicinity, for fear of artillery shelling and bombing by aircraft.
> After burning the village, the officers and mercenaries

assembled near the entry of the cave. They collected wood, and after sprinkling the wood with petrol, they set fire to it. The cries of the children and the women began rising to God. They were shooting at the entry of the cave so that no one could escape, and so were burnt, 67 children and women [died] in the cave.[90]

Following this attack, and for the first time, the Kurdish Democratic Party of Mustafa Barzani issued an official plea to the United Nations for the appointment of a U.N. commission of Inquiry with power to end the war and mediate a peaceful solution to the Kurdish question. The plea stated that the "Dakan incident" was not an isolated act, but was, rather, the pattern followed by Iraqi regulars and mercenaries. The accusation of genocide was explicit. However, the bearer of the plea received no hearing and "at the U.N. the Kurdish war remains forgotten because there was no government willing to speak out on the Kurds' behalf."[91] The bearer of the plea, Shafik Qazzar, a political science student completing his doctoral studies at the American University in Washington, told a correspondent of the *New York Post:* "It's not just a question of fighting for our rights, now it's fighting for survival."[92]

An official statement of the Kurdish Democratic Party issued in September, 1969, reported that over 3,000 Kurdish villages had been destroyed in the eight-year war, 200,000 people had been made homeless, and that 3,000 Kurdish soldiers and 20,000 civilians had been killed. It was estimated that the various Iraqi governments during this period had spent the equivalent of approximately $1.4 billion in weapons and supplies to continue the war, with greater amounts expended for the support of the mercenaries, who were considered traitors and the enemies of the Kurdish people, and that "The *Ba'ath* have played the most wicked and dangerous role in the war in the years 1963, 1968 and 1969 as they have given it the character of a racist war of extermination."[93]

Yet *again* within months a "peaceful settlement" was forecast from Baghdad and talks between the Government and Mustafa Barzani were held in January 1970, and it was reported that agreement had been reached concerning:

(1) inclusion of four Kurdish ministers in the Iraqi cabinet;

(2) retention of 10,000 armed Kurds—whose salaries would be paid by Baghdad [!]—as a Kurdish national guard;

(3) dissolution of the mercenary forces;

(4) release of all pro-Kurdish political prisoners; and

(5) proportional representation guaranteed for the Kurds in a national legislative assembly.

It would appear that a negotiated settlement was imminent. An end to the war was actually announced on March 11, 1970. The basis for settlement on this occasion was based upon a new 15-point program replacing the twelve-point program of 1966. There are obvious similarities, yet the new program provided for a number of administrative and other reforms. The major proposals are:

> Kurdish shall be an official language, along with Arabic, in areas where Kurds constitute the majority of the population. . . .
>
> The Government will work 'to achieve . . . the participation of Kurds in the Government without discrimination. . . .
>
> Officials in the administrative units inhabited by a Kurdish majority shall be Kurds. . . .
>
> A general amnesty will be declared to cover all those accused of acts of violence in the Kurdish area. . . .
>
> Efforts will be made to raise the standard of living in the Kurdish areas. . . .
>
> One of the vice-presidents of the Republic shall be a Kurd. . . .
>
> The necessary measures shall be taken . . . to unify the districts and administrative units where Kurds form a majority. . . . The state shall seek to develop these administrative units to enable the Kurdish people to exercise their full national rights and ensure they enjoy autonomy.[94]

This would appear to be a major victory for the Kurds. Implementation of the fifteen-point program is, of course, of major importance, and upon this rests the "victory" as here represented.

Positive moves were taken in this direction early after the announcement of the fifteen-point program. A new government was announced on March 29, 1970, which included five Kurds with portfolios in the Department of Municipal and Rural Affairs, Public

Works and Housing, Agriculture, Northern Reconstruction, and a representative in the Ministry of State. A nine-man committee, including five members of the K.D.P. politburo, was formed to supervise the implementation of the program. It was even reported that members of the Kurdish army were prepared "to take up positions on the Eastern Front [against the Israelis] to confront the common enemy."[95] Further, an alliance between the K.D.P. and the *Ba'ath* Party was developed "to speed up the enforcement of the remaining provisions of the 11 March proclamation and cement Arab-Kurdish fraternity . . . "[96] In short, the K.D.P. was fully expected by mid-summer, 1970, to collaborate with the Bakr regime in the formation of a national front. This alliance received support from the Revolutionary Command Council by such actions as noted above and by granting a monthly allowance to all demobilized members of the Kurdish armed forces who had no other source of income and to give them priority in appointment to government positions. Regular meetings were held between the K.D.P. and the ruling *Ba'ath* Party leadership for the implementation of the March 1970 Declaration, and it appeared in early 1971 that the civil war between Iraq and the Kurds had subsided. One great advantage for Iraq, if the peace holds, is that a considerable number of troops previously engaged in the revolt can be diverted to other areas such as Israel, Jordan, and Iran if further trouble develops.

As the Bakr regime dealt with the Palestine question, the politics of oil and the Kurdish Revolution, President Bakr attempted to consolidate his political power base within Iraq. "The Revolution is determined to achieve national unity [and] ensure the supremacy of the law . . . " (See SOCIAL POLICY above). The internal political structure, however, continued to be of a provisional nature. The May 1964 Provisional Constitution had been twice extended, the last time to be in effect until May 1970. However, on September 22, 1968, a new 95-article Provisional Constitution was promulgated and was to remain in force until a permanent constitution could be drafted and approved. Briefly, the principal features of this new Provisional Constitution were:

> The Iraqi Republic is a popular democratic state. Islam is the state religion and the basis of its laws and constitution.
> The political economy of the state is founded in socialism.

The state will protect liberty of religion, freedom of speech and opinion. Public meetings are permitted under the law. All discrimination based on race, religion or language is forbidden. There shall be freedom of the press and the right to form societies and trade unions in conformity with the law is guaranteed.

The national rights of the Kurdish people are guaranteed within the framework of the unity of Iraq.

The highest authority in the country is the Council of Command of the Revolution, which will promulgate laws until the election of a National Assembly . . . [97]

The most significant feature of the 1968 Provisional Constitution is the continuation of the Revolutionary Command Council as the highest authority in the state. The R.C.C. was empowered to elect the President of the Republic, command the armed forces, declare war, appoint the Premier and Ministers, and to supervise all state affairs. The members of the R.C.C. were also appointed Vice-Presidents of the Republic, none of whom could be dismissed except by a two-thirds majority. The Premier, his Deputies and Ministers, were required to be of Iraqi parents coming from a family which had lived in Iraq since 1900. Political control at the top level of government remained complete.

Two amendments to the Constitution, approved by the R.C.C. in 1969, provided that the President of the Republic was also the Supreme Commander of the Armed Forces and President of the Command Council of the Revolution. Membership of the R.C.C. could be increased from five to a larger number at the President's discretion.[98] (By April of 1970 the Council had been expanded to fifteen members.)

Following the March 1970 agreement with the Kurds, it was believed advisable to re-write the 1968 Provisional Constitution which would take into account the major features of that agreement. As a consequence another "new" Provisional Constitution—the fourth in twelve years—was announced in July 1970. This "new" Constitution—in 67 articles this time—reaffirmed the major features of the 1968 Constitution, especially the strong position of the Executive, i.e., the President and the fifteen-member R.C.C., and affirms the rights of the Kurdish people, providing that the Iraqi people consist of two main nationalities—Arab and Kurdish.

Kurdish became an official language in addition to Arabic in the Kurdish areas. The new Constitution also provided for the establishment of a National Assembly to *review* legislation passed by the Revolutionary Command Council and even have the right to question ministers on proposed legislation, provided the President of the Republic so approved. (The National Assembly, which was to consist of representatives of Iraq's various political, economic and social groups with its formation and qualification of membership to be determined by special law, had not been formed at the time of this writing, although the R.C.C. issued a law on December 23, 1970 for the establishment of a 100-member National Assembly.)[99]

Although freedom of the press was guaranteed by the 1968 and 1970 Provisional Constitutions, all private newspapers are required by law to obtain cabinet permission prior to their establishment. Various private newspapers have been closed down during the period of the Bakr regime, and generally only government-controlled newspapers have been in continuous publication. The Kurdish language newspaper *al-Taahki* was allowed to resume publication in 1968. Some fifteen magazines and weeklies are published by the Ministry of Culture and Information.

Political party activity has been limited to the *Ba'ath* Party, and, more recently, the Kurdish Democratic Party, which on numerous occasions has been banned depending upon the status at the time of the Kurdish Revolution. The Iraqi Communist Party has been banned but continues to operate underground. The Iraqi Communist Party, in fact, claims persecution of communists by the Government. In a statement published in Beirut, Lebanon on January 21, 1971, the Party alleged that the authorities in Southern Iraq "had launched a campaign of arrests against scores of communists and 'democratic elements' and that . . . authorities were using 'various methods of psychological and physical torture.'"[100]

In summary, what has been called the "paranoia of Iraqi politics" during the Bakr regime has revolved around the issues of the Palestine question, the attempts to realize greater control of Iraq's oil resources, the complementary problem of the Kurdish Revolution and consolidation of political power based primarily on Iraqi interests as seen by the leadership of the *Ba'ath* Party. This has seen the continuation of control of the country by whomever controls the major factions in the military services. Although it is difficult to evaluate Iraq's leadership primarily because of "the absence of public instruments of policy making and institutional checks on the exercise of power [which] have thoroughly personalized politics in Iraq . . . "[101] certain conclusions can be drawn from events and statements as they have become known to the Western world.

First, there is an obvious continuing strict censorship of news concerning events in the country.

Second, Cabinets are re-shuffled with regularity. This is not a new phenomenon in Iraqi politics. "In the pre-1958 period there were twenty cabinets with 92 ministers, 39 of them in top level positions; in the post-1958 period, there have been 14 cabinets [not including all changes during the Bakr regime] with 161 ministers, 37 of them at the top."[102]

Third, and related to the second, key portfolios, such as Defense, Interior, Treasury, have nearly always been held by a member of the military establishment.

Fourth, the use of the Provisional Constitution on an extended basis is the basic pattern of constitutional law.

Finally, all major decisions are made by the Revolutionary Command Council, which is controlled by the President of the Republic.

NOTES

[1]Majid Khadduri, *Republican Iraq* (New York: Oxford University Press, 1969), p. 262.

[2]Khalidi, *op. cit.*, 1964, p. 151.

[3]*Mideast Mirror*, April 23, 1966, p. 2.

[4]*Ibid.*, p. 3.

[5]Khadduri, *op. cit.*, p. 265–66.

[6]*Mideast Mirror*, April 30, 1965, p. 5.

[7]Khadduri, *op. cit.*, pp. 278–79.

[8]Nadav Safran, *From War to War: The Arab-Israeli Confrontation, 1948–1967* (New York: Pegasus, 1969), p. 236.

[9]*Ibid.*, p. 238.

[10]As quoted in *Arab Report and Record*, 1967, Issue 1, p. 3.

[11]*Arab Report and Record*, 1967, Issue 3, p. 34.

[12]*Mideast Mirror*, March 11, 1967, p. 19.

[13]As quoted in *Arab Report and Record*, 1967, Issue 6, p. 78.

[14]*Al-Manar*, March 20, 1967.

[15] *Sawt al-Arab*, April 2, 1967.

[16] *Arab Report and Record, 1967*, Issue 7, p. 94.

[17] *Sawt al-Arab*, April 8, 1967.

[18] *Mideast Mirror*, May 13, 1967.

[19] Keesings' Research Report, *The Arab Israeli Conflict: The 1967 Campaign* (New York: Charles Scribner's Sons, 1968) There is no attempt here to describe the events or campaigns of the June War except as involved Iraq. There are numerous such accounts among which are:

Ibrahim Abu-Lughod (ed.), *The Arab World: Special Issue*, "The Arab-Israeli Confrontation of June, 1967";

Randolph S. and Winston S. Churchill, *The Six Day War* (Boston: Houghton Mifflin, 1967);

Moshe Dayan, *Diary of the Sinai Campaign* (New York: Harper and Row, 1969);

Theodore Draper, *Israel and World Politics: Roots of the Third Arab-Israeli War* (New York: Viking, 1968);

Walter Z. Laqueur, *The Israel-Arab Reader: A Documentary History of the Middle East Conflict* (New York: Citadel Press, 1968);

Fred J. Khouri, *The Arab-Israeli Dilemma* (New York: Syracuse University Press, 1968);

M.T. Mehdi, *Peace in the Middle East* (New York: New World Press, 1967).

[20] Safran, *op. cit.*, p. 270.

[21] *Ibid.*

[22] Keesing, *op. cit.*, p. 25.

[23] Safran, *op. cit.*, p. 324.

[24] *Ibid.*, p. 329.

[25] *Ibid.*, p. 364.

[26] Khadduri, *op. cit.*, pp. 160–61.

[27] *Ibid.*, p. 162.

[28] *Ibid.*, p. 164.

[29] *Ibid.*

[30] *Ibid.*, p. 239.

[31] *Mideast Mirror*, December 16, 1966, p. 2.

[32] *Arab Report and Record, 1967*, Issue No. 3, p. 35.

[33] As quoted in *Mideast Mirror*, February 11, 1967.

[34] *Mideast Mirror*, February 25, 1967, p. 12.

[35] *Ibid.*, March 4, 1967, p. 2.

[36] *al-Thawra al-Arabiya*, March 3, 1967.

[37] As quoted in *Mideast Mirror*, March 11, 1967, p. 7.

[38] Khadduri, *op. cit.*, p. 292.

[39] *Arab Report and Record, 1967*, Issue No. 11, p. 198.

[40] *Ibid.*, Issue No. 12, p. 208.

[41] Khadduri, *op. cit.*, p. 293.

[42] Full text of the Khartoum Summit Resolutions can be found in *Arab Report and Record, 1967*, Issue No. 17, p. 286.

[43] As quoted in *Arab Report and Record, 1967*, Issue No. 22, p. 359.

[44] *Al-Jumhouriya*, December 11, 1967.

[45] *Mideast Mirror*, December 30, 1967, p. 12.

[46] As quoted in *Arab Report and Record, 1968*, Issue No. 7, p. 88.

[47] Khadduri, *op. cit.*, p. 294.

[48] Walter J. Levy, "Oil Power," *Foreign Affairs* XXXXIX (July 1971) pp.

652–53.

[49]C.J. Edmonds, "The Kurdish War in Iraq: The Constitutional Background," *World Today*, XXIV, December 1968, p. 515.

[50]*Ibid.*, p. 517.

[51]*Arab Report and Record*, 1966, Issue No. 9, pp. 110–11.

[52]See (London) *Guardian*, June 6, 1966, and (London) *Daily Telegraph*, June 14, 1966.

[53]Edmonds, *op. cit.*, p. 517.

[54]*Ibid.*, pp. 517–18.

[55]*Arab Report and Record*, 1967, Issue No. 3, p. 31.

[56]As quoted in *Mideast Mirror*, May 6, 1967, p. 10.

[57]"The Kurds and the Concept of Iraqi Unity," *The Kurdish Journal*, VI No. 3, September 1968, p. 2.

[58]Edmonds, *op. cit.*, p. 518.

[59]*Arab Report and Record*, 1968, Issue No. 7, p. 88.

[60]*Al-Thawra*, July 18, 1968.

[61]*Baghdad Observer*, July 18, 1968.

[62]*Arab Report and Record*, 1968, Issue No. 14, p. 204.

[63]*Mideast Mirror*, July 20, 1968, p. 3.

[64]*Arab Report and Record*, 1968, Issue No. 14, p. 204.

[65]*Der Spiegel*, September 30, 1968.

[66]*Al-Thawra*, October 17, 1968.

[67]*Arab Report and Record*, 1968, Issue No. 23, p. 391.

[68]*Ibid.*, Issue No. 24, p. 412.

[69]"Report from the Dark Ages," *Near East Report*, February 4, 1969, p. 10.

[70]*Ibid.*

[71]*The Department of State Bulletin* LX February 17, 1969, pp. 145–46.

[72]*Al-Ahram*, January 29, 1969.

[73]*The Arab Report and Record*, 1970, Issue No. 2, p. 60.

[74]*Al-Thawra*, June 4, 1970.

[75]*Arab Report and Record*, 1970, Issue No. 14, p. 409.

[76]*Ibid.*, Issue No. 15, p.

[77]*Al-Thawra, al-Thawra*, August 10, 1970.

[78]*Arab Report and Record*, 1970, Issue No. 23, p. 663.

[79]*Al-Nahar*, April 9, 1971.

[80]*Ibid.*

[81]al-Bakr, "Armed Struggle Only Way to Victory," *Iraq News Bulletin* March, 1971, p. 3.

[82]*Arab Report and Record*, 1968, Issue No. 21, p. 349.

[83]*Ibid.*, 1970, Issue No. 13, p. 382.

[84]*Ibid.*, 1971, Issue No. 2, p. 56.

[85]Saeed K. Hindawi, "Iraq Oil Industry," *Iraq News Bulletin* March, 1971, pp. 10–11. (This was a speech delivered by His Excellency, Mr. Hindawi, Ambassador of the Republic of Iraq in India, at the Kanpur International Centre on 6 March, 1971.)

[86]*Mideast Mirror*, August 10, 1968, p. 7.

[87]*Arab World*, November 11, 1968.

[88]Gershon Solomon, "The Kurds Are Fighting Again," *New Outlook* XII p. 36.

[89]"The Kurds and the Shelling of Kirkuk Oil Installations," *Kurdish Affairs Bulletin* No. 1, 1969.

[90]"Tragedy at Dakan Village," *Kurdish Affairs Bulletin* No. 6, 1969.

[91]*Ibid.*

[92]*New York Post*, October 13, 1969.

[93]"Statement by K.D.P. on the Eighth Anniversary of the Kurdish Revolution," *The Kurdish Journal*, VI, No. 3, September, 1969, p. 119.

[94]As quoted in *Arab Report and Record, 1970*, Issue No. 5, p. 144.

[95]*Arab Report and Record, 1970*, Issue No. 6, p. 174.

[96]*Al-Taakhi*, July 14, 1970.

[97]Europa Publications, *The Middle East and North Africa* (17th Ed.) (London: Europa Publications, Ltd., 1970–71), p. 318.

[98]*Ibid.*

[99]*Arab Report and Record, 1970*, Issue No. 24, p. 685.

[100]*Arab Report and Record, 1971*, Issue No. 2, p. 56.

[101]Phebe Ann Marr, "Iraq's Leadership Dilemma: A Study in Leadership Trends, 1948–1968," *The Middle East Journal* XXIV (Summer, 1970), p. 283.

[102]*Ibid.*

CHAPTER 10
RETROSPECT

While the old political, economic and social order in Iraq has undergone drastic changes during the past few decades, and while the future defies prediction, one cannot dispute the fact that the net result of these changes is the emergence of Iraq as a fully sovereign state. Recent events reviewed in the preceding chapters conclusively illustrate that the Iraqi leaders now feel free to choose and develop their own forms of government, society and economic life without the controlling hand of a mandatory, foreign master. By refusing to accept direct pressure from foreign powers, and equally by rejecting Western-oriented institutions, independence is being realized as a new condition which must take its own course under the leadership of local, nationalist-oriented elites who hopefully can attune themselves to the needs of the nation. While it is obvious that local nationalism pre-empts Arab nationalism in Iraq, the fact that Iraqi leaders find it necessary to pay so much tribute to Arab nationalism must be commented on. There are continued attempts on the part of Arab nationalist adherents to relate current events as they occur in the Middle East to concepts as they existed in the early Arabic-Islamic period. The mistake here is to try to revive ancient concepts and place them into context as reality. It would better suit their purposes to concentrate on attempts to create a common Arab community in terms of economic cooperation, cultural and social exchange, and educational programs from which they could build a unified Arab political system. Instead of recognizing the foundation from which they could realistically proceed, they seem to engage in an exercise of polemics designed to motivate unification without sufficient concern for what could be considered a grass-roots approach to the problem. Apparently, the euphoria of the past suffices in their pursuit of their goals, while at the same time they seem to ignore what is happening at the local level in terms of developing loyalties, attachment to new symbols and a need for material improvement. As these trends continue to develop it will become even more difficult to achieve Arab unity.

Ancient Mesopotamia flourished in a pre-Islamic era which saw great civilizations of antiquity in their fullest glory and development. The modern Iraqi nationalist can look to the past great agricultural societies in the land of the two rivers for its own cultural and social legacy and to identify with an ancient history. The Abbasid Empire, centered in Baghdad, provided the highest standard of living and cultural development which had no match anywhere, East or West, at the time of its greatest glory. As the capital of Islam, Baghdad also provided a religious legacy which continues to influence individual Iraqis even today.

Although the Abbasid power was demolished by the invasion of the Mongol hordes who advanced out of the East, the legacy of a great historical past was not obliterated by this tragic event. Latent potentialities were aroused by the Ottoman Turks during their long period of rule. Competition for the control of Iraq between the Ottomans and the Western powers resulted in European penetration into the area, especially during the nineteenth century when modern technology involved the Middle East. The introduction of Western products, the exchange of culture and education and the accompanying rise in expectations for a higher standard of living motivated a growing demand for change. New means of communication and transportation facilitated, albeit at a slow pace, the process of modernization and the aspirations which developed for self-government and an independent national identity without any reference to the political boundaries which, as is well known, were imposed on Iraq under the terms of agreements reached in London and Paris in which the Iraqis had no part.[1]

Consequently, it was the impact of World War I and the disintegration of the Ottoman Empire which resulted in the emergence of Iraq as a modern nation-state. Allied military operations in Mesopotamia as early as November 1914 were conducted by the British with the primary objective of protecting the British-controlled oil industry in the Persian Gulf area. The British government followed two contradictory policies which were responsible for the chaotic conditions of the post-war years. The first, motivated by immediate needs and military considerations, was to support the cause of Arab nationalism against the Central powers. This policy, adopted in 1914, found expression in the McMahon Agreement reached between Sherif Hussein of Hejaz and the British High Commissioner in Cairo, Egypt.[2] The second policy, motivated by long-range considerations and based on the protection of British Empire interests in the area after World War I, resulted in the conclusion of the Sykes-Picot Treaty (May 9, 1916) the St. Jean de Maurienne agreement (April 21, 1917), and the Balfour Declaration (November 2, 1917).[3]

On the strength of the McMahon agreements Sherif Hussein gave the signal for an Arab Revolt on June 5, 1916. Many Iraqis actively supported the British with a view towards future independence. However, British duplicity, as revealed both by the secret Sykes-Picot Treaty of 1916 and the Balfour Declaration of 1917 gave rise to growing resentment against the British. Iraqi nationalists demanded an independent government at Baghdad but were faced instead with a British mandate assigned at the San Remo Peace Conference in the spring of 1920. An Arab insurrection had to be quelled by British military forces and the people of Mesopotamia had to accept a peace settlement imposed by foreigners.

The final arrangements for British control were made by the British Colonial Office headed at the time by Winston Churchill. A general British Conference was convened in Cairo (March 12-24, 1921) where it was decided that one of Sherif Hussein's sons, Faisal, would be offered the kingship of Iraq and, in order to appease Iraqi nationalists, the mandate would be replaced by a treaty of alliance. Faisal was subsequently declared King of Iraq on July 11, 1921. The foundation for a new order in Iraq was established by a foreign power with but minor and nominal concessions to the Iraqi nationalists. This was hardly the independence which had been hoped for, but it did mark an important advance toward eventual freedom from foreign domination. This, however, did not materialize without bloody and violent events marking the history of Iraq since 1921.

Local nationalism was the immediate force behind the strong opposition to the new regime. This forced the British to compromise and permit the gradual emancipation of the country through a series of bilateral agreements which culminated in Iraq's admission to the League of Nations on October 3, 1932. Complete severance from Britain was obviously impossible even though Anglo-Iraqi relations deteriorated steadily. The premature death of pro-British King Faisal and the accession to the throne of an irresponsible son, King Ghazi, resulted in a period of political instability and national frustration. The members of the ruling oligarchy generally favored continued cooperation with the British authorities and this made them the target of accusations and attack by anti-British nationalists. The 1936 *coup d'etat* was a direct result of this conflict and revealed the growing strength of the anti-British forces in Iraq. World War II, however, provided an interlude in the conflict and Iraq, or at least its government, formally joined the allied cause against Germany. Popular opposition to this policy, however, was great as evidenced by internal incidents. Anti-British elements led by Rashid Ali al-Gailani engineered a *coup d'etat* and managed temporarily to establish a pro-German government in Baghdad. During the short life of this regime, Iraq became a center of pro-Axis intrigues. This government was overthrown on May 31, 1940, after forty days of fighting which followed British intervention.

Allied victory in World War II restored the pro-British elements to power and the early years of the 1950's were marked with a struggle for power in which the political forces of the ruling conservative oligarchy fought against the growing threat posed to their privileged positions by the activities of both the nationalists and the socialists whose ranks had been strengthened considerably in the post-war years. The inevitable involvement of Iraq in the international politics of the Cold War added to the country's problems by making the government of Iraq the target of new attacks from the leaders of other Arab countries. Under the rule of the conservative elements, Iraq collaborated with the West, and joined Turkey, Pakistan, Iran and Great Britain in the ill-fated Baghdad Pact. Iraq's adherence to the Pact, while establishing a new link with the West, isolated the country from other Arab states, and actually marked the final phase of monarchy in Iraq. The July

Revolution of 1958 which ended the British supported regime of King Faisal II was an inevitable consequence of this alliance.

The military dictatorship which resulted from this Revolution introduced into Iraq a series of unstable regimes which primarily relied on the army for the exercise and the continuation of their political power. During this period, any attempt to criticize or control the ruling elite, if possible at all, had to be carried out either by the army or, at the very least, with its support. General Kassem ruled with a strong hand from July 14, 1958, until his assassination on February 8, 1963. His regime was marked by (1) ruthless subjugation of any opposition through a special tribunal called the People's Court; (2) numerous crises over relations with President Nasser of the United Arab Republic; (3) communist disturbances; (4) an armed revolt of Iraqi army officers; and (5) a rebellion of the Kurdish minority. Kassem met these major problems head-on and dealt with them as effectively as possible under most difficult circumstances. His efforts failed, however, because in the long run he was unable to secure his power in terms of a loyal army, a sound economic system, and the establishment of a modern state. He vacillated in his foreign relations with the Great Powers, quarreled with his neighbors, and became hopelessly bogged down in an internal war with the Kurds. His antagonism towards a large segment of the army insured his fall. Perhaps one of the most significant aspects of President Kassem's rule was the independent nature of government policies which did not tolerate any interference from the outside in internal affairs of the country even if the outsider happened to be President Nasser of the United Arab Republic. Internally the contest for power and policy orientation centered upon the issue of Arab nationalism versus national interest as perceived by Kassem. Kassem removed the pro-Nasser elements from a position of power in Iraq, which resulted in deterioration of his relations with the United Arab Republic and the intensive propaganda war which was waged between the two countries until Kassem's death in 1963. To underline the seriousness of his intentions, Kassem even used the Iraqi Communists to advance his cause against the Nasserites before disposing of them in the interest of Iraqi nationalism. The attack on the Communists was precipitated by the Kirkuk massacres of mid-July, 1959,[3] which led him to condemn and suppress the Communists whom he called "the forces of anarchy." The ultimate result of these policies was not without irony; while Kassem successfully repelled all attempts from outside Iraq aimed at the control of his country, he failed to consolidate his own regime and to maintain his own power which he had acquired through so much bloodshed in 1958. By 1963 his regime was isolated, shaky and in a state of decline. A new and determined effort by the army ended its precarious life.

The new revolutionary wave which overthrew President Kassem was accomplished by a coalition of a Pan-Arab faction of the army in cooperation with the *Ba'ath* or the Renaissance Party, which had its roots in neighboring Syria. This coalition originally was dedicated to the principles of Arab unity and socialism and sought rapprochement with the United Arab Republic with a view towards the ultimate realization of Arab nationalism. A proposed federation to this end, including Iraq, Syria and Egypt, proved to be merely facade behind which President Nasser hoped to gain greater power. The attempt was abortive in its formative stages and never reached fruition. The conflict took the form of Nasserism versus *Ba'athist* socialism with Iraq essentially in the middle. This led to a series of political moves aimed at the creation of a bond between the ruling *Ba'athist* group in Iraq and their Syrian counterparts, but again rival factions in the army rose to prevent outside control of internal affairs. Internal dissension within the Iraqi *Ba'athist* regime contributed to its own downfall.[4] It is also significant that the Kurdish problem remained unresolved during this brief experiment with coalition forces. The *Ba'ath* regime was overthrown on November 18, 1963, after only eight months in power. During this time it contributed virtually nothing constructive to the country, but in a negative sense proved once again that the internal affairs of a state with a growing national consciousness of its own would brook no interference from external forces and that in any struggle for power local nationalism would prevail.

Exasperation best summarizes the atmosphere at the time of the counter-coup led by Staff Marshal Abdul Salam Aref. The ideas and practices of collective leadership resolved none of the major problems facing the nation. President Aref established personal rule based in support of the army. He had been a key figure in the July 14, 1958 Revolution and had been nominally installed as a Presidential figure-head in the *Ba'ath* regime. However, his rule too followed the revolutionary wave of turmoil. The Aref regime attempted to create a one-party system dedicated to the concept of

Arab socialism on the model of Nasserism, but extended to include Islam as a foundation. His immediate aims could better be described as Iraqi socialism. President Aref, however, made an attempt to reconcile Iraq's objectives with President Nasser's United Arab Republic. A unified political command was envisioned by the leaders which was to act as the highest authority in Iraq and Egypt. A joint communique issued by the two leaders outlined the ambitious program with a tentative timetable for accomplishment. Again, however, the Iraqi leadership continued to stress internal affairs as having primary importance[5] and unification with Egypt was treated as a secondary goal. Once more, national unity, rather than Arab unity, dominated the thoughts and actions of the ruling elite. Plans for unification with Egypt never passed the theoretical stage.

Although the Kurdish problem continued in much the same pattern, a significant move was made by President Aref in entrusting the Premiership to a civilian politician in hopes that the army might eventually be isolated from politics. His hopes were not realized because after his death in a helicopter crash in April 1966, rule passed to his brother, Abdul al-Rahman Aref, the former Army Chief of Staff. The army continued to be a force in the struggle for power in Iraq.

The rule of President Aref, the elder, was consolidated, and full power was asserted by August of 1966. The regime of Aref lasted until July 17, 1968, when he became the victim of a bloodless *coup* which brought to power again the Ba'ath Party under the leadership of Major-General Ahmad Hassan al-Bakr, who had served as Premier during the *Ba'ath* rule of February-November, 1963. Presidents Aref and Bakr were plagued by the difficulties presented by the June 1967 War with Israel, conflicts with foreign oil interests, the Kurdish Revolution, and the problem of maintaining themselves in power. It can be said at this writing that President Bakr has made significant progress in the resolution of the Kurdish War, he has been suddessful in realizing greater control of and more revenue realized from the country's oil resources, and he has gained—for Iraq—a semblance of political stability not attained by his predecessors in the Republic. Iraq remains, however, a firm supporter of the Palestine Liberation movement and continues to reject a "peaceful settlement" of the Palestine question. This has put President Bakr in a tenuous position as regards the U.A.R.,

Syria, and Jordan. On the other hand, he has successfully concluded the Kurdish Revolution and has reached accommodation with Iran concerning the major problem of navigational rights on the *Shatt al-Arab*.

Given the explosive nature of Iraqi politics (assassinations and attempted assassinations, plotted *coups*, and political executions continue to be reported), the Bakr regime must be evaluated in terms of unusual progress in the settlement of major problems during the last year and a half (1970–71). To predict that this will continue would be folly, but is must be stressed that the signs of reasonable resolution of major issues is at least encouraging.

Conclusions

This study of the struggle for political power in Iraq has as its central thesis the concept that the forces in conflict are complex, they have their roots in an ancient historical and religious heritage, and that they have been more complicated by foreign intervention in the modern era. Although the study is limited by the data available to the author the following conclusions can be drawn from the arguments presented herein.

First, there are two compelling sides of Arab nationalism, its unifying aspect and its divisive force, both of which simultaneously influence Arab politics. Arab nationalism agitates throughout the Arab world with enormous vocal strength and as such has provided its leaders with a strong propaganda force which it exploits at every opportunity. However, as such, it does not provide sufficient motivation for the Arab political and social unity which is desired by its most vocal exponents. Each experiment in modern times with Arab political unity has failed. Even attempts by the Arab states to unify militarily against a common enemy, Israel, have failed miserably.

Perhaps the most common integrating factors in the Arab world are the Arabic language, culture and religion. Yet even here Islam is a divided house. The basic religious schism between the *Sunnis* and the *Shi'ites* pre-dates modern times and the split has had far-reaching social and political consequences. Further, the binding force of Islamic law has broken down with the introduction of new legal concepts from the West. For example. constitutions based on the Western models provide for a division of powers, whereas, under Islamic law, power was once concentrated in the hands of the sultan-caliph.

The strongest element of Arab unity is unquestionably the Arabic language. Its importance is repeatedly expressed by writers and politicians in the Arab world, but language alone cannot provide the basis of a nation. But here again, the Arabic language is one language only in the sense of a classical language, the language of the Qu'ran, which has limited application to political problems of modern times. The language has lost its uniformity insofar as the ordinary people are concerned. Scores of dialects and sub-dialects separate one Arab group from another. The unifying aspect of language is a limited one.

Arab nationalism has proved to be more of a divisive force as it takes on different interpretations, depending on the political views of the man in power.

Second, the impact of the West upon the Arab world in modern times has accentuated this divisive feature of Arab nationalism. The introduction of Western technology, economic competition and cultural penetration has caused a drive for modernization in Arab areas. The resulting direct competition with neighbors has caused a desire for material benefits which were not previously available in a decadent society.

Third, as a direct result of these divisive features of Arab nationalism, there has developed in Iraq a local nationalism, or particularism, inherent in the Western conception of "the nation." It is argued that perhaps for the first time in modern history, a nation-state has emerged from the artificial creation of a political entity by foreign elements. Although it was expected by many observers that Arab unity was only one step away after the Revolution of July 14, 1958, subsequent events proved that national interest predominated when attempts were made towards union, federation or confederation with other Arab states. Each attempt was a failure. Two features aggravate these attempts for unification: first, the strong competition between Arab leaders for dominance in the Arab world, and second, the competition for control of each Arab nation by the Great Powers, primarily the United States and the U.S.S.R.

The centrifugal force behind local nationalism is secularism which removes much of the theoretical force behind Arab nationalism. The leadership in Iraq since the time of its creation as a nation-state after World War I has concerned itself with the national interest as the leaders saw it, not with a mythical Arab unity based on a common historical-religious legacy. New loyalties have been generated, new communities of interest have been born, local political thinking has developed based on material expectation has reached the grass-roots level of a new nation-state and is exerting itself in Iraqi nationalism.

Finally, the struggle for power during the past two decades has centered in the Iraqi army. Conspiracies and *coups d'etat* are born and fostered by competing forces within the military structure. Once the monopoly of power by a privileged class was successfully challenged and direct foreign domination removed, the national army emerged as the only remaining political force. The army is also of recent origin and, with independence, it became a symbol of national pride and dignity. The military establishment very soon became a center of nationalist activity with a clear distinction emerging between the older and higher-ranking officers who were identified with the old leadership based on British support, and the younger junior officers who rebelled against the *status quo*. The clash between these two elements resulted in a series of political and military upheavals which have been reviewed in this study.

To seize power, however, is one thing and to preserve it is quite another. It is this problem of maintaining power on a legitimate basis that has not been resolved as yet in Iraq. Military dictatorship, based on usurpation of power, has neither institutional foundations nor legitimacy; it must necessarily depend on the loyalty of the army for the preservation of its life. Without the emergence of competent leadership, Iraq will be likely to continue on a course of internal eruptions for the foreseeable future.

The experience in Iraq as here discussed is more of a common occurrence in the Arab World rather than the exception. Military *coups* have taken place in Egypt (1881, 1952, 1957); a dozen more attempted in Syria since 1949, four in the Sudan (1958, 1964, 1969, 1971); three in Yemen (1949, 1955, 1962); two in Algeria (1962, 1965); and one in Libya (1969), to name only a few of the major events. This has led to the conclusion that the military coup is regarded as the "natural course" of political development in the contemporary Arab States.* Following many of these military "take-overs" there were attempts to allow civilians to rule, but invariably the military has either seen fit to take over the machinery of government themselves and to rule the country directly, or direct the rule of the country by civilians from behind the scenes. The military has not always agreed upon the policies to be followed, and there has been and will continue to be factional strife within the military with civilians providing a "balance" force which determines which military faction will emerge victorious. The strong army officer in the victorious faction then rules in an authoritarian manner, disposing of rivals by the methods of retirement from military service, exile or liquidation, usually on the basis of treason, i.e., disagreement with the man or group in power.

Why has praetorianism become so prevalent in the Middle East, to say nothing of Latin America and Africa? Huntington discounts the simplistic view that military aid by the major powers to the developing countries as the sole or principal course of the intervention of the military in politics. Rather, he suggests "that military interventions are only one specific manifestation of a broader phenomenon in underdeveloped societies: the general politicization of social forces and institutions. In such societies, politics lack autonomy, complexity, coherence and adaptability. All sorts of social forces and groups become directly engaged in general politics. Countries which have political armies also have political clergies, political universities, political bureaucracies, political labor unions, and political corporations. Society as a whole is out of joint, not just the military."* However, in these societies it has become evident, very nearly a "rule of law," that nearly all aspects of society have become dominated, or at least influenced, by the military and the institutions, political, economic, religious and social, which are subordinate to and supportive of the dominant force in being. In short, *Militarism* has become the strongest force in countries such as Iraq, if not even on a much broader scale, although not so noticeable, in not only the developing countries of the world, but even in the major powers of the world today. Nationalism, whether it be regional (the Arab homeland), local (Iraq, etc.), secular, or religious, as well as its concomitant concept "patriotism," has become the tool of the predominant

---

*see Eliezer Be'eri, *Army Officers in Arab Politics and Society* (New York: Frederick A. Praeger, Inc., 1970) for a full discussion of this theory.

force—*Militarism*. Unless this trend is arrested and reversed, the conditions of a "police state" will not be found in "isolation," or a rarity, if it is that now, but will become the way of life for all humanity.

*See Samuel P. Huntington, *Political Order in Changing Societies* (New Haven: Yale University Press, 1968), especially Chapter 4, pp. 192–263.

NOTES

[1]See Chapter 4 above.

[2]See George Lenczowski, *The Middle East in World Affairs* (New York: Cornell University Press, 1962), pp. 67–83 for discussion of wartime agreements concerning the Middle East.

[3]*Ibid*. The St. Jean de Maurienne agreement included Italy's claim to a sphere of influence in the area. The Balfour Declaration provided British approval for the establishment of a national home for Jewish people in Palestine.

[3]See pages 158–63 above.

[4]See pages 177–84 above.

[5]See Appendix P, Provisional Constitution of April 29, 1964, which again reiterates the theme of Iraqi unity.

BIBLIOGRAPHY

A. BOOKS

Abu-Lughod, Ibrahim. (ed.). *The Arab World: Special Issue*, "The Arab-Israeli Confrontation of June, 1967."

al-Razzaz, Munif. *The Evolution of the Meaning of Nationalism*. Trans. Ibrahim Abu-Lughod. New York: Doubleday and Company, Inc., 1963.

Antonius, George. *The Arab Awakening*. London: Hamish Hamilton, 1938.

Atiya, Aziz S. *Crusade, Commerce and Culture*. Bloomington: Indiana University Press, 1962.

Be'eri, Eliezer. *Army Officers in Arab Politics and Society*. New York: Frederick A. Praeger, Inc., 1970.

Bell, Lady D.B.E. (ed.). *The Letters of Gertrude Bell*. New York: Boni and Liveright, 1927.

Brockelmann, Carl. *History of the Islamic Peoples*. New York: Capricorn Books, 1960.

Browne, Edward G. *A Literary History of Persia*. 2 vols. Cambridge: The University Press, 1956.

_____. *The Persian Revolution, 1905–1909*. Cambridge: The University Press, 1910.

Churchill, Randolph S. and Winston S. *The Six Day War*. Boston: Houghton-Mifflin, 1967.

Cressey, George B. *Crossroads, Land and Life in Southwest Asia*. New York: J.B. Lippincott Company, 1960.

Dahl, Robert A. *Modern Political Analysis*. Englewood Cliffs, N.J.: Prentice-Hall, Inc., 1965.

Dayan, Moshe. *Diary of the Sinai Campaign*. New York: Harper and Row, 1969.

De Jouvenal, Bertrand. *On Power: Its Nature and The History of Its Growth*. Boston: Beacon Press, 1962.

Deutsch, Karl W. *Nationalism and Social Communication: An Inquiry Into the Foundations of Nationality*. New York: John Wiley and Sons, Inc., 1953.

Draper, Theodore. *Israel and World Politics: Roots of the Third Arab-Israeli War*. New York: Viking, 1968.

Durant, Will. *The Age of Faith*. New York: Simon and Schuster, 1950.

Europa Publications. *The Middle East and North Africa*. 12th ed. London: Europa Publications, Ltd., 1965.

————. *The Middle East and North Africa*. 17th ed. London: Europa Publications, Ltd., 1970-71.

Everyman's United Nations. New York: United Nations, 1964.

Fisher, Sydney N. *The Middle East: A History*. New York: Alfred A. Knopf, 1959.

Gallman, Waldemar J. *Iraq Under General Nuri: My Recollections of Nuri al-Said, 1954-1958*. Baltimore: The Johns Hopkins Press, 1964.

Harari, Maurice. *Government and Politics of the Middle East*. Englewood Cliffs, N.J.: Prentice-Hall, Inc., 1962.

Harris, George L. *Iraq*. New Haven: Human Relations Area Files Press, 1958.

Hayes, Carlton J. H. *Essays on Nationalism*. New York: The Macmillan Company, 1928.

Hitti, Philip K. *History of the Arabs*. New York: St. Martin's Press, 1967.

————. *The Near East in History*. Princeton: D. Van Nostrand and Company, Inc., 1961.

Houtsma, M. Th. *et al. The Encyclopaedia of Islam*. 4 vols. London: Luzac & Co., 1936.

Huntington, Samuel P. *Political Order in Changing Societies*. New Haven: Yale University Press, 1968.

Hurewitz, J.C. *Diplomacy in the Near and Middle East*. 2 vols. Princeton: D. Van Nostrand and Company, Inc., 1956.

Ireland, Philip W. *Iraq: A Study in Political Development*. London: Jonathan Cape, 1937.

Jeffrey, Arthur. *Muhammad and His Religion*. New York: The Liberal Arts Press, 1958.

Kedourie, Elie. *Afghani and 'Abduh*. London: Frank Cass & Co., Ltd., 1966.

Keesing's Research Report. *The Arab Israeli Conflict: The 1967 Campaign*. New York: Charles Scribner's Sons, 1968.

Khadduri, Majid. *Independent Iraq 1932–1958: A Study in Iraqi Politics*. London: Oxford University Press, 1960.

————. *Political Trends in the Arab World*. Baltimore: The Johns Hopkins Press, 1970.

————. *Republican Iraq*. New York: Oxford University Press, 1969.

Khalidi, Walid and Yusuf Ibish (eds.). *Arab Political Documents, 1963*. Beirut:

Political Studies and Public Administration Department of the American University, 1963.

Khalil, Muhammad (ed.). *The Arab States and the Arab League: A Documentary Record.* 2 vols. Beirut: Khayats, 1962.

Khouri, Fred J. *The Arab-Israeli Dilemma.* New York: Syracuse University Press, 1968.

Kohn, Hans. *TheIdea of Nationalism: A Study in its Origin and Background.* New York: The Macmillan Company, 1961.

Laqueur, Walter. *The Soviet Union and the Middle East.* New York: Frederick A. Praeger, 1959.

_____. *The Israel-Arab Reader: A Documentary History of the Middle East Conflict.* New York: Citadel Press, 1968.

Lasswell, Harold D. *Power and Personality.* New York: The Viking Press, 1962.

_____. , and Daniel Lerner (eds.). *World Revolutionary Elites.* Cambridge: The M.I.T. Press, 1966.

Lawrence, Thomas E. *Revolt in the Desert.* New York: Doran, 1927.

Lenczowski, George. *The Middle East in World Affairs.* New York: Cornell University Press, 1966.

Lewis, Bernard. *Emergence of Modern Turkey.* New York: Oxford University Press, 1961.

_____. *The Arabs in History.* New York: Harper and Row, 1960.

Longrigg, Stephen H. *Iraq, 1900 to 1950: A Political, Social and Economic History.* London: Oxford University Press, 1953.

Macdonald, Robert W. *The League of Arab States.* Princeton: Princeton University Press, 1965.

MacIver, R. M. *The Web of Government.* New York: The Free Press, 1965.

Mehdi, M.T. *Peace in the Middle East.* New York: New World Press, 1967.

Merriam, Charles E. *Political Power.* New York: Collier Books, 1964.

Mills, C. Wright. *The Power Elite.* New York: Oxford University Press, 1959.

Mostofi, Khosrow. *Aspects of Nationalism: A Sociology of Colonial Revolt.* Salt Lake City: Institute of Government, University of Utah, 1964.

Nuseiheb, Hazem Zaki. *The Ideas of Arab Nationalism.* New York: Cornell University Press, 1956.

Oppenheim, Felix E. *Dimensions of Freedom: An Analysis.* New York: St. Martin's Press, 1961.

Oppenheim, L. *International Law: A Treatise.* Ed. H. Lauterpacht. 2 vols. New York: David McKay Company, Inc., 1955.

Rivlin, Benjamin and Joseph S. Szyliowicz (eds.). *The Contemporary Middle East.* New York: Random House, 1965.

Rosenthal, E.I.J. *Political Thought in Medieval Islam.* Cambridge: The University Press, 1962.

Russell, Bertrand. *Power: A New Social Analysis.* New York: W.W. Norton and Company, 1938.

Safran, Nadav. *From War to War. The Arab-Israeli Confrontation, 1948–1967.* New York: Pegasus, 1969.

Sayegh, Fayez A. *Arab Unity: Hope and Fulfillment.* New York: The Devin-Adair

Company, 1958.

Shwadran, Benjamin. *The Middle East, Oil and the Great Powers 1959.* New York: Council for Middle Eastern Affairs Press, 1959.

_____. *The Power Struggle in Iraq.* New York: Council for Middle Eastern Affairs Press, 1960.

Sharabi, Hisham. *Nationalism and Revolution in the Arab World.* Princeton: D. Van Nostrand and Company, Inc., 1966.

Sykes, Sir Percy. *A History of Persia.* 2 vols. London: Macmillan and Company, Ltd., 1951.

Tutsch, Hans E. *Facets of Arab Nationalism.* Detroit: Wayne State University Press, 1965.

Ward, Barbara. *Five Ideas that Changed the World.* New York: W. W. Norton and Company, Inc., 1959.

Zeine, Zein N. *The Emergence of Arab Nationalism.* Beirut: Khayats, 1966.

B. PERIODICALS

Al-Bakr, Hassan Ahmad. "Armed Struggle Only Way to Victory," *Iraq News Bulletin* (March 1971), pp. 1–3.

"Announcement of Coup d'Etat in Iraq," *Middle Eastern Affairs,* IX (August-September 1958), p. 267.

"A Question of Motive," *New Statesman,* June 30, 1961, p. 1032.

Birdwood, Lord. "Nuri, Nasser and the Middle East," *Contemporary Review,* XV (June 1959), 335–37.

Childers, Erskine B. "Iraq After Aref," *New Statesman,* December 13, 1958, pp. 839–40.

_____. "Kassem and Kuwait," *The Spectator,* July 7, 1961, p. 7.

"Complaint by Kuwait Against Iraq and by Iraq Against UK," *International Organization,* XV (Fall 1961), p. 652–55.

"Coup d'Etat in Iraq," *Middle Eastern Affairs,* XIV (March 1963), 78–80.

Edmonds, C.J. "The Kurds and the Revolution in Iraq," *The Middle East Journal,* XIII (Winter 1959), p. 1–10.

_____. "The Kurdish War in Iraq: The Constitutional Background," *World Today,* XXIV (December 1968), pp. 512–520.

Hindawi, Saeed K. "Iraq Oil Industry," *Iraq News Bulletin* (March 1971), pp. 10–11.

Jenkins, Roy. "Kassem and Pan-Arabism" *The Spectator,* November 14, 1958, pp. 637–39.

Langley, Kathleen M. "Iraq: Some Aspects of the Economic Scene," *The Middle East Journal,* XVIII (Spring 1964), pp. 180–88.

Laqueur, Walter. "As Iraq Goes Communist: Days of Decision in Baghdad," *Commentary,* XXVII (May 1959), pp. 369–76.

Lenczowski, George. "Iraq: Seven Years of Revolution," *Current History*, XLVIII (May 1965), pp. 283–87.

_____. "Radical Regimes in Egypt, Syria and Iraq," *The Journal of Politics*, XXVIII (February 1966), pp. 30–35.

Levy, Walter J. "Oil Power," *Foreign Affairs*, (July 1971), pp. 652–668.

Marr, Phebe Ann, "Iraq's Leadership Dilemma: A Study in Leadership Trends, 1948–1968," *The Middle East Journal*, XXIV (Summer 1970), pp. 283–301.

Naamani, Israel T. "The Kurdish Drive for Self-Determination," *The Middle East Journal*, XX (Summer 1966), pp. 279–95.

Perlman, N. "Midsummer Madness," *Middle Eastern Affairs*, IX (August-September 1958), pp. 246–61.

"Politics in Iraq," *New Statesman* (July 19, 1958), pp. 74–75.

Priestly Vito. "The Political Situation in Iraq," *Middle Eastern Affairs*, XIII (May 1962), pp. 139-45.

Solomon, Gershon. "The Kurds Are Fighting Again," *New Outlook*, XII (May 1969), pp. 35–37.

"Statement by KDP on the Eighth Anniversary of the Kurdish Revolution," *The Kurdish Journal*, VI (September 1969), pp. 117–120.

Stewart, Desmond. "Iraq's Political Maze," *The Spectator* (October 24, 1958), pp. 537–38.

_____. "The Mood in Iraq," *The Spectator* (December 6, 1963), p. 748.

"The Iraqi Tragedy," *Economist* (April 4, 1959), p. 47.

"The Kurds and the Concept of Iraqi Unity," *The Kurdish Journal*, V (September 1968), pp. 1–3.

"The Kurds and the Shelling of Kirkuk Oil Installations," *Kurdish Affairs Bulletin*, No. 1, 1969, p. 1

Torrey, Gordon H. and John F. Devlin. "Arab Socialism," *Journal of International Affairs*, XIX (January 1965), pp. 47-62.

"Tragedy at Dakan Village," *Kurdish Affairs Bulletin*, No. 6, 1969, p. 1.

Walter, E.V. "Power and Violence," *American Political Science Review*, LVIII (June 1964), pp. 350–60.

Westerman, William Linn. "Kurdish Independence and Russian Expansion," *Foreign Affairs*, XXIV (July 1946), pp. 675–86.

Wormuth, Francis D. "Matched-Dependent Behavioralism: The Cargo Cult in Political Science," *Western Political Quarterly*, XX (December 1967), pp. 809–40.

C. ESSAYS AND ARTICLES IN COLLECTIONS

Glubb, Sir John Bagot. "The Role of the Army in the Traditional Arab State," *Modernization of the Arab World*, Princeton: D. Van Nostrand Company,

Inc., 1966, pp. 52–60.

Heller, Herman. "Political Power," *Encyclopedia of the Social Sciences*, XII, pp. 300–305. New York: Macmillan Company, 1937

Neumann, Franz L. "Approaches to the Study of Political Power,' *Contemporary Politics*, Homewood, Ill.: The Dorsey Press, 1964. pp. 65-75.

D. DOCUMENTS AND STATEMENTS

"Communique of the Military Governor-General in Iraq Announcing the execution of General Abdul Karim Kassem," *Arab Political Documents 1963*. Walid Khalidi and Yusuf Ibish, Editors. Beirut: American University of Beirut, 1963. p. 7.

"Declaration of the Tripartite Union: Announcement of the Creation of the Federal State of the United Arab Republic," *Arab Political Documents 1963*. Walid Khalidi and Yusuf Ibish, editors. Beirut: American University of Beirut, 1963. pp. 227–46.

Great Britain. *Parliamentary Debates, House of Commons*. Vol. 398, February 24, 1943.

"Joint Syrian-Iraqi Communique Issued on Visit of President Aref to Syria," *Arab Political Documents 1963*. Walid Khalidi and Ibish Yusuf, editors. Beirut: American University of Beirut: 1963. pp. 370–71.

"Ministerial Programme of the Iraqi Government, December 24, 1963," *Arab Political Documents 1963*. Walid Khalidi and Yusuf Ibish, editors. Beirut: American University of Beirut, 1963. pp. 506-7.

"Nui As-Sa'id's Fertile Crescent Project 1943," *The Arab States and the Arab League*, Vol. II. Muhammad Khalil, editor. Beirut: Khayats, 1962. pp. 9–12.

"Pact of Mutual Cooperation Between Iraq and Turkey (the Baghdad Pact)," *The Arab States and the Arab League*, Vol. II. Muhammad Khalil, editor. Beirut: Khayats, 1962, pp. 368–70.

"President J. 'Abd an-Nasir's Speech on the Occasion of the Visit to Damascus by the Leaders of the Iraqi Revolution, July 19, 1958," *The Arab States and the Arab League*, Vol. II. Muhammad Khalil, editor. Beirut: Khayats, 1962, p. 289.

"Resolutions of the Sixth National Congress of the Arab Ba'ath Socialist Party," *Arab Political Documents 1963*. Beirut: American University of Beirut, 1963, p. 438.

"Statement of the Iraqi National Revolution Council on the Barzani Movement," *Arab Political Documents 1963*. Walid Khalidi and Yusuf Ibish, editors. Beirut: American University of Beirut, 1963. pp. 285-8 8.

"Statement Regarding the Resumption of Diplomatic Relations Between the Iraqi Republic and the Soviet Union," *The Arab States and the Arab League*, Vol. II. Muhammad Khalil, editor. Beirut: Khayats, 1962. pp. 376–77.

"The Alexandria Protocol, October 7, 1944," *The Arab States and the Arab League*, Vol. II. Muhammad Khalil, editor. Beirut: Khayats, 1962. pp. 53-56.

"The Covenant of the League of Arab States," *The Arab States and the Arab League*, Vol. II. Muhammad Khalil, editor. Beirut: Khayats, 1962. pp. 56–61.

"The Iraqi National Guard Law, May 18, 1963," *Arab Political Documents 1963*. Walid Khalidi and Yusuf Ibish, editors. Beirut: American University of Beirut, 1963. pp. 273–74.

United Nations. Security Council Official Records, S/PV, 830, 16 July, 1958.

United Nations. Security Council Official Records, S/PV, 838, 7 August, 1958.

————. Security Council Official Records, S/PV, 840, 25 November, 1958.

United Nations. Security Council Official Records, S/PV, 957, 2 July, 1961.

————. Security Council Documents S/4844, S/4845.

"U.S. Statement Supporting the Baghdad Pact," *The Arab States and the Arab League*, Vol. II. Muhammad Khalil, editor. Beirut: Khayats, 1962. p. 376.

E. NEWSPAPERS AND NEWS ANALYSES

Al-Ahram
Al-Jumbouriya
Al-Manar
Al-Nahar
Arab Report and Record
Al-Thawrah Al-Arabiya
Baghdad Observer
Daily Telegraph (London)
Der Spiegel
Guardian (London)
London Times
Mideast Mirror
Near East Report
New York Post
Sawt al-Arab
Washington Post

F. UNPUBLISHED MATERIALS

Dorton, Maurice K. "The Relationship Between the Department of State and the American Oil Companies Operating in the Middle East." Unpublished Master's thesis, University of Utah, Salt Lake City. 1964.

Hanna, Sami. "Socialism and the *Ahali* Movement in Iraq." (Article prepared for publication in the *Middle East Journal*.)

APPENDICES

A. Treaty of Alliance: Great Britain and Iraq, 10 October 1922

B. Treaty of Alliance Between the United Kingdom and Iraq (Baghdad, June 30, 1930), Together with Exchange of Notes on a Separate Financial Agreement

C. Nuri As'Sa'id's Fertile Crescent Project

D. Pact of Mutual Co-operation Between Iraq and Turkey (The Baghdad Pact) Baghdad, February 24, 1955

E. The Coup d'Etat in Iraq: First Statement Proclaiming the Revolution and Abolishing the Monarchy, July 14, 1958

F. Provisional Constitution of the Republic of Iraq

G. Statements Made by Premier Abdul Karim Kassem to a Lebanese Journalist on Iraq's Arab Policy, February 5, 1963

H. Counter-Coup, February 8, 1963

I. Communique of the Military Governor-General in Iraq Announcing the Execution of General Abdul Karim Kassem, February 9, 1963

J. Law Establishing the National Revolutionary Council in Iraq, April 4, 1963

K. The Iraqi National Guard Law, May 18, 1963

L. Statement of the National Command of the Ba'ath Party on its Assumption of Power in Iraq, Baghdad, November 14, 1963

M. Official Statement No. 1 of President Aref, Commander-in-Chief of the Iraqi Armed Forces, Baghdad, November 18, 1963

N. Official Statement No. 1 of the Iraqi National Revolutionary Council, Baghdad, November 18, 1963

O. Ministerial Programme of the Iraqi Government, Baghdad, December 24, 1963

P. Provisional Constitution, April 29, 1964

APPENDIX A

TREATY OF ALLIANCE: GREAT BRITAIN AND IRAQ
10 October 1922
(Ratifications exchanged, Baghdad, 19 December 1924)
[Great Britain, Parliamentary Papers, 1925,
Treaty Series No. 17, Cmd. 2370]

Article I. At the request of His Majesty the King of Iraq, His Britannic Majesty undertakes subject to the provisions of this Treaty to provide the State of Iraq with such advice and assistance as may be required during the period of the present Treaty, without prejudice to her national sovereignty. His Britannic Majesty shall be represented in Iraq by a High Commissioner and Consul-General assisted by the necessary staff.

Article II. His Majesty the King of Iraq undertakes that for the period of the present Treaty no gazetted official of other than Iraq nationality shall be appointed in Iraq without the concurrence of His Britannic Majesty. A separate agreement shall regulate the numbers and conditions of employment of British officials so appointed in the Iraq Government.

Article III. His Majesty the King of Iraq agrees to frame an Organic Law for presentation to the Constituent Assembly of Iraq and to give effect to the said law, which shall contain nothing contrary to the provisions of the present Treaty and shall take account of the rights, wishes and interests of all populations inhabiting Iraq. This Organic Law shall ensure to all complete freedom of conscience and the free exercise of all forms of worship, subject only to the maintenance of public order and morals. It shall provide that no discrimination of any kind shall be made between the inhabitants of Iraq on the ground of race, religion or language, and shall secure that the right of each community to maintain its own schools for the education of its own members in its own language, while conforming to such educational requirements of a general nature as the Government of Iraq may impose, shall not be denied or impaired. It shall prescribe the constitutional procedure, whether legislative or executive, by which decisions will be take 1 on all matters of importance, including those involving questions (*i* fiscal, financial and military policy.

Article IV. Without prejudice to the provisions of Articles XVII and XVIII of this Treaty, His Majesty the King of Iraq agrees to be guided by the advice of His Britannic Majesty tendered through the High Commissioner on all important matters affecting the international and financial obligations and interests of His Britannic Majesty for the whole period of this Treaty. His Majesty the King of Iraq will fully consult the High Commissioner on what is conducive to a sound financial and fiscal policy and will ensure the stability and good organization of the finances of the Iraq Government so long as that Government is under financial obligations to the Government of His Britannic Majesty.

Article V. His Majesty the King of Iraq shall have the right of representation in London and in such other capitals and places as may be agreed upon by the High Contracting Parties. Where His Majesty the King of Iraq is not represented he agrees to entrust the protection of Iraq nationals to His Britannic Majesty. His Majesty the King of Iraq shall himself issue exequaturs to representatives of

Foreign Powers in Iraq after His Britannic Majesty has agreed to their appointment.

Article VI. His Britannic Majesty undertakes to use his good offices to secure the admission of Iraq to membership of the League of Nations as soon as possible.

Article VII. His Britannic Majesty undertakes to provide such support and assistance to the armed forces of His Majesty the King of Iraq as may from time to time be agreed by the High Contracting Parties. A separate agreement regulating the extent and conditions of such support and assistance shall be concluded between the High Contracting Parties and communicated to the Council of the League of Nations.

Article VIII. No territory in Iraq shall be ceded or leased or in any way placed under the control of any Foreign Power; this shall not prevent His Majesty the King of Iraq from making such arrangements as may be necessary for the accommodation of foreign representatives and for the fulfillment of the provisions of the preceding Article.

Article IX. His Majesty the King of Iraq undertakes that he will accept and give effect to such reasonable provisions as His Britannic Majesty may consider necessary in judicial matters to safeguard the interests of foreigners in consequence of the non-application of the immunities and privileges enjoyed by them under capitulation or usage. These provisions shall be embodied in a separate agreement, which shall be communicated to the Council of the League of Nations.

Article X. The High Contracting Parties agree to conclude separate agreements to secure the execution of any treaties, agreements or undertakings which His Britannic Majesty is under obligation to see carried out in respect of Iraq. His Majesty the King of Iraq undertakes to bring in any legislation necessary to ensure the execution of these agreements. Such agreements shall be communicated to the Council of the League of Nations.

Article XI. There shall be no discrimination in Iraq against the nationals of any State, member of the League of Nations, or of any State to which His Britannic Majesty has agreed by treaty that the same rights should be ensured as it would enjoy if it were a member of the said League (including companies incorporated under the laws of such State), as compared with British nationals or those of any foreign State in matters concerning taxation, commerce or navigation, the exercise of industries or professions, or in the treatment of merchant vessels or civil aircraft. Nor shall there be any discrimination in Iraq against goods originating in or destined for any of the said States. There shall be freedom of transit under equitable conditions across Iraq territory.

Article XII. No measure shall be taken in Iraq to obstruct or interfere with missionary enterprise or to discriminate against any missionary on the ground of his religious belief or nationality, provided that such enterprise is not prejudicial to public order and good government.

Article XIII. His Majesty the King of Iraq undertakes to co-operate, in so far as social, religious and other conditions may permit, in the execution of any common policy adopted by the League of Nations for preventing and combating disease, including diseases of plants and animals.

Article XIV. His Majesty the King of Iraq undertakes to secure the enactment within twelve months of the coming into force of this Treaty, and to ensure the execution of a Law of Antiquities based on the rules annexed to Article 421 of the Treaty of Peace signed at Sevres on the 10th of August, 1920. This Law shall replace the former Ottoman Law of Antiquities, and shall ensure equality of treatment in the matter of archaeological research to the nationals of all States members of the League of Nations, and of any State to which His Britannic Majesty has agreed by treaty that the same rights should be ensured as it would enjoy if it were a member of the said League.

Article XV. A separate agreement shall regulate the financial relations between the High Contracting Parties. It shall provide, on the one hand, for the transfer by His Britannic Majesty's Government to the Government of Iraq of such works of public utility as may be agreed upon and for the rendering by His Britannic Majesty's Government of such financial assistance as may from time to time be considered necessary for Iraq, and, on the other hand, for the progressive liquidation by the Government of Iraq of all liabilities thus incurred. Such agreement shall be communicated to the Council of the League of Nations.

Article XVI. So far as is consistent with his international obligations His Britannic Majesty undertakes to place no obstacle in the way of the association of the State of Iraq for customs or other purposes with such neighbouring Arab States as may desire it.

Article XVII. Any difference that may arise between the High Contracting Parties as to the interpretation of the provisions of this Treaty shall be referred to the Permanent Court of International Justice provided for by Article 14 of the Covenant of the League of Nations. In such case, should there by any discrepancy between the English and Arabic texts of this Treaty, the English shall be taken as the authoritative version.

Article XVIII. This Treaty shall come into force as it has been ratified by the High Contracting Parties after its acceptance by the Constituent Assembly, and shall remain in force for twenty years, at the end of which period the situation shall be examined, and if the High Contracting Parties are of opinion that the Treaty is no longer required it shall be terminated. Termination shall be subject to confirmation by the League of Nations unless before that date Article VI of this Treaty has come into effect, in which case notice of termination shall be communicated to the Council of the League of Nations. Nothing shall prevent the High Contracting Parties from reviewing from time to time the provisions of this Treaty, and those of the separate Agreements arising out of Articles VII, X and XV, with a view to any revision which may seem desirable in the circumstances then existing, and any modification which may be agreed upon by the High Contracting Parties shall be communicated to the Council of the League of Nations.

APPENDIX B

TREATY OF ALLIANCE BETWEEN THE UNITED KINGDOM AND IRAQ
(BAGHDAD, JUNE 30, 1930), TOGETHER WITH EXCHANGE OF
NOTES ON A SEPARATE FINANCIAL AGREEMENT

His Majesty the King of Great Britain, Ireland and the British Dominions beyond the Seas, Emperor of India,

And His Majesty the King of 'Iraq,

Whereas they desire to consolidate the friendship and to maintain and perpetuate the relations of good understanding between their respective countries; and

Whereas His Britannic Majesty undertook in the Treaty of Alliance signed at Baghdad on the thirteenth day of January, One thousand nine hundred and twenty-six of the Christian Era, corresponding to the twenty-eighth day of Jamadi-al-Ukhra, One thousand three hundred and forty-four, Hijrah, that he would take into active consideration at successive intervals of four years the question whether it was possible for him to press for the admission of 'Iraq into the League of Nations; and

Whereas His Majesty's Government in the United Kingdom of Great Britain and Northern Ireland informed the 'Iraq Government without qualification or proviso on the fourteenth day of September, One thousand nine hundred and twenty-nine that they were prepared to support the candidature of 'Iraq for admission to the League of the Nations in the year One thousand nine hundred and thirty-two and announced to the Council of the League on the fourth day of November, One thousand nine hundred and twenty-nine, that this was their intention; and

Whereas the mandatory responsibilities accepted by His Britannic Majesty in respect of 'Iraq will automatically terminate upon the admission of 'Iraq to the League of Nations; and

Whereas His Britannic Majesty and His Majesty the King of 'Iraq consider that the relations which will subsist between them as independent sovereigns should be defined by the conclusion of a Treaty of Alliance and Amity;

Have agreed to conclude a new Treaty for this purpose on terms of complete freedom, equality and independence which will become operative upon the entry of Iraq into the League of Nations, and have appointed as their Plenipotentiaries:

His Majesty the King of Great Britain, Ireland and the British Dominions beyond the Seas, Emperor of India:

For Great Britain and Northern Ireland:

Lieutenant-Colonel Sir Francis Henry Humphrys, Knight Granc Cross of the Royal Victorian Order, Knight Commander of the Mos Distinguished Order of Saint Michael and Saint George, Knigh Commander of the Most Excellent Order of the British Empire Companion of the Most Eminent Order of the Indian Empire, Higl Commissioner of His Britannic Majesty in Iraq; and

His Majesty the King of 'Iraq:

General Nuri Pasha al Sa'id, Order of the Nadha, Second

Class, Order of the Istiqlal, Second Class, Companion of the Most Distinguished Order of Saint Michael and Saint George, Companion of the Distinguished Service Order, Prime Minister of the 'Iraq Government and Minister for Foreign Affairs;

who having communicated their full powers, found in due form, have agreed as follows:

Article 1. There shall be perpetual peace and friendship between His Britannic Majesty and His Majesty the King of 'Iraq.

There shall be established between the High Contracting Parties a close alliance in consecration of their friendship, their cordial understanding and their good relations, and there shall be full and frank consultation between them in all matters of foreign policy which may affect their common interests.

Each of the High Contracting Parties undertakes not to adopt in foreign countries an attitude which is inconsistent with the alliance or might create difficulties for the other party thereto.

Article 2. Each High Contracting Party will be represented at the Court of the other High Contracting Party by a diplomatic representative duly accredited.

Article 3. Should any dispute between 'Iraq and a third State produce a situation which involves the risk of a rupture with that State, the High Contracting Parties will concert together with a view to the settlement of the said dispute by peaceful means in accordance with the provisions of the Covenant of the League of Nations and of any other international obligations which may be applicable to the case.

Article 4. Should, notwithstanding the provisions of Article 3 above, either of the High Contracting Parties become engaged in war, the other High Contracting Party will, subject always to the provisions of Article 9 below, immediately come to his aid in the capacity of an ally. In the event of an imminent menace of war the High Contracting Parties will immediately concert together the necessary measures of defence. The aid of His Majesty the King of 'Iraq in the event of war or the imminent menace of war will consist in furnishing to His Britannic Majesty on 'Iraq territory all facilities and assistance in his power including the use of railways, rivers, ports, aerodromes and means of communication.

Article 5. It is understood between the High Contracting Parties that responsibility for the maintenance of internal order in 'Iraq and, subject to the provisions of Article 4 above, for the defence of 'Iraq from external aggression rests with His Majesty the King of 'Iraq. Nevertheless His Majesty the King of 'Iraq recognises that the permanent maintenance and protection in all circumstances of the essential communications of His Britannic Majesty is in the common interest of the High Contracting Parties. For this purpose and in order to facilitate the discharge of the obligations of His Britannic Majesty under Article 4 above His Majesty the King of 'Iraq undertakes to grant to His Britannic Majesty for the duration of the Alliance sites for air bases to be selected by His Britannic Majesty at or in the vicinity of Basra and for an air base to be selected by His Britannic Majesty to the west of the Euphrates. His Majesty the King of 'Iraq further authorises His Britannic Majesty to maintain forces upon 'Iraq territory at the above localities in accordance with the provisions of the Annexure of this Treaty on the understanding that the presence of those forces shall not constitute in any manner an occupation and will in no way prejudice the sovereign rights of 'Iraq.

Article 6. The Annexure hereto shall be regarded as an integral part of the present Treaty.

Article 7. This Treaty shall replace the Treaties of Alliance signed by Baghdad on the tenth day of October, One thousand nine hundred and twenty-two of the Christian Era, corresponding to the nineteenth day of Safar, One thousand three hundred and forty-one, Hijrah, and on the thirteenth day of January, One thousand nine hundred and twenty-six, of the Christian Era, corresponding to the twenty-eighth day of Jamadi-al-Ukhra, One thousand three hundred and forty-four, Hijrah, and the subsidiary agreements thereto, which shall cease to have effect upon the entry into force of this Treaty. It shall be executed in duplicate, in the English and Arabic languages, of which the former shall be regarded as the authoritative version.

Article 8. The High Contracting Parties recognise that, upon the entry into force of this Treaty, all responsibilities devolving under the Treaties and Agreements referred to in Article 7 hereof upon His Britannic Majesty in respect of 'Iraq will, in so far as His Britannic Majesty is concerned, then automatically and completely come to an end, and that such responsibilities, in so far as they continue at all, will devolve upon His Majesty the King of 'Iraq alone.

It is also recognised that all responsibilities devolving upon His

Britannic Majesty in respect of 'Iraq under any other international instrument, in so far as they continue at all, should similarly devolve upon His Majesty the King of Iraq alone, and the High Contracting Parties shall immediately take such steps as may be necessary to secure the transference to His Majesty the King of 'Iraq of these responsibilities.

Article 9. Nothing in the present Treaty is intended to or shall in any way prejudice the rights and obligations which devolve, or may devolve, upon either of the High Contracting Parties under the Covenant of the League of Nations or the Treaty for the Renunciation of War signed at Paris on the twenty-seventh day of August, One thousand nine hundred and twenty-eight.

Article 10. Should any difference arise relative to the application or the interpretation of this Treaty and should the High Contracting Parties fail to settle such difference by direct negotiation, then it shall be dealt with in accordance with the provisions of the Covenant of the League of Nations.

Article 11. This Treaty shall be ratified and ratifications shall be exchanged as soon as possible. Thereafter it shall come into force as soon as 'Iraq has been admitted to membership of the League of Nations.

The present Treaty shall remain in force for a period of twenty-five years from the date of its coming into force. At any time after twenty years from the date of the coming into force of this Treaty, the High Contracting Parties will, at the request of either of them, conclude a new Treaty which shall provide for the continued maintenance and protection in all circumstances of the essential communications of His Britannic Majesty. In case of disagreement in this matter the difference will be submitted to the Council of the League of Nations.

In faith whereof the respective Plenipotentiaries have signed the present Treaty and have affixed thereto their seals.

Done at Baghdad in duplicate this thirtieth day of June, One thousand nine hundred and thirty, of the Christian Era, corresponding to the fourth day of Safar, One thousand three hundred and forty-nine, Hijrah.

F. H. Humphrys.
Noury Said.

ANNEXURE TO TREATY OF ALLIANCE

1.

The strength of the forces maintained in 'Iraq by His Britannic Majesty in accordance with the terms of Article 5 of this Treaty shall be determined by His Britannic Majesty from time to time after consultation with His Majesty the King of 'Iraq.

His Britannic Majesty shall maintain forces at Hinaidi for a period of five years after the entry into force of this Treaty in order to enable His Majesty the King of 'Iraq to organise the necessary forces to replace them. By the expiration of that period the said forces of His Britannic Majesty shall have been withdrawn from Hinaidi. It shall be also open to His Britannic Majesty to maintain forces at Mosul for a maximum period of five years from the entry into force of this Treaty. Thereafter it shall be open to His Britannic Majesty to station his forces in the localities mentioned in Article 5 of this Treaty, and His Majesty the King of 'Iraq will grant to His Britannic Majesty for the duration of the Alliance leases of the necessary sites for the accommodation of the forces of His Britannic Majesty in those localities.

2.

Subject to any modifications which the two High Contracting Parties may agree to introduce in the future, the immunities and privileges in jurisdictional and fiscal matters, including freedom from taxation, enjoyed by the British forces in 'Iraq will continue to extend to the forces referred to in Clause 1 above and to such of His Britannic Majesty's forces of all arms as may be in 'Iraq in pursuance of the present Treaty and its annexure or otherwise by agreement between the High Contracting Parties, and the existing provisions of any local legislation affecting the armed forces of His Britannic Majesty in 'Iraq shall also continue. The 'Iraq Government will take the necessary steps to ensure that the altered conditions will not render the position of the British forces as regards immunities and privileges in any way less favourable than that enjoyed by them at the date of the entry into force of this Treaty.

3.

His Majesty the King of 'Iraq agrees to provide all possible facilities foɪ the movement, training and maintenance of the forces referred to in Clause 1 above and to accord to those forces the same facilities for the use of wireless telegraphy as those enjoyed by them at the date of the entry into force of the present Treaty.

4.

His Majesty the King of 'Iraq undertakes to provide at the request and at the expense of His Britaɪɪnic Majesty and upon such conditions as may be agreed between the High Contracting Parties special guards from his own forces for the protection of such air bases as may, in accordance with the provisions of this Treaty, be occupied by the forces of His Britannic Majesty, and to secure the enactment of such legislation as may be necessary for the fulfillment of the conditions referred to above.

5.

His Britannic Majesty undertakes to grant whenever they may be required by His Majesty the King of 'Iraq all possible facilities in the following matters, the cost of which will be met by His Majesty the King of 'Iraq.

1. Naval, military and aeronautical instruction of 'Iraqi officers in the United Kingdom.

2. The provision of arms, ammunition, equipment, ships and aeroplanes of the latest available pattern for the forces of His Majesty the King of 'Iraq.

3. The provision of British naval, military and air force officers to serve in an advisory capacity with the forces of His Majesty the King of 'Iraq.

6.

In view of the desirability of identity in training and methods between the 'Iraq and British armies, His Majesty the King of 'Iraq undertakes that, should he deem it necessary to have recourse to foreign military instructors, these shall be chosen from amongst British subjects..

He further undertakes that any personnel of his forces that may be sent abroad for military training will be sent to military schools, colleges and training centres in the territories of His Britannic

Majesty provided that this shall not prevent him from sending to any other country such personnel as cannot be received in the said institutions and training centres

He further undertakes that the armament and essential equipment of his forces shall not differ in type from those of the forces of His Britannic Majesty.

7.

His Majesty the King of 'Iraq agrees to afford, when requested to do so by His Britannic Majesty, all possible facilities for the movement of the forces of His Britannic Majesty of all arms in transit across 'Iraq and for the transport and storage of all supplies and equipment that may be required by these forces during their passage across 'Iraq. These facilities shall cover the use of the roads, railways, waterways, ports and aerodromes of 'Iraq, and His Britannic Majesty's ships shall have general permission to visit the Shatt-al-Arab on the understanding that His Majesty the King of 'Iraq is given prior notification of visits to 'Iraq ports.

(Initialled)
F.H.H.
N.S.

NOTES EXCHANGED
I.

The Residency,
Baghdad, Dated the 30th June, 1930.

SIR,

I have the honour to inform you, with regard to Article 2 of the Treaty which we have signed to-day, that it is intended that His Britannic Majesty's diplomatic representative at the Court of His Majesty the King of 'Iraq shall have the status of Ambassador.

I have etc.,
(Signed) F.H. Humphrys

His Excellency Nuri Pasha al Sa'id, C.M.G., D.S.O.,
Prime Minister and Minister for Foreign Affairs, Baghdad.

*   *   *

Ministry of Foreign Affairs,

Baghdad, Dated the 30th June, 1930

SIR,

In reply to your Note of to-day's date I have the honour to inform you that the 'Iraq Government, anxious to mark the satisfaction which the appointment of His Britannic Majesty's representative as the first Ambassador in 'Iraq affords them, intend that his precedence in relation to the representatives of other Powers shall extend to his successors. The 'Iraq Government also intend that the diplomatic representative of His Majesty the King of 'Iraq at the Court of St. James shall have the status of Minister Plenipotentiary during the currency of this Treaty.

I have, etc.,

(Signed) Noury Said.

His Excellency Sir F. H. Humphrys, G.C.V.O., K.C.M.G., K.B.E., C.I.E.,

His Britannic Majesty's High Commissioner in 'Iraq.

*   *   *

II.

The Residency
Baghdad, the 30th June, 1930.

SIR,

In connection with the Treaty signed by us to-day I have the honour to place on record that it has been agreed that all outstanding financial questions, such a those relating to the 'Iraq Railways and the Port of Basra and those which it is necessary to settle for the purpose of the operation of the Treaty and of its Annexure, shall form the subject of a separate agreement which shall be concluded as soon as possible and which shall be deemed an integral part of the present Treaty and shall be ratified simultaneously therewith.

I have, etc.,

(Signed) F. H. Humphrys.

His Excellency, Nuri Pasha al Sa'id, C.M.G., D.S.O.,

Prime Minister and Minister for Foreign Affairs, Baghdad.

*   *   *

Ministry of Foreign Affairs,
Baghdad, the 30th June, 1930.

SIR,

In connection with the Treaty signed by us to-day I have the honour to place on record that it has been agreed that all outstanding financial questions, such as those relating to the 'Iraq Railways and the Port of Basra and those which it is necessary to settle for the purpose of the operation of the Treaty and of its Annexure, shall form the subject of a separate agreement which shall be concluded as soon as possible and which shall be deemed an integral part of the present Treaty and shall be ratified simultaneously therewith.

I have, etc.,

(Signed) Noury Said.

His Excellency Sir. F. H. Humphrys, G.C.V.O., K.C.M.G., K.B.E., C.I.E.,

His Britannic Majesty's High Commissioner in 'Iraq.

* * *

III.

Ministry of Foreign Affairs,
Baghdad, dated the 30th June, 1930.

SIR,

In connection with the Treaty signed by us to-day I have the honour to inform Your Excellency that in view of the close friendship and alliance between our two countries the 'Iraq Government will normally engage British subjects when in need of the services of foreign officials. Such officials will be selected after consultation between our two Governments. It is understood that this shall not prejudice the freedom of the 'Iraq Government to engage non-British foreign officials for posts for which suitable British subjects are not available.

I have also the honour to inform Your Excellency that nothing in the Treaty which we hve signed to-day shall affect the validity of the contracts concluded and in existence between the 'Iraq Government and British officials.

I have, etc.,
(Signed) Noury Said.
His Excellency Sir F. H. Humphrys, G.C.V.O., K.C.M.G.,
K.B.E., C.I.E.,
His Britannic Majesty's High Commisioner in 'Iraq.

*   *   *

The Residency,
Baghdad, dated the 30th June, 1930.
SIR,
I have the honour to acknowledge the receipt of Your
Excellency's Note of to-day's date regarding the engagement of
foreign officials, and to confirm the statement therein recorded of the
understanding which we have reached.
I have, etc.,
(Signed) F. H. Humphrys.
His Excellency, Nuri Pasha al Sa'id, C.M.G., D.S.O.,
Prime Minister and Minister for Foreign Affairs, Baghdad.

*   *   *

IV.

Ministry of Foreign Affairs,
Baghdad, 30th June, 1930.

SIR,
I have the honour to inform Your Excellency that it is the
intention of the 'Iraq Government, in view of their desire to improve
the efficiency of their land and air forces, to ask for a British
Advisory Military Mission, the numbers of which shall be decided
before the Treaty comes into force and the conditions of service of
which shall be similar to those of the existing Military Mission.
I have, etc.,
(Signed) Noury Said.
His Excellency Sir F. H. Humphrys, G.C.V.O., K.C.M.G.,
K.B.E., C.I.E.,
His Britannic Majesty's High Commissioner in 'Iraq.

*   *   *

The Residency,
Baghdad, 30th June, 1930.

SIR,

I have the honour to acknowledge the receipt of Your Note of to-day's date on the subject of the British Advisory Military Mission which the 'Iraq Government intend to invite to 'Iraq.

I have, etc.,
(Signed) F. H. Humphrys.

His Excellency, Nuri Pasha al Sa'id, C.M.G., D.S.P.O.,
Prime Minister and Minister for Foreign Affairs, Baghdad.

NOTES EXCHANGED WITH THE 'IRAQ PRIME MINISTER EMBODYING THE SEPARATE AGREEMENT ON FINANCIAL QUESTIONS REFERRED TO IN THE SECOND EXCHANGE OF NOTES APPENDED TO THE ANGLO-'IRAQ TREATY OF 30th JUNE, 1930.

I.

London,
19th August, 1930.

SIR,

With reference to our conversations in London, I have the honour to propose that the following provisions shall be considered as embodying the separate agreement on all financial questions referred to in the second exchange of Notes between Your Excellency and myself at the time of the signature of the Treaty of Alliance on the 30th June, 1930.

It is understood that the agreement constituted by this note and by Your Excellency's reply thereto shall be included in the instruments of ratification of the Treaty of Alliance and shall become operative on the exchange of ratifications.

1   The Government of the United Kingdom of Great Britain and Northern Ireland shall transfer to the 'Iraq Government, within the period stipulated in Clause 1 of the Annexure to the Treaty of Alliance signed on the 30th of June, 1930, the aerodromes and encampments at Hinaidi and Mosul at present occupied by the Forces of His Britannic Majesty, and the 'Iraq Government shall accept the transfer thereof (less two "A" type steel hangars and the

ice plants at Hinaidi and Mosul to be removed by the Government of the United Kingdom) at one-third of the cost price certified as correct by the Air Ministry of the Government of the United Kingdom, of the permanent buildings, plant and structures thereon, no account being taken of the mud buildings which shall be transferred to the Iraq Government free of cost. The 'Iraq Government shall pay this sum to the Government of the United Kingdom not later than the date upon which the aforesaid transfer is completed.

During the maximum period stipulated in Clause 1 of the Annexure to the Treaty of Alliance the Forces of His Britannic Majesty shall remain in undisturbed occupation of their present stations of Hinaidi and Mosul and at Shaiba and in the use of their existing emergency landing grounds, and the Government of the United Kingdom shall not be called upon to pay higher rental charges in respect thereof than those at present paid.

2. If upon the withdrawal of the Forces of His Britannic Majesty from Hinaidi and Mosul in accordance with Clause 1 of the Annexure to the Treaty of Alliance, the Government of the United Kingdom should decide to establish a British air base in the neighbourhood of Habbaniya, then the 'Iraq Government shall take all possible steps, at no cost to either Government, to arrange for the construction of a railway to connect such air base with the railway system of 'Iraq.

3. The lease of the sites for air bases to be granted to His Britannic Majesty, in accordance with the provisions of Article 5 of the Treaty of Alliance, shall, in so far as such sites are on waste Government land, be free of all rental charges, and, in so far as they are on non- Government land, every facility shall be given for their acquisition on reasonable terms, such acquisition being effected by the 'Iraq Government at the request and at the cost of the Government of the United Kingdom. The leased lands shall be free of all taxes and rates and the leases shall continue so long as these bases remain in the occupation of the Forces of His Britannic Majesty in accordance with the provisions of the aforesaid Treaty of Alliance or of any extension thereof. On the final termination of the leases of the said sites, or of any one of them, the 'Iraq Government shall either themselves take over the buildings and permanent structures thereon at a fair valuation, having regard to the use to which they have been put, or shall afford such facilities as may

reasonably be necessary to enable the Government of the United Kingdom to dispose thereof to the best advantage.

After the expiry of the maximum period stipulated in Clause 1 of the Annexure to the Treaty of Alliance and so long as the said Treaty of Alliance remains in force the Government of the United Kingdom shall not be called upon to pay any charges in respect of the use of any of the existing emergency landing grounds in 'Iraq.

4. The following arrangements for the disposal and administration of the 'Iraq railways system shall be carried into effect as soon as possible and in any case within a maximum period of one year from the entry into force of the Treaty of Alliance:

(a) Legal ownership of the railways system shall be transferred by the Government of the United Kingdom to the 'Iraq Government and registered in the name of the 'Iraq Government and simultaneously with such transfer full beneficial ownership shall be vested, by lease or otherwise and at a nominal rent and on terms satisfactory to the Government of the United Kingdom, in a special body or corporation having legal personality, to be constituted by a special Statute of the 'Iraq Legislature, the terms of which shall have been agreed upon by both Governments.

(b) The above-mentioned Corporation shall be wholly responsible for the administration and management of the 'Iraq railway system, and subject to such limitations as may be imposed in the Statute referred to above, shall have sole and exclusive authority to raise new capital by public issue or private loan and to dispose of the revenues of that system.

(c) The capital of the said Corporation shall comprise:

(1) Rs. 275 Lakhs of Preferred Stock, bearing interest at 6 percent, such interest being non-cumulative for a period of twenty years from the date of the transfer of the ownership of the system and thereafter cumulative, to be allotted to the Government of the United Kingdom, of which Rs.25 Lakhs represents the capitalized value of the debt of the railways to the Government of the United Kingdom on liquidation account;

(2) Rs. 45.85 Lakhs of similar Preferred Stock, to be allotted to the 'Iraq Government, being an amount equal to the loans which the 'Iraq Government have made to the railway on which interest charges have been waived; and

(3) Rs. 250 Lakhs of Deferred Stock also to be allotted to the 'Iraq Government.

The 'Iraq Government shall have the option to buy at any time at par the Stock allotted to the Government of the United Kingdom.

(d) The Board of the Corporation shall consist of five Directors of whom two shall be appointed by the Government of the United Kingdom and two by the 'Iraq Government, and the fifth, who shall be the Chairman, shall be appointed by both Governments in agreement. The first Chairman shall be the present Director of the 'Iraq Railways.

(e) The Corporation shall be responsible for raising loan capital required for the reconditioning and development of the 'Iraq railway system, and neither Government shall be under any obligation to guarantee such loan capital either in respect of interest or of capital.

(f) Any loan capital raised by the Corporation for the reconditioning or development of the 'Iraq railway system shall rank before the Stock allotted to the two Governments in accordance with Clause (c) above.

(g) The 'Iraq Government, as owners of the equity of the system, shall accept ultimate responsibility for any liabilities relating thereto, not devolving upon the Corporation, that may subsequently come to light and in consideration thereof the Government of the United Kingdom shall transfer to the 'Iraq Government an amount of Preferred Stock of a nominal value equal to the amount of any irrecoverable disbursements that the 'Iraq Government may have to make in the discharge of any of the aforesaid liabilities, the validity of which may have been established to the satisfaction of the Government of the United Kingdom.

(h) In anticipation of the transfer of the railway system and the establishment of the Corporation, the 'Iraq Government shall forthwith grant three-year contracts, on "Treaty" conditions, to such British railway officials as may be recommended therefor by the Director of the 'Iraq Railways, and shall not terminate any such contracts when granted except with the agreement of the Government of the United Kingdom. The question of granting these officials contracts of longer duration shall be left for the decision of the corporation when constituted.

5. The property in the port of Basra at present held by the Government of the United Kingdom shall be transferred to the 'Iraq

Government and the port shall be administered by a Port Trust. For this purpose legislation in terms agreed with the Government of the United Kingdom shall be enacted in 'Iraq for the establishment of a Port Trust having legal personality and such legislation shall not be amended, except by agreement with the Government of the United Kingdom, so long as any part of the debt owing to the Government of the United Kingdom in respect of the port is still outstanding.

Upon the enactment of the above legislation and the establishment of the Port Trust, the property in the port shall be transferred to the 'Iraq Government in whose name it will then be registered, and, simultaneously with such transfer, full beneficial ownership shall be conferred by lease, concession or other appropriate instrument, the terms of which shall be subject to the approval of the Government of the United Kingdom, upon the Port Trust for the period during which any part of the debt owing to the Government of the United Kingdom in respect of the port remains outstanding.

I have, etc.,

(Signed) F. H. Humphrys

His Excellency, Nuri Pasha al Sa'id, C.M.G., D.S.O.,
    Prime Minister and Minister for Foreign Affairs, 'Iraq.

*   *   *

II.

London,
19th August, 1930.

SIR,

I have the honour to acknowledge the receipt of your note of to-day's date setting out the provisions to be considered as embodying the separate agreement on all financial questions referred to in the second exchange of Notes between Your Excellency and myself at the time of signature of the Treaty of Alliance on the 30th June, 1930, and to confirm that your Note accurately sets out the agreement at which we have arrived

I have, etc.

(Signed) Noury Said.

His Excellency, Sir F. H. Humphrys, G.C.V.O., K.C.M.G., K.B.E., C.I.E.,
    His Britannic Majesty's High Commissioner in 'Iraq.

APPENDIX C

NURI AS-SA'ID'S FERTILE CRESCENT PROJECT

The following proposals of mine are based on the close and firm ties between Iraq and all the Arabs inhabiting historical Syria. The States of the Arabian Peninsula have an economic system which differs from our own, though they are very close to us in respect of language, customs and religion. On the other hand, Egypt has a bigger population than that of backward States. It also has its (own) problems in the Sudan and elsewhere. Because of this, I have assumed that these States are not inclined to join an Arab federation or an Arab League from the start. But if the union (ittihad) of Iraq and Syria does materialize, it may then be very likely that these States mentioned may in the course of time show their desire to join this union. But I expect that this union—even if confined to Iraq and Syria—will at the very beginning lead to the facilitation of joint consultation among all the Arab States and to all these States acting in concert, whether they are inside the union or outside it. For many of our problems are common, and we all belong to one civilization; thus, we generally have the same (way of) thinking and are moved by the same ideals, namely, the principles of freedom of conscience, freedom of expression, equality before the law, and the fundamental human brotherhood.

Conclusion

In my view, the only equitable solution—indeed the only hope of securing permanent peace, reassurance and progress in these Arab areas, is for the United Nations to declare now the following:

(1) That Syria, Lebanon, Palestine and Transjordan be reunited into one State.

(2) That the inhabitants of this State themselves shall decide upon the type of government to be adopted by this State, whether monarchal, republican, unitary or federal.

(3) That there shall be created an Arab League to which Iraq and Syria shall adhere at once, provided that the other Arab States are

permitted to adhere to it whenever they please.

(4) That this Arab League shall have a permanent Council nominated by the States Members of this League and presided over by one of the heads of States concerned.

(5) That the Council of the Arab League shall be responsible for the following matters:

(a) Defence

(b) Foreign Affairs

(c) Currency

(d) Communications

(e) Customs

(f) Protection of Minority Rights

(g) Education

(6) The Jews in Palestine shall be granted a semi-autonomous administration in the area wherein they form a majority. They shall also be given the right to their own rural and urban administration, including schools, health institutions and police, provided that these health institutions and police shall be under the general supervision of the Syrian State.

(7) Jerusalem shall be a city to which members of all faiths shall have free access for the purpose of pilgrimage or worship. A special commission composed of the representatives of the three prevailing religions shall be set up to ensure this.

(8) That the Maronites in Lebanon shall, if they so desire, be granted a privileged administration such as the one they enjoyed during the last years of the Ottoman Empire. This special administration, like those to be set up in accordance with paragraphs (6) and (7), above, shall rest on an international guarantee.

Should it be possible, as is (proposed) above, to create a Confederation of the Arab States comprising Iraq, Syria, Palestine and Transjordan at the beginning, to which the other Arab States may later adhere, then a great many of the difficulties faced by Great Britain and France in the Near East during the past twenty years will disappear.

We see that the Arabs of Palestine are at present afraid that they may become a minority in a Jewish State. For this, we see that they are strongly opposed to granting special rights to the Jews. This hostility will, however, diminish if Palestine becomes part of a large strong Arab State. The Jews can establish their national home in those parts of Palestine where they are now a majority. They will, thus, feel more reassured as to their safety, since their Arab neighbours will show good will towards them, and in addition, their economic opportunities will increase when they become a semi-autonomous religious community in a much larger State than they had hoped for.

The British Empire is not founded on negative bases, but on positive ideals. Free institutions and free co-operation will give it greater life and vigour. On the basis of this free co-operation a real union comprising many diverse peoples and countries has been established. This union depends on noble and firm principles which are inscribed in the heart and conscience of Man. If the Arab peoples are given the opportunity to establish such a free co-operation among themselves, they will then be able to deal tolerantly with all the Jews living in their midst, whether these Jews are in Palestine or in (any) other country. Admittedly, conditions must be made and guarantees secured. But these conditions and guarantees must be practicable, lest they should become a dead letter, as has been the case with many provisions concerning minorities in European countries during the past twenty years.

Should these proposals meet with approval they will require meticulous study until it becomes possible to take the appropriate measures at the suitable time and in the right order. Naturally enough, the union of the various parts of historical Syria must first be effected. On the one hand, this union may at the beginning (take the form of) a federation comprising Syria, Lebanon, Palestine and Transjordan, provided that each Member State continues to manage its own internal affairs, leaving defence, foreign affairs, currency and customs to the Central Government. On the other hand, it may be possible to unite Syria at once and at the same time to make whatever provisions may be necessary for the Jewish enclaves and the administration of the City of Jerusalem. Measures should be taken at once to fix the boundaries of these enclaves. This will necessitate the drawing up of an accurate ethnographical map of Palestine, which will show the number of Arabs and Jews in each district and town, as also the drawing up of another map on the same scale as that of the (first) map, which will show the lands under cultivation as well as the lands which can be intensely cultivated in the future. In addition, an inquiry should be made into the number of Jews who have settled (in Palestine) since the outbreak of war in September 1939.

The achievement of unity may necessitate sacrificing the rights of sovereignty and the traditional interests. The British Dominions have made similar sacrifices. It is also possible to require the Arab leaders to make sacrifices like these.

I have throughout this Memorandum presumed that, as France declared before the War that she was willing to grant independence to Syria and Lebanon, she will not be given the chance to repudiate her undertaking, nor to place obstacles in the way of every union that may be created for the Arab countries by insisting on retaining old privileges and antiquated rights.

APPENDIX D

PACT OF MUTUAL CO-OPERATION BETWEEN IRAQ AND TURKEY
(THE BAGHDAD PACT) Baghdad, February 24, 1955

Whereas the friendly and brotherly relations existing between Iraq and Turkey are in constant progress, and in order to complement the contents of the Treaty of Friendship and Good Neighbourhood concluded between His Majesty the King of Baghdad Iraq and His Excellency the President of the Turkish Republic signed in Ankara on March 29, 1946, which recognised the fact that peace and security between the two countries is an integral part of the peace and security of all the nations of the world and in particular the nations of the Middle East, and that it is the basis for their foreign policies;

Whereas article II of the Treaty of Joint Defence and Economic Co-operation between the Arab League States provides that no provision of that treaty shall in any way affect, or is designed to affect, any of the rights and obligations accruing to the Contracting Parties from the United Nations Charter;

And having realised the great responsibilities borne by them in their capacity as members of the United Nations concerned with the maintenance of peace and security in the Middle East region which necessitate taking the required measures in accordance with article 51 of the United Nations Charter;

They have been fully convinced of the necessity of concluding a pact fulfilling these aims, and for that purpose have appointed as their plenipotentiaries:

His Majesty King Faisal II,
    King of Iraq;
His Excellency Al Farik Nuri As-Said,
    Prime Minister;
His Excellency Burhanuddi Bash-Ayan,
    Acting Minister for Foreign Affairs;
His Excellency Jalal Bayar,
    President of the Turkish Republic;
His Excellency Adnan Menderes,
    Prime Minister;
His Excellency Professor Fuat Koprulu,
    Minister for Foreign Affairs;

who have communicated their full powers, found to be in good and due form, have agreed as follows:

Article 1 Consistent with article 51 of the United Nations Charter the High Contracting Parties will co-operate for their security and defence. Such measures as they agree to take to give effect to this co-operation may form the subject of special agreements with each other.

Article 2 In order to ensure the realization and effect application of the co-operation provided for in article 1 above, the competent authorities of the High Contracting Parties will determine the measures to be taken as soon as the present pact enters into force. These measures will become operative as soon as they have been approved by the Governments of the High Contracting Parties.

Article 3 The High Contracting Parties undertake to refrain from any interference whatsoever in each other's internal affairs. They will settle any dispute between themselves in a peaceful way in accordance with the United Nations Charter.

Article 4 The High Contracting Parties declare that the dispositions of the present pact are not in contradiction with any of the international obligations contracted by either of them with any third State or States. They do not derogate from and cannot be interpreted as derogating from, the said international obligations. The High Contracting Parties undertake not to enter into any international obligation incompatible with the present pact.

Article 5 This pact shall be open for accession to any member of the Arab League or any other State actively concerned with the security and peace in this region and which is fully recognised by both the High Contracting Parties. Accession shall come into force from the date of which the instrument of accession of the State concerned is deposited with the Ministry for Foreign Affairs of Iraq.

Any acceding State party to the present pact may conclude special agreements, in accordance with article 1, with one or more States parties to the present pact. The competent authority of any acceding State may determine measures in accordance with article 2. These measures will become operative as soon as they have been approved by the Governments of the parties concerned.

Article 6 A permanent Council at ministerial level will be set up to function within the framework of the purposes of this pact when at least four Powers become parties to the pact.

The Council will draw up its own rules of procedure.

Article 7 This pact remains in force for a period of five years renewable for other five-year periods. Any Contracting Party may withdraw from the pact by notifying the other parties in writing of its desire to do so six months before the expiration of any of the above-mentioned periods, in which case the pact remains valid for the other parties.

Article 8 This pact shall be ratified by the contracting parties and ratifications shall be exchanged at Ankara as soon as possible. Thereafter it shall come into force from the date of the exchange of ratifications.

In witness whereof, the said plenipotentiaries have signed the present pact in Arabic, Turkish and English, all three texts being equally authentic except in the case of doubt when the English text shall prevail..

Done in duplicate at Baghdad this second day of Rajab 1374 Hijri corresponding to the twenty-fourth day of February 1955.

NURI AS-SAID
For His Majesty the King of Iraq.
BURHANUDDIN BASH-AYAN
For His Majesty the King of Iraq.

ADNAN MENDERES
For the President of the Turkish Republic.
FUAT KÖPRÜLU
For the President of the Turkish Republic.

APPENDIX E

THE COUP d'ETAT IN IRAQ:
FIRST STATEMENT PROCLAIMING THE REVOLUTION
AND ABOLISHING THE MONARCHY
July 14, 1958

Depending on God, and (with) the support of the faithful sons of the people, and the (assistance) of the national armed forces, we have accomplished the liberation of the beloved fatherland from the domination of the corrupt clique that was installed by imperialism to rule the people and to tamper with their fortunes in the interest of (imperialism) and for personal interests.

Brethren: The army stems from you and is for you. It has already realized your wishes and has got rid of the despotic class which grossly neglected the rights of the people. All you have to do is to support it [in its bullets, its bombs, and the wrath that it is pouring on the Rihab Palace and on the (residence) of Nuri as-Sa'id]. All you have to do is to support (the army). And be assured that victory cannot be achieved except by supporting it and by protecting it against the conspiracies and the stooges (of imperialism). For this reason we call on you to inform the authorities about any evil-doer, offender or traitor, so that we may eradicate them. And we ask you to unite in order to destroy these criminals and to rid (yourselves) of their vices.

Compatriots: Whilst appreciating your eager patriotic spirit and your noble deeds, we would appeal to you to be calm and disciplined, and to adhere to order, unity and co-operation for the sake of fruitful work and in the interest of the fatherland—one fatherland and one people.

Ye people: We have vowed to sacrifice our blood and everything that is dear to us for your sake. You can, thus, be confident and reassured that we will continue to work for you.

Authority must be entrusted to a government that stems from the people and is inspired in its work by your wishes. This cannot be achieved except by setting up a popular Republic that will adhere to (the policy of) the all-embracing Iraqi unity—north, south, east and west—comprising Sulaymaniyya, Rutba, Mosul, Faw, and Baghdad, as well as all the other parts of the country. (This Republic) will maintain brotherly ties with the Islamo-Arab States, will work in conformity with the principles of the United Nations, and will adhere to (all) obligations and pacts in accordance with the interests of the country and the resolutions of the Bandung Conference.

In view of the above, this national government will be henceforward known as the (*Iraqi Republic*). May you, brave people, (accept our) congratulations on (the establishment of) this young Republic of yours, as it stems from you and is for you and in your service.

And in response to the wishes of the people, we have provisionally entrusted the presidency of (this Republic) to a Council of Sovereignty which will enjoy the powers of the President of the Republic until a popular referendum is held for the election of the President.

Let us pray to God to grant us success in our work in the service of our beloved fatherland. May He grant us this prayer.

The Acting Commander-In-Chief
of the Armed Forces

APPENDIX F

PROVISIONAL CONSTITUTION OF THE REPUBLIC OF IRAQ

Whereas the national movement undertaken by the Iraqi Army on July 14th (1958), with the co-operation and support of the people, aims at realising the sovereignty of the people and endeavours to prevent its usurpation as well as to safeguard and maintain the rights of the citizens.

And whereas the former regime in the country, which has been finally eradicated, rested on political corruption, as power was assumed by individuals who ruled the country contrary to the will of the majority and against the interests of the people, when the purpose of that rule to satisfy their (own) interests and protect those of colonialism and carry out its objectives as was stated in the first Proclamation addressed to the people on July 14, 1958, at the beginning of the national movement and which incorporated the downfall of the Monarchy and the establishment of the Iraqi Republic.

We, therefore, in the name of the people hereby declare the annulment of the Iraqi Organic Law (together with) all its amendments, as from July 14, 1958.

And in order to lay firm the foundations of government and to regulate the rights and duties for all citizens, we hereby proclaim this Provisional Constitution which will remain in force during the transitional period until (the new) Constitution is enacted.

CHAPTER I

The Iraqi Republic

Article 1. The Iraqi State is an independent and fully sovereign Republic.

Article 2. Iraq is part of the Arab Nation.

Article 3. The structure of Iraq is based on co-operation among all citizens, on respect for the rights, and on the protection of their liberty.

Arabs and Kurds are considered partners in this fatherland, and their national rights within the unity of Iraq are acknowledged by this Constitution.

Article 4. Islam is the religion of the State.

Article 5. The Capital of the Iraqi Republic is Baghdad.

Article 6. The Iraqi Flag and the National Emblem of the Iraqi Republic, together with all matters relating to these, shall be regulated by law.

CHAPTER II

Source of Powers, Public Rights and Duties

Article 7. The people are the source of all powers.

Article 8. Iraqi nationality shall be regulated by law.

Article 9. The citizens are equal before the law in regard to public rights and duties; there shall no be discrimination between them on account of race, origin, language, religion, or belief.

Article 10. Freedom of belief and expression is guaranteed and shall be regulated by law.

Article 11. Personal liberty and the inviolability of places of residence are guaranteed; they shall not be by-passed except in accordance with the requirements of public security; this shall be regulated by law.

Article 12. Freedom of religious belief is inviolable, and religious rites shall be respected, provided they are not repugnant to public order or contrary to public morals.

Article 13. Private property is inviolable. Its social function shall be regulated by law; it shall not be expropriated save for public utility and in return for fair compensation in accordance with the law.

Article 14. (a) Agricultural ownership shall be limited and regulated by law. (b) The rights of agricultural ownership shall remain inviolable in accordance with the laws in force until (new) legislations are issued and the necessary measures are taken for their implementation.

Article 15. No tax or fee (rasm) shall be imposed, altered or abolished except by law.

Article 16. The defence of the fatherland is a sacred duty, and military service is an honour for the citizens; its provisions shall be regulated by law.

Article 17. The armed forces in the Iraqi Republic belong to the people; their function is to protect the sovereignty of the country and the integrity of its territory.

Article 18. The State alone can create armed forces; no organization or group may set up military or paramilitary formations.

Article 19. The extradition of political refugees is prohibited.

CHAPTER III

The System of Government

Article 20. The Presidency of the Republic shall be vested in the Council of Sovereignty which shall consist of a President and two members.

Article 21. The legislative power shall be vested in the Council of Ministers with the approval of the Council of Sovereignty.

Article 22. The executive power shall be vested in the Council of Ministers and the Ministers, each in so far as he is concerned.

Article 23. Judges are independent and, within their jurisdiction, shall not be subject except to law. No authority or individual shall interfere in the independence of the judiciary or in the affairs of justice. The judicial machinery shall be regulated by law.

Article 24. Sessions of the courts shall be open (to the public) unless the court decides to make them secret in deference to public order and morals.

Article 25. Judgments shall be issued and executed in the name of the people.

Article 26. Laws shall be published in the *Official Gazette*, and shall become effective from the date of their publication, unless otherwise provided therein; if the date on which they will be implemented is not mentioned they shall be implemented ten days after the day following that of publication.

CHAPTER IV

Transitional Provisions

Article 27. Decisions (Qararat), Orders, Proclamations, and Decrees issued by the Commander-in-Chief of the Armed Forces, the Prime Minister, or the Council of Sovereignty during the period July 14, 1958, to the date of the implementation of this Provisional Constitution, shall have the force of law; they shall modify the provisions of any laws in force before their publication if (these) conflict with their provisions.

Article 28. Everything established by legislation in force before July 14, 1958, shall remain in force; this legislation may be repealed or amended in the manner indicated in the manner indicated in this Provisional Constitution.

Article 29. This Provisional Constitution shall be put into operation from the date of its publication in the *Official Gazette*.

Article 30. The Ministers of the State shall implement this Constitution.

Written in Baghdad on Muharram 9, 1378 A.H., corresponding to July 27, 1958.

(Signatures of the President and the two Members of the Council of Sovereignty, as well as those of the Prime Minister and the eleven Ministers, follow. E.D.)

APPENDIX G

STATEMENTS MADE BY PREMIER ABDUL KARIM KASSEM TO A LEBANESE JOURNALIST ON IRAQ'S ARAB POLICY FEBRUARY 5, 1963

(*Al-Zaman*, February 5, 1963 and Iraqi Press Release)

Brigadier Abdul Karim Kassem told the Lebanese reporter Muhammad Amin Dughan, "Convey my warm salutations to my brother, President Fouad Chehab. The Iraqis have respect and love for President Chehab and would like to assure him that they feel that Lebanon is a dear brother. However they do not believe that Lebanon would like them to neglect or overlook their interests because these interests are linked with Lebanon's interests. On the other hand, the interests of the Kuwaiti Sheikhs are linked with those of the imperialists, and whoever serves them will be serving the imperialists. There is no way of holding a neutral position between Iraq and Kuwait.

It is the Arabs' duty to co-operate with each other sincerely to abolish the foundations of imperialism in the world, not to strengthen them."

His Excellency denied accusations made against Iraqi policy towards Kuwait. He said that this policy did not lead to the isolation of Iraq from the Arab world. Diplomatic representation still existed between Iraq and the Arab countries. Iraq withdrew its ambassadors only from the countries that recognized Kuwait, as a way of protesting against their stand. He added that all the Arab countries have a high esteem for Iraq because it had not got involved in the abusive battles going on between the Arab countries. Iraq had not insulted anyone.

When Premier Kassem was asked about Iraqi-British relations, he said that they were the same as they had been since the Revolution of July 14. The English were continuing their imperialist game. They wanted to attack the Iraqis from their base in Kuwait. Since they had lost their bases here in Iraq, they had been trying to harm the country through their newspapers, magazines and business deals. The Iraqis were beginning to defend themselves by counter-attacking through their economy. Iraq used to import everything from Britain but now it imported only 50% from it and the rest from all over the world.

Concerning the reasons for the Iraqi delay in recognizing the new regime in Yemen, His Excellency said that Iraq believed in making a long and thorough consideration of policy and did not make quick decisions. Just as Iraq had delayed its recognition of Syria after the last Revolution for 12 days, it was now delaying recognition of Yemen. In both cases, Iraq had decided on the recognition as early as the second day.

APPENDIX H

COUNTER-COUP, FEBRUARY 8, 1963

From the Revolutionary Command Council;
In the name of God, the Merciful, the Compassionate;
Esteemed Iraqi People:

With the help of God we have destroyed 'Abdul Karim Kassem, the enemy of the people, and his gang which has exploited the country's resources to spread its cause and realize its interests. Freedom was suppressed, dignity trampled upon, trust betrayed, laws suspended, and the people persecuted. The July 14 revolution had been executed to free our country from imperialism entrenched in the monarchical regime, to get rid of feudal domination, and to put an end to the policy of submission. [We aimed at] establishing a democracy under which the people could enjoy peace and dignity, but the treacherous criminal, God's enemy and yours, took advantage of his position and employed all criminal means to establish his black rule. . . .

O esteemed people:

This movement undertaken by both the people and the army [aims at] continuing the victorious course of the revolution of July 14, which must realize two goals:

First, national unity, and

Second, the people's participation in the government.

In order to realize these two goals it is imperative that public freedoms and supremacy of the law be re-established. . . .

The [new] government shall strive to re-establish the democratic freedoms, bolster the supremacy of law, realize national unity, and strengthen the ties of Arab-Kurdish brotherhood. It shall work to safeguard national interests, strengthen the common struggle against imperialism, and strengthen respect for the rights of the minorities so that they may be better able to participate in national life. . .

APPENDIX I

COMMUNIQUE OF THE MILITARY GOVERNOR-GENERAL IN IRAQ ANNOUNCING THE EXECUTION OF GENERAL ABDUL KARIM KASSEM
February 9, 1963

(*Al-Hayat*, February 10, 1963)

The Armed Forces have arrested the enemy of the people, Abdul Karim Kassem, and the following people: Fadel Abbas Al-Mahdawi, Taha Al-Sheikh Ahmad and Kan'an Khalil Haddad. A military tribunal was formed for their trial and passed a death sentence upon them. They were executed by a firing squad today at 1:30 p.m.

APPENDIX J

LAW ESTABLISHING THE NATIONAL REVOLUTIONARY COUNCIL IN IRAQ
(April 4, 1963)

(The Iraqi Official Gazette, April 25, 1963)

In the name of the people.

The Presidency of the Republic

Pursuant to Statement No. 15 of 1963 issued by the National Revolutionary Council the same Council hereby issues the following law:

THE NATIONAL REVOLUTIONARY COUNCIL AND ITS FORMATION

Article I—1. The National Revolutionary Council is the organ of revolutionary command that led the masses and the national armed forces on the 14th of Ramadan (February 8, 1963), overthrew Kassem's regime and established in the name of the people and in its interest the existing revolutionary authority in Iraq. It consists of not more than 20 members.

2. With a two-thirds majority vote, the Council has the right to choose one or more members temporarily or permanently. In any case the number of members must not exceed 20.

3. With a majority of two-thirds, the Council has the right to retire one or more members.

THE POWERS OF THE COUNCIL

Article II—The National Revolutionary Council is empowered to:

1. Assume legislative powers. It has the right to make law and regulations, and to amend and abrogate them.

2. Conclude treaties and agreements, and ratify them.

3. Declare war and make peace.

4. Assume the general command of the armed forces, the police and the national guard. It exercises the authority of Commander-in-Chief of the Armed Forces as and where mentioned in laws, regulations, instructions, orders, etc.

5. Supervise the Chief-of-Staff of the army, defence affairs, military intelligence machinery and public security.

6. Form the Cabinet and accept the resignation or dismiss any or all of the members.

7. Ratify the Cabinet's decrees.

8. Appoint by decree civil and military personnel above a certain rank. It has the right to dismiss and retire military and civil personnel.

9. Confirm death sentences. The Council has the right to change, or reduce or annul a sentence by special legislation.

10. Supervise, in general, the affairs of the Iraqi Republic in order to protect the Revolution and help it achieve the goals stated in the official Statement which announced its outbreak and in others which have been and will be issued from time to time. The Council will direct and help the Revolution until it achieves all its aims. This applies to the transitional period.

Article III—Decrees and orders issued by the National Revolutionary Counci since February 8 shall have the power of laws, regulations, instructions, decrees or orders by virtue of such legislation as may be issued for their classification as laws, regulations, instructions, decrees and orders respectively.

IMMUNITY OF MEMBERS OF THE COUNCIL

Article IV—1. Every member of the National Revolutionary Council has complete freedom of speech. No measures may be taken against him, for his manner of voting or for expressing an opinion.

2. No member of the Council may be questioned about any matter than concerns his work in the Council. He may not be arrested, interrogated or tried without a decree issued by a two-thirds majority of the members of the Council.

3. In the event of a member of the Council committing, or being alleged to have committed, a crime, the Council shall form a committee of investigation from amongst its members to investigate the allegation and present the result of its investigations, with the dossier, to the Council. The case shall be decided by a resolution issued by a two-thirds majority of the Council.

MEETINGS OF THE COUNCIL AND VOTING PROCEDURE

Article V—The Council shall appoint each of its members in rotation to be chairman for a period of two months. His duties are restricted to taking the chair and calling meetings.

Article VI—1. The Council shall hold a regular meeting once a week.

2. The chairman of the session or 4 members of the Council can

call for a meeting to be held. In this case the meeting must be held not later than two days from the date of the request.

Article VII—Meetings shall be held only if a majority of Council members are present.

Article VIII—Resolutions in the Council are passed by a majority of members with the exceptions stated in the law. If the votes are equal, the side that includes the chairman of the session shall prevail.

Article IX—Laws are approved by a majority of two-thirds.

THE SECRETARIAT

Article X—The Council shall form a secretariat. Its president shall be called "Secretary-General of the National Revolutionary Council." He shall be appointed by a decree of the Council.

Article XI—The Secretariat shall be responsible for administrative work, correspondence, the keeping of the files, records, dossiers and other documents of the Council, and it shall carry out whatever orders it receives from the Council.

Article XII—Letters and documents issued by the National Revolutionary Council shall be signed by the Secretary-General or his official deputy and sealed with the seal of the Secretary-General of the National Revolutionary Council.

SALARY AND ALLOCATIONS

Article XIII—The salary and allocations of a member of the Council are the same as those of a minister as fixed by such laws as may be in force.

Article XIV—A member of the Council is entitled to pension in the event of resignation, dismissal, death or inability to continue work for any reason. If he has served the term specified by such laws as may be in force, his pension shall be not less than half the salary and allocations he used to earn as a member of the Council. If he has not served the term specified by the law he is entitled to a pension and allocations which amount to half of what he used to earn as a member of the Council.

THE PRESIDENCY OF THE REPUBLIC AND THE NATIONAL REVOLUTIONARY COUNCIL

Article XV—The President of the Republic is the supreme head of state and the supreme commander of the National Armed Forces. He exercises powers which are defined by such laws as may be in force and in particular he does the following:

1. He concludes treaties and agreements ratified by the National

Revolutionary Council.

2. He appoints heads of diplomatic missions accredited to foreign countries and the U.N. and accepts the credentials of heads of missions accredited to the Iraqi Republic.

3. He signs the laws ratified by the National Revolutionary Council.

4. He issues the decrees forming the Cabinet, accepting its resignation or dismissing it, appointing one or more ministers, accepting the resignation or dismissing one or more ministers, according to the decision of the Council.

5. The Decrees of the Republic are issued in his name.

Article XVI—If the President does not approve of a law, regulation, decree or decision made by the National Revolutionary Council, he may submit his opinion to the Council within a week. In this case, the Council will hold a meeting, discuss the issue and vote again on this law, regulation, decree, or decision. If it is approved by a two-thirds majority, the decision shall be considered final.

Article XVII—The National Revolutionary Council may issue regulations and instructions concerning the implementation of this law.

Article XVIII—This law shall be considered a constitutional law.

Article XIX—This law shall be considered effective as from Ramadan 14, 1382 (February 8, 1963).

Article XX—All ministers shall implement this law.

Signed:

Abdul Salem Aref—President of the Republic and Cabinet, and the Members of the National Revolutionary Council.

APPENDIX K

THE IRAQI NATIONAL GUARD LAW
May 18, 1963

(Iraqi Official Gazette, June 2, 1963)

In the name of the people.
The Presidency of the Republic.

In accordance with the Constitutional Law of the National Revolutionary Council and in pursuance of the proposal of the Premier, and with the approval of the cabinet and after ratification by the National Revolutionary Council, the following law is hereby promulgated:

Article 1. An armed national organization shall be formed; it shall be called the National Guard Forces. They shall have an independent command attached to the Chief of General Staff or to such other authority as may be designated by the National Revolutionary Council.

Article 2. The National Guard is an organized popular force trained to use arms. It consists of members who believe in their right to a free and honourable life. Its duties are:

A. To protect the Arab movement in Iraq and ·assist its progressive revolutionary advance.

B. To aid the armed forces in civil defence and to defend the country in case of war or external aggression.

C. To assist in the maintenance of internal security.

D. To assist in public service and economic and social development.

E. To perform the duties entrusted to them by the competent authorities.

Article 3. The National Guard Forces shall consist of:

A. Iraqi volunteers.

B. Privates and non-commissioned officers, and reserve officers who are not on active service in the army, (when there is no general mobilization).

C. Volunteers from the Arab states with the Chief of General Staff's approval.

D. Soldiers seconded from the army for service in the National Guard on the request of the National Guard Command and with the approval of the Chief of General Staff.

Article 4. A volunteer for the National Guard must be:

A. Free from disease and physical defects which might prevent him from executing his duties.

B. Of good character and morals.

C. Not less than 25 years old and not more than 50.

Article 5. The volunteers shall undertake to serve in the National Guard for one year including the training period, which shall be fixed by the Chief of General Staff. Service may be extended at the end of one year on a new contract if the commander of the volunteer's unit certifies that his service was satisfactory.

Article 6. The National Guard Command may cancel contracts at any time it wishes.

Article 7. A. Service in the National Guard is on a voluntary basis and unpaid.

B. The National Guard Command may grant a fixed monthly financial stipend to certain members of these forces, if necessary or for some special reason, in accordance with instructions issued by the National Guard Command and with the approval of the Chief of General Staff.

C. If the volunteer is a government employee and is called for service during official working hours, with the approval of the department concerned, he shall be paid his basic salary by that department.

D. Service in the National Guard—when volunteers are called up for duty—shall be considered by their employers as service in their ordinary jobs as regards promotion, retirement and indemnity.

Article 8. The Headquarters of the General Staff shall be responsible for the training, equipment and arming of the National Guard in accordance with instructions it shall issue.

Article 9. Retirement and indemnity rights of the members of the National Guard shall be defined by a special law.

Article 10. Matters of discipline and punishment shall be defined in a special law.

Article 11. The Ministry of Defence shall be responsible for the National Guard's expenditures in accordance with such instructions as it may issue without regard to the financial laws in force for the year 1963 and 1964.

Article 12. The Chief of General Staff shall issue special instructions concerning the enactment of all articles of this law.

Issued in Baghdad on March 18, 1963.

In the public interest and for the protection of the Revolution of Ramadan 14 and in order to define the rights and duties of the National Guard in the Iraqi Republic, this law has been passed.

APPENDIX L

STATEMENT OF THE NATIONAL COMMAND
OF THE BA'ATH PARTY ON ITS
ASSUMPTION OF POWER IN IRAQ
BAGHDAD, NOVEMBER 15, 1963

(Al-Ba'ath, November 15, 1963)

During the past crisis your Party has given proof of its profound respect for Party values and its adherence to the principle of legality which derives from properly organized elections. Any disregard of these values, must expose to the greatest dangers the existence of the Party, of the Revolution and of the Arab people's cause in Unity, Freedom and Socialism. Democracy in the Arab Ba'th Socialist Party is not a mere matter of form; it is the Party's basic and distinguishing characteristic which is linked with the interests of the toiling masses—the workers, the peasants, the military, and educated revolutionaries.

Democracy as exercised by the Party in drafting its policy and plans and in electing its Commands is the true.and sound course for the achievement of the Party's objectives. It is not strange that we should see the masses giving proof of their profound awareness by supporting Party values and calling on the National Command to exercise its legal authority to find a solution of the crisis.

Since the outbreak of the Revolution the Party has fallen into errors caused by: the difficulty of the circumstances which characterized the past phase, lack of experience on the part of its Command, and the attempts of certain members of the Command to run things single-handedly. Our Party has criticized its own errors and made them public at its Regional Congresses and at its Sixth National Congress, in the belief that by this self-criticism, it would be able to avoid further mistakes and establish sound values in its constructive battle, as it has always done during its long history of struggle.

At the Regional Congress held on November 11, 1963, advantage was taken of the goodness of certain officers who in the past had not had the opportunity of expressing their opinions in a correct form, and improper, non-Party procedures were resorted to. Thus the

Regional Command that was elected by that Congress does not express the will of the Party.

The Party insists on the correction of the mistakes made by some of its political members. However, mistakes can only be corrected by following sound Party methods within the Party organization, by strict adherence to legality and democracy and by being in close contact with the people and listening to their opinions and demands.

Fully aware of the seriousness of the part played by the Revolution of the 14th of Ramadan in the Arab nationalist struggle and of the necessity of consolidating the unity of the civilian and military sectors of the Party, on the one hand, and of maintaining the fusion of the Party with the masses, on the other, and in its desire to ensure circumstances favourable for the election of a new Iraqi Regional Command, the National Command of the Arab Ba'ath Socialist Party has decided the following:

1. To consider the Regional Congress held in Baghdad on November 11, as illegal and to dissolve the Regional Command which it elected.

2. To dissolve the Regional Command which was in power when the Congress was held.

3. To invest the National Command with all prerogatives of the Regional Command in Iraq.

4. To investigate the mistakes made during this last period and to take decisive Party measures with regard to them.

5. To restrict the power of passing sentences on Iraqi Party members to the National Command.

6. To hold Party elections in the Iraqi Region and to hold a Regional Congress for the election of a new Regional Command within a period of four months.

The National Command salutes the makers of the Revolution of the 14th Ramadan and declares that the Iraqi Region has passed through this last crisis safely because of the discipline of the military and civilian members of the Party and because of the understanding of the masses of the necessity for strengthening the unity of Party ranks. The National Command reaffirms its determination to hasten the implementation of the resolutions of the Sixth National Congress in order to achieve the objectives of our nation which are Unity, Liberty and Socialism.

The National Command

APPENDIX M

OFFICIAL STATEMENT NO. 1 OF PRESIDENT AREF, COMMANDER-IN-CHIEF OF THE IRAQI ARMED FORCES BAGHDAD, NOVEMBER 18, 1963

(*Al-Jumhuriyah*, November 26, 1963)

In accordance with the powers vested in us, and in pursuance of the resolutions passed by the National Revolutionary Council in response to the appeals of the people and the Army, we order the following:

1. The Armed Forces, including the Air Force, are to control Baghdad and its suburbs and stifle any resistance aimed at opposing the Government and harming the people. The General Chief of Staff is entrusted with the carrying out of all military operations and with the execution of the plan that includes all the Armed Forces.

2. The National Guard and its Command and Organizations are to be dissolved immediately. Its members are ordered to surrender their arms to the nearest Army unit. Whoever does not obey this order will be considered a traitor and will be executed on the spot.

3. Unit commanders are to sign the sentences of execution and to execute all traitors and rebels on the spot.

4. Units, branch units, and troops are to open fire on all rebels and they are to give orders to their subordinates to do the same.

5. The Security Forces are to be immediately attached to the General Chief of Staff for Military Operations.

6. Ministers and officials are to implement his order.

Staff Marshal Adbul Salem Aref
President of the Iraqi Republic
and Commander-in-Chief of the
Armed Forces
November 18, 1963

APPENDIX N

/

OFFICIAL STATEMENT NO. 1 OF THE IRAQI NATIONAL REVOLUTIONARY COUNCIL
Baghdad, November 18, 1963

(Al-Jumhuriyah, November 26, 1963)

The attacks on the people's freedoms carried out by the *shu'ubis* (anti-Arab racialists) and blood-thirsty members of the National Guard, their violation of things sacred, their disregard of the law, the injuries they have done to the State and the people, and finally their armed rebellion on November 13, 1963, have led to an intolerable situation which is fraught with grave dangers to the future of this people which is an integral part of the Arab nation. We have endured all we could to avoid bloodshed. But as our patience increased the non-National Guard's acts of terrorism also increased. The Army has answered the call of the people to rid them of this terror. The National Revolutionary Council has therefore decided the following in response to the call of the people and the demands of the Army and the Armed Forces:

1. Staff Marshal Aref, President of the Iraqi Republic, is elected President of the National Revolutionary Council.

2. President Aref is appointed Commander-in-Chief of the Armed Forces and will exercise all authorities vested in him.

3. Staff Brigadier of the Air Force, Hardan Abdul Ghaffar, is appointed Deputy Commander-in-Chief of the Armed Forces in addition to his present post.

4. Staff Marshal Aref is granted special powers for one year, to be renewed automatically if necessary.

5. The National Guard is dissolved and all laws, regulations, instructions and orders issued concerning it are rescinded.

6. The formation of the National Revolutionary Council is as follows:

    a. The President: The President of the Republic.

    b. Members: The Commander-in-Chief of the Armed Forces; the Vice-President of the Republic; the Deputy Commander-in-Chief of the Armed Forces; the Chief of General Staff and his Assistants; commanders of Units; the Commander of the

Air Force; the Military Governor General; such officers as shall be appointed by the Council.

c. The Council shall elect a Secretary who may be a member of the Council or may be appointed from outside it. The President may authorize him to sign statements and orders issued by the Council.

d. The National Revolutionary Council shall form an Advisory council from citizens of good reputation, qualification, and experience.

7. The Council will take immediate legal action against the rebels who caused the November 13, 1963 rebellion.

Issued in Baghdad, November 18, 1963
Signed by
Staff Marshal Abdul Salam Aref
President of the National
Revolutionary Council

APPENDIX O

MINISTERIAL PROGRAMME OF THE IRAQI GOVERNMENT BAGHDAD, DECEMBER 24, 1963

(*Al-Jumhuriyah*, December 25, 1963)

The Revolution of July 15 was made in response to the appeal of the people who had been maltreated by the imperialists and their agents. The Revolution of 14th Ramadan was the result of the nationalist struggle against the racialist regime which had brought corruption to the country. The Revolution of November 18, made by your Army in response to your appeal, was necessary to achieve the goals aimed at by the July and the Ramadan Revolutions, to correct deviations by restoring the sovereignty of law, to protect the freedoms and the property of the citizens, to put an end to chaos and to permit the Arab people to recover their authentic Arab personality by removing all obstacles from the path of their complete unity, which is the hope of all Arabs everywhere.

This is why the Government will try its best to achieve the people's demands for repair of the damage done by past malpractices. It will stress in particular the unity of the national ranks, the sovereignty of laws, the realization of social justice in accordance with Arab socialism, and the ensuring of the basic freedoms which will guarantee the citizen his dignity, protect him from tyranny and help him to advance towards progress and prosperity.

The Government will use all possible means to achieve these goals in the fields of military, social, economic and general policy.

I—General Policy:

1. Internal Policy:

The grievous events that have taken place over the years in our homeland and the attempts of one political party or another to control its destiny at the expense of the majority, have led to party conflicts subversive to the foundations of society and accompanied by deviations from the advance towards the fundamental objectives of the nation. This created a gap between the government and the people, broke the unity of the national forces, implanted mutual hatred in the hearts of the citizens and left deep wounds in their souls. Because we believe that the unity of the nationalist ranks is necessary and because we want to avoid relapses, we welcome every sincere call for the formation of a nationalist front in which all desirable elements, without distinction, can co-operate, in working to achieve social justice and the sovereignty of law.

Your government will shortly promulgate the Provisional Constitution which will define the principles of government, including the State Council, during the transitional period that will be defined by the Constitution. The Provisional Constitution will guarantee for all citizens equality of rights and obligations and will secure for them the freedoms, including the freedoms of belief, opinion, press and association. It will safeguard their personal dignity from all arbitrary conduct so that every citizen may enjoy security and stability.

One of the most important reforms which the Government intends to bring about is the strengthening of the judiciary and the securing of its independence and non-partisanship with a view to the establishment of justice ruled by law. The independence of the judiciary always leads to the implementation of the principle of the sovereignty of law which may be considered as one of the major aims of the Revolution of November 18.

In order to implement this, the Government is determined:

A. To establish a State Council which will be independent in the same way as are similar councils in progressive countries in so far as its methods of procedure and its powers are concerned.

B. To amend criminal, commercial, maritime, property and other laws in a manner consonant with the public interest, and to make them reflect the reality of our Republic and its development in order to guarantee justice, secure the rights of individuals and facilitate transactions.

The Government will encourage organizations and committees that really serve the people and will give them every opportunity to develop and progress towards the achievement of their objectives. The Government will also try to improve its administrative system and will apply decentralized administration more widely in order to make citizens participate actively in public administration. This is why administrative laws will be re-examined in the interest of the achievement of these objectives. The Government is, in addition, intent on raising the · ndards of the police, on providing them with technical aid and on ensuring that the force consists only of desirable elements.

2. Arab Policy:

Our Arab policy stems from the fact that Iraq is an integral part of the Arab homeland and that the Iraqi people is a part of the Arab nation and that the Arab people's persistent desire to unite is a categorical imperative dictated by the will of the people because it is the very foundation of Arab existence. The Cairo Charter of April 17 is the starting point of the advance towards unity. The Government will try its best, in collaboration with the other Arab states, to liberate Palestine and to provide the Palestinians with the means of fighting their own battle. We shall actively assist them in carrying the burdens of the struggle. The Government will also support the struggle of the people of Oman, Occupied South Yemen and the other usurped parts of the Arab homeland until they win their freedom and independence. The Government supports the Arab League and believes that it is a useful instrument through which the sincere efforts to defend the Arab cause may be unified.

3. Foreign Policy:

The bonds of neighbourhood and religion lead us to strengthen our relations with the two Moslem countries which are our neighbours in particular and with the Moslem world in general. We are also intent on strengthening our relations with the Afro-Asian countries in accordance with the Bandung Charter.

The Government adheres to the policies of positive neutrality, of non-alignment and of dealing with friendly countries on an equal footing and on the basis of reciprocation in matters of mutual interest. It adheres to the U.N. Charter and supports all its organs and departments. It also tries its best to combat imperialism and to help the nations that are struggling for their independence. It denounces racial discrimination, which it considers a degradation of human dignity. It supports the efforts that are being made for disarmament, for opposing war, for the avoidance of violence in solving international disputes and for peaceful co-existence.

II—Economic Policy:

1. Planning will be the basis of our economic policy. That is why the first thing we shall attend to will be the organization of the departments in the light of past experience in order to prepare a sound five-year economic plan based on the securing of the necessary resources for its implementation and the guaranteeing of equilibrium in the developing of the different sectors. We aim at:

A. Development of the agricultural sector by speeding up the implementation of irrigation and desalinization projects, the implementation of the Eski Mosul and Upper Euphrates projects, and the reclamation of soil and forests.

B. The development of the public and private industrial sectors so as to profit from the country's natural resources in the best possible way. The Government will give all its attention to the execution of the following projects: generation and distribution of electric power, chemical fertilizers, artificial silk, spinning and weaving, production of agricultural machines and electrical equipment, extraction of sulphur and exploitation of natural gas.

C. The execution of the agricultural and industrial development programmes will be carried out through the improvement and extension of the means of transport (railway, land, air and water) and the means of communication (telephone, telegraph and wireless).

2. The Government will provide suitable conditions for the encouragement of capital investment in the different branches of the private sector, commerce, industry and agriculture.

3. In the field of trade policy, the Government will try to achieve

the following:

A. To develop trade relations with all the Arab countries on the basis of the Arab Economic Union Agreement and with the foreign countries on the basis of mutual interests. It will encourage exports and will decrease the restrictions placed on the imports of essential foodstuffs and on capital equipment.

B. To provide the necessary protection for local production, especially the new industries, from unfair foreign competition.

C. To lower the prices of essential foodstuffs without harming legitimate economic interests. In order to execute this, the Government will assist distribution, increasing amounts of bread and foodstuffs at a low price.

4. To support the policy of economic planning, the government will balance the regular budget by restricting administrative expenditure in order to save enough money for the implementation of the projects of the economic plan. It will also re-examine tax regulations with a view to relieving the burdens of the poorer classes, revivifying economic activity and increasing the country's resources. The Central Bank will co-operate with the other banks to establish a regular money market, to make available the facilities necessary for extending insurance operations by the commercial and specialized banks and to strengthen the Dinar by diversifying its monetary coverage.

The Government affirms that it welcomes Arab investors who wish to invest their capital in Iraq and announces that it will provide the necessary guarantees for the transfer of capital and profits.

5. The Government will establish a national oil industry that will be the basis for its future oil activity in exploiting the areas the rights for which were recovered in accordance with Law No. 80 of 1961, profiting from the services and experience available in the world oil industry. The Government will start this year the implementation of the Iraqi National Oil Company Project and the Oil Exploitation Law. At the same time it will develop the existing oil industry and will solve its problems in accordance with the spirit of the present time and in conformity with our basic interests. It will aim at producing a greater quantity, especially from the oil companies' present concession areas which are capable of producing much greater quantities for export.

Iraq belongs to the Organization of the Petroleum Exporting Countries (OPEC) and thinks that this Organization must start using its dormant powers to protect the interests of its members and to gain just and reasonable profits from its oil.

III—Social Policy:

Our social policy stems from the sound concepts of Arab Socialism that are based on social justice and equal opportunities for all citizens. It will be implemented through increasing income, organizing the national wealth, preventing exploitation, and raising the individual's standard of living. We have in our Arab legacy and Islamic Shari'a all that is needed to give our system meaning and content, without recourse to imported principles. On this basis our Government is trying to give every individual the opportunity to obtain all he requires in the fields of education, medical treatment, housing, clothing nutrition, and spiritual instruction. In order to implement this policy, the following is being done:

1. The Government is directing educational policy towards the formation of a generation that believes in God, is loyal to the homeland, and confident of its nation's right to live the free, unified life that is based on the Arab Charter for Cultural Union. This requires increased opportunities for primary, secondary and university education so as to make it possible for every citizen to obtain the education that is adapted both to his abilities and to the country's needs. The Government intends to eliminate illiteracy, to make primary education compulsory, and to extend secondary education and diversify it culturally and technically in accordance with the requirements of social and economic development. The Government also intends to raise both the educational standards and the salaries of teachers so that they may fulfill their duties loyally and conscientiously. In the field of higher education the Government intends to raise the standard of education in colleges and higher institutes, and to diversify the fields of specialization, giving special care to applied research in response to the requirements of social and economic development. This requires the guaranteeing of the freedom of thought and adherence to sound university standards so that the university may be able to fulfill its mission. It requires also the drafting of a special law for service in the universities. The Government will support all scientific and technical research institutes including the Academy of Science.

2. The Government is determined to make every effort to raise the standard of health. It will increase the number of clinics and health centres, and of institutions that deal with mother and child

care, and school health; it will combat tuberculosis and will provide health services for the rural areas and for the whole of Iraq.

3. The Government is determined to extend the following public services throughout Iraq: artesian wells, electricity, sewerage, street paving and public transport. In order to execute these projects, the Government is developing the departments responsible for them, in particular the Municipality Offices. These offices will be given a large measure of administrative freedom which will enable them to complete their work quickly.

4. The *Wakf* Administration is building new mosques, restoring old ones and aiding religious institutes so that they may fulfill their mission to perfection. It is investing its income in construction, industrial and philanthropic projects.

5. The Government is working on the issue of legislation that will guarantee the workers a decent life, stressing in particular wages, working hours, and protection from industrial accidents and disease. The Government will also issue legislation which will support the organization of trade unions insofar as this is in conformity with the public interest, on a just basis which will take into account the interests of both the workers and the employers. The Social Security Law will be re-examined in order to establish it on a basis that will provide the workers and their families with old age, permanent disability and death pensions. The Social Security Law will be gradually made to include other sectors of the people. The institutions for the aged, orphans and the disabled will be increased in number. The Government intends to organize the co-operative movement and extend it in all fields so that the co-operative organizations may be able to support the movement towards social and economic development in all popular sectors. It also intends to encourage tourism, summer resorts, and the protection of antiquities.

6. The Government is at present drawing up a comprehensive plan for housing which will ensure a healthy dwelling for every citizen. To implement this, every family will receive a piece of land either free or for a very small sum (depending on the family's financial circumstances) on which it will be able to build a house with the help of credit companies subsidized by the Government.

IV. Agrarian Reform:

The Government is determined to implement the Agrarian Reform Law, fully and finally benefiting from experience and taking the just measures necessary to complete the operations of confiscation and distribution during the coming three years. The Government is determined to complete the supplementary activities necessary for the success of the Agrarian Reform project in order that the peasants may make use of their new land in the best possible way. This will be done through the establishment of agricultural co-operatives and the mechanization of agriculture by extending the networks of mechanical units throughout all agricultural areas. In addition, it will extend the policy of agricultural loans, will stress directed loans, and improvement of the irrigation system, will undertake desalination projects and encourage animal husbandry, will provide improved seeds and implement the Rural Development Project which includes the establishment of modern villages equipped with public utilities and the necessary social services.

V. Military Policy:

The Government is determined to make the Army worthy of the nationalist responsibility laid on its shoulders by our Arab Nation in these critical circumstances of our history. To achieve this it has decided:

1. To ensure discipline and self-sacrifice in the fulfillment of duties and the execution of orders. Orders must be obeyed only if they come from the proper military authorities.

2. To keep the armed forces away from party politics so that they may devote themselves to their military duties.

3. To do everything to raise the standard of training and to benefit from other armies experience in this field.

4. To eliminate illiteracy in the Army and give lectures on religion, morals and the heritage of our nation.

5. To obtain the most modern arms and equipment that will enable our armed forces to perform their duty to the full.

6. To establish arms factories to meet the Army's requirements.

7. To achieve harmony and co-operation with the other Arab armies that together form the single Arab army which will achieve our national objectives.

8. To raise the standard of living of all members of the Army and police and provide housing and medical treatment.

Citizens:

The media of information have in the past been exploited by imperialists, racialists and deviationists. These created confusion, spread false concepts in the minds of the people, and contributed to the disintegration of national unity. We must ensure that these media provide the people with sound national, Arab, and Islamic guidance. This requires:

A. Raising the standard of the press by amending the Press Law in such a way as to ensure that journalism becomes a respectable profession, the only aim of which is the service of the people.

B. To develop the broadcasting system and improve it in both the administrative and technical fields so that it may provide guidance and knowledge to all the citizens, and discover talents, develop them and benefit from them.

C. To improve the television station so that programmes may be received in all parts of Iraq.

D. To revive popular arts, encourage Arab and Islamic arts and provide guidance offices in the majority of the cities.

People of Iraq, your Government submits to you its programme, praying that God will help it and support its steps in establishing stability and security.

Your Government declares before God and before you that its rule is based on the sovereignty of law, respect for the freedoms and the establishment of authority on sound constitutional foundations derived from our Shari'a and our glorious national heritage.

We repeat the appeal made by President Abdul Salem Aref in his historic statement to the Kurds on 28/11/63, in which he pardoned them and offered forgiveness to all who repented. We repeat this appeal so that life may return to normal, so that we may have the opportunity of building up the North and so that the Kurds may assist us in the development of the homeland, and in working for its independence and National Unity, and so that peace and security may be enjoyed by all without discrimination. We hope that the Kurds will respond to this noble appeal that aims at unifying the national ranks so that all may enjoy peace and security.

The grievous responsibilities that have been laid on the shoulders of the Government under these circumstances require that all good elements in this country should unite their efforts and rally around the Government. Citizens are invited to offer their constructive criticism of all fields of activity. The authorities will always be ready to consider any constructive criticism so long as it is supported by facts.

APPENDIX P

PROVISIONAL CONSTITUTION, APRIL 29, 1964

The Iraqi Republic is a democratic socialist state deriving the rudiments of its democracy and socialism from the Arab heritage and the spirit of Islam. The Iraqi people are a part of the Arab nation and its aim is total Arab unity. The government binds itself to achieve this unity as soon as possible, starting with unity with the U.A.R.

Private property is inviolable. . . . The law determines the [maximum] of agricultural ownership in such a manner as to prevent the establishment of a feudal system. . . .

The incumbent president of the republic shall continue to perform the functions of his post until a new president is elected in accordance with the provisions of the permanent constitution. The interim period shall not exceed three years from the date this transitional constitution comes into force. The president of the republic shall appoint the premier, the deputy premier, and the ministers and shall accept their resignations and relieve them of their posts. He shall have the power to declare martial law and a state of emergency with approval of the Revolutionary Command Council.

The President of the Republic, in cooperation with the government, shall lay down the general policy of the state in all the military, political, economic, and social aspects and shall supervise its implementation. The cabinet shall exercise the legislative powers during the transitional period, while observing the provisions of the law of the Revolutionary Command Council. The President of the Republic shall rectify the laws and promulgate them. (Articles, 1, 12, 13, 43, 48, 59, 63, 100, 101)

SUDAN
Texts in Khalil, I, pp. 359–361.

INDEX